PUBLICATIONS MANAGEMENT: ESSAYS FOR PROFESSIONAL COMMUNICATORS

Edited by

O. JANE ALLEN
New Mexico State University

and

LYNN H. DEMING
New Mexico Institute of Mining & Technology

Baywood's Technical Communications Series
Series Editor: JAY R. GOULD

Baywood Publishing Company, Inc.
Amityville, New York

Copyright © 1994, Baywood Publishing Company, Inc.
Amityville, New York. All rights reserved.

Library of Congress Catalog Number: 94-14936
ISBN: 0-89503-163-9 (Cloth)
ISBN: 0-89503-164-7 (Paper)

Library of Congress Cataloging-in-Publication Data

Publications management : essays for professional communicators /
    edited by O. Jane Allen and Lynn H. Deming.
        p. cm. - - (Baywood's technical communications series)
     Includes bibliographical references (p.) and index.
     ISBN 0-89503-163-9. - - ISBN 0-89503-164-7 (pbk.)
     1. Technical publishing- -United States- -Management.
    2. Corporations- -United States- -Publishing- -Management.   I. Allen.
    O. Jane.   II. Deming, Lynn H. III. Series: Baywood's technical
    communication series (Unnumbered)
    Z479.P835 1994
    070.5'0973- -dc20   94-14936
                                                                  CIP

Printed in the United States of America
on acid-free paper

Acknowledgments

We gratefully acknowledge the support provided for this project by the Department of English, New Mexico State University, and the Department of Humanities, New Mexico Institute of Mining and Technology.

Special thanks go to Ann Macbeth for meticulously editing and preparing the illustrations, and to Isabel Villaseñor for editorial and research assistance.

An earlier version of David Armbruster's "Hiring and Managing Editorial Freelancers" appeared as "Hiring and Managing Editorial Consultants" in *Technical Communication, 33*:4, pp. 243-246, 1986. The Society for Technical Communication Code for Communicators in Chapter 15 is reprinted with permission from the Society for Technical Communication, Arlington, VA. We thank Gerald Cohen for permission to reprint his Dial-A-Buzzword illustration in Chapter 11.

We are especially grateful to all our contributors who made this book possible and to our anonymous reviewers for their valuable critiques. Finally, we thank Jay R. Gould, our series editor, for his continuing wise counsel.

Table of Contents

Introduction

O. JANE ALLEN

and

LYNN H. DEMING

The growing number of academic programs in technical and professional communication and the increasing interaction between communication professionals in the workplace and teachers in the classroom is resulting in a better understanding of the complex roles of communicators in the industrial context and a growing sophistication of the literature in the field. The 1983 publication of *New Essays in Technical and Scientific Communication: Research, Theory, Practice*, edited by Paul V. Anderson, R. John Brockmann, and Carolyn R. Miller [1], reflected an increasingly research-oriented approach to the field of technical and professional communication. More recent collections that continue to build on this research emphasis are Lee Odell and Dixie Goswami's *Writing in Nonacademic Settings* [2], Carolyn B. Matalene's *Worlds of Writing: Teaching and Learning in Discourse Communities of Work* [3], Charles Bazerman and James Paradis' *Textual Dynamics and the Professions* [4], Mary M. Lay and William M. Karis' *Collaborative Writing in Industry: Investigations in Theory and Practice* [5], and Nancy Roundy Blyler and Charlotte Thralls's *Professional Communication: The Social Perspective* [6].

An important theme in these collections is the significance of the social context in which written communication takes place and the reciprocal role of communication in shaping that context. Paradis, David Dobrin, and Richard Miller argue that documents not only reflect the social context in which they are produced, but they may help to shape that context [7]. Discussing the social implications of writing in organizations, Paradis, Dobrin, and Miller point to some of the roles of written communication in managing the work of an organization and helping it meet objectives. They credit written communication with enabling employees to promote their "physical and intellectual labor" and to clarify their own roles in individual projects. Written communication, along with formal oral presentations, helps to further interaction among groups within an organization by breaking down boundaries between research groups and between levels of organization. Moreover, written communication is useful in maintaining accountability within an organization, in generating new ideas, and in providing background information for new employees, thus maintaining continuity and encouraging employees to construct a knowledge base from which to write their own documents.

J. C. Mathes, also concerned with the role of written communication in reflecting and shaping its social context, discusses the importance of understanding the industrial context as a "prerequisite to the teaching and mastery of technical-communication skills" [8, p. 222]. Mathes notes the failure of typical communication models to define the flow of communication within the organizational structure, to anticipate how decisions are made in particular organizations, to reflect functional differences among various types of organizations, and to anticipate some of the relationships that exist between units within organizations.

Blyler and Thralls bring together a collection of work by scholars who explore various social dimensions of professional communication. In their book, for example, James E. Porter explores the importance of ethics in corporate composing processes. Humanistic values, he notes, may not "generate answers, but they are necessary elements of serious inquiry" [9, p. 143].

Lay and Karis contribute to an ongoing dialogue that focuses on collaboration, including in their collection essays that address theoretical and practical issues of collaboration in the workplace and in the academy. These essays identify and investigate difficulties experienced by collaborative groups and offer suggestions for managing the collaborative process in industry.

This focus on the social aspects of communication calls attention to both the range of responsibility and the potential of the communication professional in the workplace.

THE COMMUNICATION SPECIALIST AS MANAGER

When we observe the organizational environment, we find that entry-level technical writers frequently spend only a small portion of their time writing and editing. They may, for example, spend much of their time in conference with others, gathering information and coordinating various aspects of document production, including document testing and details of printing and publication.

As they move beyond entry level, they often have to assume responsibility for the work of others.

Most of us are aware that management skills are important to even the simplest communication project. Whether we write a short memorandum report to an immediate supervisor or a proposal for a multimillion dollar project, we must consider audience and purpose, and we must collect information and arrange and deliver it appropriately if we are to achieve our purpose. As projects become larger and more complex, the role of the manager may involve developing libraries and/or databases of product documentation, even hiring, training, and managing specialists who produce the documentation.

A manager's responsibilites for publications staff may include ensuring that their needs and potential within the organization are communicated to other managers so that publications staff receive the esteem and the resources they need to do their jobs. The manager must also be concerned with communication channels within the organization that guarantee access to people and information critical to the performance of publications staff. Good managers are also aware, and communicate their awareness, of the importance of publications in marketing products and in conveying the attitudes and values of an organization to its public. In summary, management skills are critical to effective communication in the workplace.

ESSAYS ON PUBLICATIONS MANAGEMENT

We have collected these essays for students in academic programs in technical and professional communication and for communication professionals in the workplace. The contributors include publications managers in the workplace and academics who teach in technical and professional communication programs around the country. Their multiple perspectives offer a broad introduction to some of the important issues publications professionals face. We have encouraged contributors to include, when possible, a wide range of references to literature in the field, thereby expanding the resource nature of the collection.

As teachers of technical and professional communication, we look forward to using the essays in the classroom—to discussing with students the varied responsibilities of communication specialists in complex organizational environments, as well as examining the different writing styles and the academic versus workplace foci and approaches to topics. Moreover, we hope this book elicits discussion that will contribute to the research on communication and the workplace and that will enrich the dialogue that already exists between the two spheres.

The book has five sections. The first, Communication and the Manager, looks at the changing responsibilities of publications managers and some of the intraorganizational communication challenges they face. The second section,

Management and Supervision, includes essays to help managers meet their responsibilities for recruiting and training publications staff. Section three, Project Management and the Information Development Cycle, includes discussions, guidelines, worksheets, and information for smooth, efficient document production and project management. Section four, Legal and Ethical Issues, provides essential and provocative information on ethics and legal matters. The final section, Pedagogy, offers a discussion of the use of corporate boards to assist academic programs, and descriptions of publications management courses taught at Miami University (Ohio) and New Mexico State University.

For the most part, these essays offer a practical, experiential approach to publications management. Moreover, they point to the ever-increasing scope of responsibility of publications units and to the substantial contributions communications professionals make to the organizations in which they work. Although we realize that this collection is no substitute for years of experience and/or formal management education and training, we hope it offers students and professionals perspectives from which to view the challenges of the workplace and a starting point for further study. Most of all, we hope this book instills a sense of responsibility in professional communicators, who influence both the environment in which they work and the image of that environment.

REFERENCES

1. P. V. Anderson, R. J. Brockmann, and C. R. Miller (eds.), *Essays in Technical and Scientific Communication: Research, Theory, Practice,* Baywood Publishing Company, Amityville, New York, 1983.
2. L. Odell and D. Goswami (eds.), *Writing in Nonacademic Settings,* Guilford Press, New York, 1985.
3. C. B. Matalene (ed.), *Worlds of Writing: Teaching and Learning in Discourse Communities of Work,* Random House, New York, 1989.
4. C. Bazerman and J. Paradis (eds.), *Textual Dynamics of the Professions: Historical and Contemporary Studies of Writing in Professional Communities,* University of Wisconsin Press, Madison, 1991.
5. M. M. Lay and W. M. Karis (eds.), *Collaborative Writing in Industry: Investigations in Theory and Practice*, Baywood Publishing Company, Amityville, New York, 1991.
6. N. R. Blyler and C. Thralls (eds.), *Professional Communication: The Social Perspective,* Sage Publications, Newbury Park, California, 1993.
7. J. Paradis, D. Dobrin, and R. Miller, Writing at Exxon ITD: Notes on the Writing Environment of an R&D Organization, in *Collaborative Writing in Industry: Writing in Nonacademic Settings,* L. Odell and D. Goswami (eds.), Guilford Press, New York, pp. 281-307, 1985.

8. J. C. Mathes, Written Communication: the Industrial Context, in *Worlds of Writing: Teaching and Learning in Discourse Communities of Work*, C. B. Matalene (ed.), Random House, New York, pp. 222-246, 1989.
9. J. E. Porter, The Role of Law, Policy, and Ethics in Corporate Composing: Toward a Practical Ethics for Professional Writing, in *Professional Communication: The Social Perspective*, N. R. Blyler and C. Thralls (eds.), Sage Publications, Newbury Park, California, pp. 128-143, 1993.

PART I

Communication and the Manager

Publications managers, like other managers in an organization, must communicate effectively with upper management and with their own staff. And because they are communication professionals, they often are seen as a resource for advice on communication matters throughout an organization. The three essays in this section deal with some of the specific intraorganizational communication challenges encountered by managers of publications units.

The first chapter, by the late James W. Souther, professor emeritus of technical communication, University of Washington, points to the increased responsibllity publications managers have assumed in the last decade, in part as a result of computer technology. In "Managing Technical Publications: A Growing and Changing Responsibility," Souther responds to common misconceptions about the relationship between technical and publications staff responsibilities and suggests an effective approach for directing the writing/publishing processes, an approach that encourages collaboration between technical and publications staff.

Publications managers are necessarily concerned with interpersonal communication within the publications unit. They may also find themselves contributing to improved written and oral communication throughout an organization. In "Designing Noise Audits to Improve Managerial-Employee Communication," Renee B. Horowitz and Robert V. Peltier, professors in the Department of Manufacturing and Industrial Technology at Arizona State University, suggest ways to combat psychological noise in manager-employee communication. They provide a checklist that can be used to audit noise levels and improve communication.

Another challenge for the publications manager is conducting cost-effective meetings. According to Marian G. Barchilon, assistant professor in the Department of Manufacturing and Industrial Technology at Arizona State University, meetings often fail to produce the right results. In "Technical Communication Models that Ensure Productive Meetings," Barchilon notes the increasing importance of meetings in the business environment and provides models for well-structured agenda and meeting minutes that will help to ensure productive, cost-effective meetings.

CHAPTER 1

Managing Technical Publications: A Growing and Changing Responsibility

JAMES W. SOUTHER

The decade of the 1980s was a significant watershed for technical publications management. Prior to the 1980s, publications activities—the basic functions of writing and editing, of graphics, and of printing and publication—were usually perceived as different processes and technologies and were frequently located in different units or departments. Technical writing, editing, printing, and publication were traditionally seen as separate functions requiring different units, staffs, and management.

Today publications functions are perceived as highly interrelated, interdependent activities in the technical publications process. These functions are frequently combined within a single technical communication or publishing department with an integrated staff and a common management. The key ingredient of this watershed was, of course, a new computer-based technology and the development of desktop publishing. As a result, publications today depend more on staff collaboration and teamwork and less on contributions of specialized individuals or units.

During the 1980s, technical publications management also experienced substantial growth and increased professional recognition. One needs only to compare the many sessions, papers, and workshops on this subject presented at the 39th International Technical Communication Conference of the Society for Technical Communication in Atlanta in May 1992 or at the October 1991 International Professional Communication Conference of the IEEE Professional Communication Society in Orlando with the few sessions at the same conferences ten years ago. Today, almost ten times more program sessions are devoted to publications management.

But even more important, the decade of the 1980s saw the rise and growth of new functions. Publications units today are just as apt to be involved in online, movie, and video presentations as with the more traditional print media. In addition, user testing has become a defined function of publications management. Again, the software industry is primarily responsible for this new development. The shift from mainframe to personal computers caused the availability of the software and the usability of its documentation to become key marketing factors for the new computers. User testing, seldom heard of ten years ago, is today an essential publications management activity. Although everyone in technical communication has reader-advocate responsibilities, publications managers who plan, direct, review, and approve documents have the greatest responsibility. User testing, as Joseph S. Dumas of the Document Design Center has pointed out, can provide significant input into future product design [1]. In other words, the reader-advocate role actually allows publications managers to contribute to the design of future products, to become change agents and contributors to the technical team.

Managing publications, of course, requires all the usual management functions and skills traditionally associated with other areas and activities. Consequently, today's publications managers need to develop the skills in working with people described by JoAnn T. Hackos in her excellent article "Managing Creative People" [2] and to apply the suggestions on managing publications presented in this collection.

In addition to developing the necessary management skills, however, publications managers must also understand how others view the writing and publications functions. Publications managers and their staff work with a variety of people— from highly specialized scientists, engineers, and health professionals, to managers, executives, and quality committees, to users and customers—many of whom often view writing and publications activities differently than do technical communication specialists, and many of whom share some common misconceptions that impact on working relationships.

In order to provide a more realistic understanding that will support effective interaction and planning, publications managers must strive to overcome these misconceptions. This chapter addresses these issues by examining the scope and responsibility of the publications unit. In addition, it outlines the major differences between the two most common modes of writing and stresses the importance of functional organization for documents; describes the interactive relationship between the technical and the writing/publishing processes; and provides suggestions for overcoming the differences between the views of the writer and reader and for developing an effective approach for directing the writing/publishing process.

PUBLICATIONS SCOPE AND RESPONSIBILITY

The scope and responsibility of publications activity are related directly to the purpose and readership of specific publications. For example, scientific, medical, or technical research articles and reports written to present findings to professional colleagues are almost always written by the technical professional. Technical writers are seldom involved, and technical editors are usually limited to a light edit at most. But as the readership shifts from technical professionals to other professionals, to management, to customers, and finally to the general public, the communication role of the *technical professional* shifts from writer, to contributor, to information source; and the role of the *technical communicator* grows from light editor, to substantive editor, to writer, to publisher.

Publications managers must understand that unlike the technical staff, technical writers do not write about their own work. They write about the work of others, a task which requires a substantial interaction between the technical writer and the technical specialist. The shifting role and responsibility of the technical professionals and communication professionals, in part, reflects the importance that the technical professionals attach to certain content and to certain audiences. Understanding the nature of this shifting responsibility and the interactive working relationship between technical professionals and communication professionals provides publications managers a basis on which they can develop effective plans for involving both parties in a realistic and effective partnership.

REFLECTIVE AND PRESENTATIONAL MODES
OF WRITING

Peter Hartley of the Colorado School of Mines provides a useful distinction between the reflective and presentational modes of writing. According to Hartley, "[t]raditional writing instruction is conceived in terms of the essay, a *reflective mode* not suited to industrial applications." Industrial writing, on the other hand, "is action oriented," requiring a *presentational mode* that focuses on "the reader's pragmatic needs in the social context of an organizational role" [3, p. 162]. Hartley's comments on the nature of the two modes are important for publications managers, and his statement that all of us, as students, are trained almost exclusively as essay writers is not only valid but most significant.

Almost all writing courses and experience, from the first grade through college, have an essay focus because the reflective mode is an essential, effective educational approach for helping students develop their ability to think, to expand their thought patterns, and to apply principles of clarity, coherence, and logic to their writing. As Hartley tells us, the focus in reflective writing is on developing the thought patterns of the writer and on the writing itself.

On the other hand, in the presentational mode—which is usually confined to college business and technical writing courses and, unfortunately, only to some of those—the emphasis shifts to communicating information to specific readers who have real informational needs and who function within an organizational or social context. This basic function of the presentational mode, which in earlier years gave rise to the concept of technical writing as a design or problem-solving process [4-9], today serves as the basis for user-testing activities.

If publications managers are aware that many of the people they work with— engineers, scientists, computer programmers, business people, social scientists, managers, executives, customers, and even their technical communication colleagues—are more apt to think of writing as reflective than as presentational, they can help writers shift from the reflective to the presentational mode with its reader-advocate role.

CHOOSING THE MOST FUNCTIONAL ORGANIZATION

Publications managers also need to develop the habit of examining alternative organizational structures for the writing they manage or review. The choice of which organizational pattern is most functional for the reader can be based only on an evaluation of the available alternatives. Publications managers who insist that functionality is an essential ingredient of effective presentation have the responsibility of identifying and evaluating alternative patterns. They also need to recognize that writers tend to choose the first sensible, logical pattern they discover and seldom consider alternatives.

Managers can save time, both for themselves and their staff, by encouraging their writers to first develop alternative patterns that concentrate only on the main topics and avoid detailed content. Having evaluated patterns and selected one, the writers should fully develop and detail the content of the document. Managers also need to realize that previously successful patterns may not serve readers well in a different situation; managers and writers should develop the habit of being wary of using such patterns without reevaluation.

UNDERSTANDING THE INTERACTIVE RELATIONSHIP OF THE TECHNICAL AND THE WRITING/PUBLISHING PROCESSES

Technical managers, technical staff, technical writers, and publications managers must understand that technical work and the communication work growing out of it are not simple sequential activities, with writing/publishing merely a tag-on activity at the end of the technical project.

Frequently, this sequential view creates an unrealistic time schedule for the writing and publication function, as the following example illustrates. When a twelve-week government contract extension was given to a well-known manufacturing company for further refining its product design before the final production contract would be awarded, the company allocated eleven weeks for completing the design work and one week for preparing the final bid report. A quick examination of the reporting task revealed that the report would be some 3000 pages, all to be written, reviewed, printed, and delivered in a week. *Tag-on planning at its very worst!* Of course, the publications people developed their own more realistic plan, which started several weeks earlier and overlapped the end of the design work.

A more realistic, interactive relationship between the technical work and publications activity is the parallel view, which provides a basis for effectively planning and managing these two highly interrelated processes. Here the two processes start out together. Frequently publications task analysis—including both the reader's informational needs assessment and document definition—grows out of insights from the analysis of the objectives and functions of the technical work itself. The task for the publications manager, then, is, first, to establish this parallel relationship between the technical work and the communication work and, second, to add the stages of the publications process, as presented in Figure 1, to the parallel relationship.

Thus, by examining Figure 1 and the following technical publications process, the publications manager may combine the elements of both the technical work and the publications process.

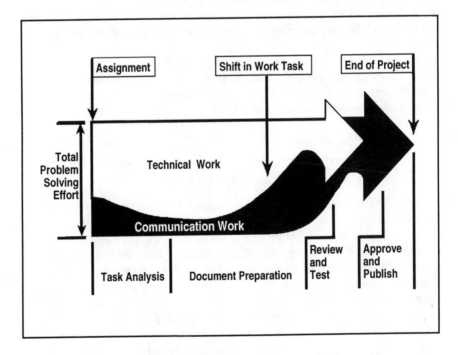

Figure 1. The technical problem and the communication problem:
an interactive model.

The Technical Publications Process

1. Task Analysis
   A. Needs Assessment—purpose, use, reader's knowledge and information needs (reader-advocate role)
   B. Document Definition—overall package, specific documents, number, size, nature, design, required content, and sources of information.
2. Document Preparation
   A. Locating and Gathering Information
   B. Selecting and Organizing Content—verbal and graphic, examining alternative structures, determining the most functional
   C. Writing and Revising (two separate activities)
   D. Reviewing, Testing, Editing
3. Approving, Publishing, Distributing

Communication task analysis and technical problem analysis, then, begin together. As the two processes continue in parallel, the amount of time, effort, and personnel devoted to the communication activity will, of course, vary throughout. Although the major writing and publishing thrust tends to come toward the end, much document preparation, such as collecting and organizing information, continues throughout the technical work. Toward the end of the process, when the technical work is nearing completion, the communication work is usually at its maximum.

This interactive view of the two processes provides the valuable insight needed for effective planning for both activities, stressing their interdependence. By truly understanding the significance of the parallel relationships of these processes, publications managers can avoid the many pitfalls associated with the tag-on view.

OVERCOMING THE DIFFERENCE BETWEEN WRITER AND READER VIEWS

Writers and readers tend to view the same piece of writing very differently. Writers read much into what they write—seeing everything they thought related to the material presented as part of it; a cloud of meaning surrounds the writing. Readers, on the other hand, see only what is on the paper or the computer screen, no more. Writers see both coordinate and subordinate organizational relationships: after all, they identified and developed these relationships. Readers see only those relationships which are actually described in the writing and which they have just read in a limited, sequential relationship (see Figure 2).

Readability depends on how well the writer reveals and explains these organizational relationships. Readers need roadmaps. They need to be told when they are moving from one topic to another and how those topics relate to each other.

Figure 2. The writer's view and the reader's view.

Although writers are responsible for providing introductions, transitions, and summaries, as well as lists of major points and conclusions, managers who review and approve documents must also recognize the readers' needs and make certain that the organizational content and maps are present as well as directions to help the reader use illustrations and tables. The one other person most apt to see the material from the writer's view is the publications manager, who has worked closely with the writer. That manager must consciously adopt the reader's view because both meaning and significance so often grow out of these organizational relationships. Contrary to the popular saying, facts do *not* speak for themselves. To be meaningful for the reader, data must be interpreted and implications stated, especially for management readers.

DIRECTING THE PUBLICATIONS PROCESS

The integration of information and product-development activities is important to the development of information as well as to the products that are being documented [10]. Hence publications managers must develop an effective approach for directing the writing/publishing process and knowing when to best enter the process. Publications managers need to

- Establish an interactive, interdependent relationship between the technical and publishing processes

- Involve both technical and publications staff at key meetings
- Enter the publications process at points where the most results can be achieved while conserving time and effort

Cooperation is not difficult when the technical and publications staff are aware of and informed about the required interaction. Planning based on the parallel relationship of the technical and communication processes is, of course, an important ingredient. But so are management's efforts to provide support, to establish standards, and to direct the communication process itself. Too often managers touch the process only at the beginning when they make a vague assignment and at the end when they review the writing produced. Such ineffective direction and input into the process often leads to less-than-satisfactory reports. More time is often wasted making changes during review than would be required to direct the process itself.

In a 1971 article in the *Journal of Technical Writing and Communication* [11], I identified the four most effective checkpoints for intervention (see Figure 3).

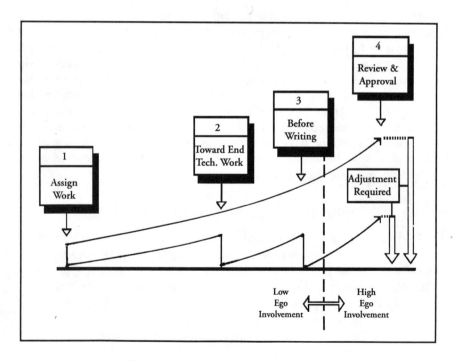

Figure 3. Checkpoints for intervention.

The first checkpoint is at the beginning of the project when work is being assigned. At this point the publications manager relates the technical and the writing assignments, focusing on task analysis, establishing deadlines, and discussing purpose, use, and readers. A memo from publications staff should define their view of the task analysis and include a needs assessment and a list of required documentation.

The second checkpoint is during the technical work but before it ends. Here publications and technical staff review the collected information and its proposed organization and determine what is important and what remains to be done before the major writing activity starts.

The third checkpoint is just before the writing starts. Publications and technical staffs agree on document content, parts, and structure. Publications staff prepare an outline of the document to be written, providing organization and emphasis and indicating staff roles.

At checkpoint four the publications staff provide a copy of the written document. Review and user-testing take place; necessary changes are identified, including additions, deletions, and reorganization. Presentational standards (style and format) are applied. A final copy is prepared for approval and publication.

The number of conferences at each checkpoint depends on project size, complexity, and importance. Nevertheless, these four checkpoints remain the most effective entry points for monitoring and managing the process. They tend to provide the greatest productivity and best control for the least amount of time and effort on the part of both staff and management.

Too often when technical work assignments also involve writing, managers tend to concentrate on the technical assignment and omit the writing assignment. When the writing and publishing are seen as the activity of a special communication group, these tasks are often totally separated from any consideration at the time the technical work is assigned. Yet, even then, managers set both processes in motion, and the highly interactive relationship between the processes requires that both be integrated from the very beginning. Publications groups must be included from the very beginning of technical work assignments if the parallel processes are to function effectively. Otherwise, writing becomes a tag-on operation. Managers also need to realize that when they make assignments, what they perceive as the work to be done often differs from the work the staff perceives. If such a difference exists at the beginning of the process, it will only become larger as the work progresses.

The four directing checkpoints provide managers with the ability

- to identify the difference in the views of the assignment that exists at the beginning of the project
- to monitor and reduce the drift between these views that occurs during the process

- to direct the process so as to reduce the amount of adjustment required at the end, during review and approval

The task is always to increase mutual understanding and to build consensus at each point during the process. All this will reduce the adjustment required during review and approval where change is always difficult and time-consuming because of the ego involvement of the writer and the pending deadline.

Both writers and managers must realize that well-directed activity saves time for everybody. Although four—or more—conferences sound rather time-consuming, the total time devoted to the problems of document overhaul during review and approval is frequently greater and certainly more emotionally charged than the time required for the conferences. But, just as important, this common view of the writing task contributes significantly to the quality of the product and the efficiency of the process—especially if publications managers at the same time add a common understanding of standards to be met and goals to be achieved. Using this particular procedure not only produces better documents, but also increases the number of documents finished on time. The emphasis on process planning and monitoring forces both managers and writers to complete work that otherwise they tend to put off, and the sharing of perspective between publications managers and staff fosters staff growth and development because it makes writing an integral part of the total work of the organization. Writing takes on a relevancy and relatedness, and technical and publications managers and staff become members of the same team.

REFERENCES

1. J. S. Dumas, Stimulating Change Through Usability Testing, *SIGCHI Bulletin, 21*:1, pp. 37-44, 1989.
2. J. T. Hackos, Managing Creative People, *Technical Communication, 37*:4, pp. 375-380, 1990.
3. P. Hartley, Writing for Industry: The Presentational Mode Versus the Reflective Mode, *Technical Writing Teacher, 18*:2, pp. 162-166, 1991.
4. J. R. Nelson, *Writing the Technical Report,* McGraw, New York (1st Edition) 1940, (2nd Edition) 1947.
5. J. W. Souther, Applying the Engineering Method to Report Writing, *Machine Design, 24*:12, pp. 114-118, December 1952.
6. J. W. Souther and M. L. White, *Technical Report Writing,* John Wiley, New York (1st Edition) 1957, (2nd Edition) 1977.
7. L. Flower and J. Hayes, Problem-Solving Strategies and the Writing Process, *College English, 39*:4, pp. 449-461, 1977.
8. L. Flower, *Problem-Solving Strategies for Writing,* Harcourt Brace Jovanovich, Inc., New York, 1981.
9. J. C. Mathes and D. W. Stevenson, *Designing Technical Reports,* Bobbs-Merrill Educational Publishing, Indianapolis, 1976.

10. R. A. Grice, Verifying Technical Information: Issues in Information-Development Collaboration, in *Collaborative Writing in Industry: Investigations in Theory and Practice*, M. M. Lay and W. M. Karis (eds.), Baywood Publishing Company, Amityville, New York, pp. 224-241, 1991.
11. J. W. Souther, The Technical Supervisor and the Writing Process, *Journal of Technical Writing and Communication, 1*:3, pp. 193-202, 1971.

CHAPTER 2

Designing Noise Audits to Improve Managerial-Employee Communication

RENEE B. HOROWITZ and ROBERT V. PELTIER

Publications managers have a responsibility that extends beyond the production of an organization's written communication. They also must be concerned with interpersonal communication within the publications unit. And where organizational policies permit, they may contribute to improved written and oral communication between managers and employees throughout an organization.

As companies move beyond the earliest stage of quality improvement, concern with manufactured products, they realize the need to expand the concept beyond its original boundaries. Many companies now are involved in simultaneous engineering, total quality management, or other programs to compete globally by improving productivity and quality. Organizations are looking at new areas of improvement such as customer service, communication in the form of technical proposals and presentations, and employee relations. To ensure the success of such programs, managers also must come to grips with the importance of improving managerial-employee communication.

More than a decade ago, Roger D'Aprix, the president of Organizational Communication Services and former manager of employee communication at Xerox, linked proactive communication with improved organizational productivity [1]. Although D'Aprix acknowledges that companies cannot entirely eliminate reactive communication, he insists that most organizations can deal with major issues or concerns of their employees proactively and offers a model for such communication. D'Aprix also includes in his book a question and answer section that pinpoints the necessity for communication professionals to lead their companies in improving managerial-employee communication.

More recent research by D'Aprix and others [2, 3] shows that management in industry is out of touch with employees and points to the relationship between communication and employee turnover [4]. Studies also indicate other areas of employee dissatisfaction with corporate communication:

> The "up" of two-way communication is still missing, resulting in a failure to build shared understanding between employees and management of what needs to be done to move the organization forward. Programs are in good shape, but the process needs attention [5, p. 101].

Conversely, researchers have found a measurable correlation between good managerial communication and employee satisfaction [6].

Thus, companies must find ways to reduce or remove factors that interfere with communication between management and employees. Experienced managers are aware that these blocks must be eliminated for their companies to achieve world-class status, but they may be unable or unwilling to change. To resolve this problem, managers must reduce adversarial relationships and achieve other communication improvements by increased training, clarification of expectations, early employee involvement in such areas as implementation of new technology and process development, and more job autonomy in decision making. These areas require changes in company policy that are beyond the reach of most technical communicators or publication managers. However, our expertise as communicators can prove valuable in limiting psychological factors that interfere with the communication process.

Publications managers must first convince upper management that the challenge of improving the communication process is also a means of effecting improvements in both productivity and quality. To do so, we need to show management that interference with the process goes beyond the physical or technical blocks generally depicted in communication models. The term "noise" is used to designate physical or technical blocks to communication such as garbled transmissions or static, but psychological noise can be a greater barrier to oral and written communication. Managers need to understand how psychological noise is created and how it can be attenuated. They also need to realize which activities tend to amplify rather than lessen psychological barriers to communication (see Figure 1).

Many companies have used communication audits as management tools since the concept was introduced nearly forty years ago by George S. Odiorne [7]. Odiorne saw communication within an organization as a new frontier and modified a National Society of Professional Engineers' format to conduct a communication audit. His purpose was to determine the effectiveness of managerial-employee communication rather than its quality. Among the audit questions were those asking whether the engineers believed they had a part in

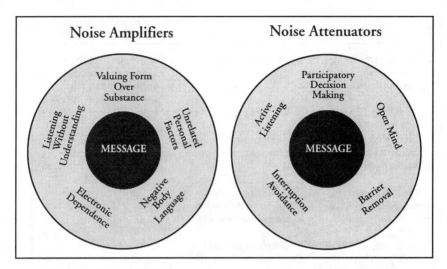

Figure 1. External influences on manager-employee communications.

management, planning, and departmental meetings. They were also asked which information channels were adequate and where improvement was needed. Management predicted employee responses, and these predictions were compared with the engineers' answers. Results of the audit showed little correlation between management predictions and employee responses [7].

Since Odiorne's attempt at a communication audit, several standardized audit instruments have become available: the LTT Audit System of the Helsinki Research Institute for Business Economics, the Organizational Communication Development (OCD) Procedure, and the International Communication (ICA) Audit System. Of these three systems, the ICA is most often used by U.S. organizations. However, communication specialists within organizations often prefer to design their own audit instruments in accordance with the specific company culture [8].

This chapter proposes that publications managers participate in designing "noise audits" to identify problem areas and successful areas in managerial-employee communication. Such noise audits will identify those elements that amplify psychological noise and those elements that attenuate it, provide feedback to managers, and promote continuous improvement in communication skills.

Figure 2 is a model checklist that can be used to audit noise levels of managerial-employee communication. The following discusses each of the items in the checklist and suggests specific ways to improve managerial-employee communication within a company.

Does the Corporation:	Does the Manager:	Does the Employee:
❑ Make the policies and procedures of the organization known?	❑ Understand and not just listen?	❑ Understand the global context and situation of the organization and the specific communication activity?
❑ Place a high priority on active communication skills and effectiveness?	❑ Communicate in a positive manner?	❑ Look for ways to short-circuit organizational communication channels?
❑ Apply the correct communication technology?	❑ Probe for resolution of verbal-nonverbal communication imbalances?	❑ Trust the organizational leaders?
❑ Use a variety of media for employee communication?	❑ Display communication situational adaptability?	❑ Understand and subscribe to the corporate goals and purpose?
❑ Solicit and seriously consider employee feedback?	❑ Legitimize employee goals?	❑ Understand the employee place in the overall organization?
❑ Seek out and remove physical, social, and other barriers to communication?	❑ Deal with perceptions as well as facts?	❑ Believe everyone is treated fairly and without prejudice?
❑ Hold managers responsible for effective employee communication?	❑ Overcome the gravitational pull of downward communication?	❑ Work to promote the organizational goals?
❑ Provide training in communication skills?	❑ Understand the importance of facial expressions and other body language?	❑ Believe managers provide information that is required to do the job?
❑ Have a method to assess organizational communication effectiveness?	❑ Achieve a balance among oral, written, and electronic communication?	❑ Believe upward communication is possible and desired?
❑ Effectively communicate the organizational vision for the future?	❑ Minimize upward-communication red tape?	❑ Believe supervisors properly recognize support of active communication?

Figure 2. A three-part check list acts as a guide to audit noise levels of managerial-employee communications.

AMPLIFICATION OF COMMUNICATION BARRIERS

Within an industrial environment, effective managers are aware of factors that tend to amplify managerial-employee barriers: valuing form over substance, the influence of factors unrelated to the message, negative body language, listening without understanding, and dependence on electronic communication. These factors are described below.

Valuing Form Over Substance

Effective managers realize the importance of providing substantial information to employees. Ineffective managers are more concerned about the medium than the message. Three-dimensional pie charts and multicolor newsletters are not as important as the factors that determine continued productivity and profits. Some managers hold lengthy meetings or write long memos to impress subordinates and superiors. It is not unusual to find little hard information in such meetings or memos. Yet, substantive communication is particularly important today to minimize deteriorating morale as companies downsize. For those employees who remain, downsizing creates stress that affects their performance. Managers must actively raise morale by establishing a dialogue with employees to make sure their anxieties are voiced and understood [9].

During the introduction of new technology, substantive communication is also necessary. One author recently interviewed a successful plant manager to find how he maintains plant productivity while introducing high technology equipment that may reduce the workforce. This manager's approach is to make himself the source of all rumors rather than to allow rumors to originate elsewhere. In other words, he immediately communicates to the workforce what is happening by personally meeting with each shift and making himself available for questions. Thus, he avoids the anticipation and anxiety that result from failure to get substantive information, anxiety that could prove more detrimental to productivity than impending layoffs.

Influence of Factors Unrelated to the Message

Effective managers are aware that delivery style, gender, ethnicity, education, culture, or language can influence the effectiveness of their message. For example, some managers may feel threatened when employees from other cultures intrude on their space. Managers who are aware that such behavior is the cultural norm for an employee avoid letting it inhibit communication. Effective managers know that stereotypes can interfere with the reception of a message. Studies have shown that when the same message supposedly originated with people of different backgrounds, the receivers of these messages interpreted them differently [8].

Another factor that may influence the way managers communicate information to their employees is the belief that information is power. As a result, some managers are uncomfortable sharing information with others in the organization [10]. Thus sales, quality, and productivity figures may be kept from employees. With today's corporate emphasis on total quality management, effective managers understand employee need for this information.

Effective managers look beyond personality and other subjective factors in evaluating employee communications. They are aware that when a message involves issues of personal importance to supervisor, employee, or both, managers must avoid becoming emotionally deaf [8].

Body Language

Effective managers are aware of the importance of positive body language. The familiar arms-crossed stance is an example of negative body language. Researchers tell of a manager who habitually rolled his eyes, shook his head, or sighed while listening to his employees [11]. Productivity suffered because employees felt this manager had no respect for them or for their opinions. Studies indicate that if "employees report organizational climates deficient in these so-called 'soft' areas, the company can expect to bear significantly higher bottom-line costs in the area of employee sickness and accident compensation costs" [11, p. 66].

The first step in overcoming negative body language is to develop self-awareness of individual gestures and facial expressions and their impact on productivity. With this awareness, managers can make a conscious effort to change to more positive body language.

Listening without Understanding

Some observers have found that effective communication between supervisors and employees goes beyond the physiological act of hearing or comprehension of the spoken word to a higher plane of understanding [12]. Understanding must include the ability to place the communication in a proper frame of reference within a societal and corporate organization; within the personalities, capabilities, and shortcomings of those involved; and within the social and personal ethics, morality, and trustworthiness the receiver of the message perceives in the players. When these elements do not exist, a breakdown between listening and understanding occurs, diminishing trust. When prior communications have been fair and equitable, resulting in successful understanding and successful results, then trust develops in the manager-employee relationship.

Dependence on Electronic Communication

Effective managers are aware of the importance of face-to-face communication. A disturbing trend is the prevalence of voice mail and e-mail in many companies today. Some managers now use voice mail as their primary medium of communication with employees, ostensibly to save time. In direct opposition to such techniques as management by walking around, this reliance on technology depersonalizes manager-employee communication. In fact, studies show that despite advances in communication technology, productive managers tend to prefer face-to-face communication [13]. Research indicates a positive relationship between productivity and media selection; managers with higher performance ratings are more aware of this relationship than other managers and tend to use face-to-face communication, particularly for equivocal situations.

Another survey asked employees which company action did most to improve communication and productivity. In their response, 41 percent targeted regular meetings with employees. The next highest category, quality-improvement programs, scored only 20 percent [14]. It is too early to determine the overall effect of limiting face-to-face communication, but clearly it is another way that management remains out of touch with employees. Thus managers should not substitute electronic for personal communication.

ATTENUATION OF
PSYCHOLOGICAL NOISE

Managers whose subordinates consider them to be excellent communicators seem to share certain characteristics. These managers tend to attenuate the psychological noise in their communications by encouraging participatory decision making, keeping an open mind and listening with a conscious positive attitude, removing obvious barriers to communication, minimizing outside interruptions, and keeping an open-door policy.

Encouraging Participatory Decision Making

Managers who are open to new ideas find their employees tend to make more suggestions and actively participate in improvement of quality and service. Much has been written recently about participatory management. Research shows that such participation is important for engineers and other technical personnel [4]. In a technical environment, a free and open flow of ideas and concerns is particularly beneficial, as technical details may be complex and tightly interrelated between disciplines. Small details ignored or unresolved can have dramatic impact on individuals and the entire organization, as the well-known story of NASA's stifling dissent about o-ring design and the resulting Challenger tragedy shows. Organizational communication channels must be open, and a free stream of information must be made available to decision makers to pinpoint technical strengths and weaknesses within the firm and to give an accurate view of its competitive position.

Keeping an Open Mind and Listening with a Conscious Positive Attitude

Managers should orient themselves toward accepting rather than rejecting employee ideas. They must learn how to listen in such a way that mutual understanding is achieved. As E. A. Herda and D. S. Messerschmitt point out, "A manager skilled in communication is one who knows how to listen and can utilise the power of language as a resource to bring employees to their full creative capacities. . . . This requires commitment and time" [12, p. 24]. We might add that good listening skills are not easy to acquire. Although some managers have developed such skills without formal training, this is a major area in which training can provide visible improvement.

Removing Obvious Barriers to Communication

One way to remove obvious communication barriers is to downplay the superior-subordinate relationship. Traditionally, communication within an organization has meant downward communication, and this is still true. Unfortunately, downward communication generally does not allow for employee feedback; it may also result in distortion of the message. On the other hand, those organizations that encourage upward communication may find improvement in employee morale [8].

The distances that organization charts place between managers and employees also block free and open communication. Such communication fences are common in larger organizations that implement systems and procedures to maintain consistency. Larger companies seem to perpetuate a legalistic environment where "send me a memo" or "call a meeting" are typical responses. One author recalls a past supervisor's favorite saying: "If it's not in writing, it doesn't exist." Such an attitude with subordinates tends to amplify the static quality of communication. Within small organizations, quick conversations with supervisors or managers can provide necessary direction. Larger organizations need to provide a similar culture where employees are not bound by strict organizational lines.

At W. L. Gore & Associates, for example, a "lattice" organization eliminates communication barriers by empowering all employees to communicate across traditional lines. Any Gore employee may communicate directly with any other individual in the organization; employees are not limited by a structured chain of command [15]. Publications managers can also help to lower communication fences by influencing management to use a more humanistic and consistent corporate style when written communication with employees is unavoidable.

Minimizing External Interruptions

By giving complete attention to the conversation, managers remove any sense that employees are competing for their attention; employees perceive that such supervisors are approachable. "Being approachable means that you are seen as receptive and concerned; that you will give people your undivided attention and that they will be 'heard,' no matter what's on their minds" [16, p. 30]. Further, employees are more likely to come to such managers with important matters that they might otherwise fear to communicate.

Keeping an Open-Door Policy

Effective managers do not allow their prejudices and emotions to interfere with open communication. When management experts first recommended the open-door policy, they used anecdotal information as the primary basis for their recommendations. Today, although we still do not find much empirical research, some studies indicate that employees consider such a climate of open communication an important factor in improving their performance [17].

Resistance to open-door communication often comes from first-level supervisors who are concerned that their subordinates will bypass them in the chain of command. One way to avoid this problem is to bring the lower-level supervisor into the picture. However, such a policy could limit employee willingness to use the open door [17].

Particularly within technical organizations, managers may resist involvement with aspects of human relations that they consider "touchy-feely." For scientific or technical white-collar professionals, researchers have shown that managers must provide autonomy or decentralized goal setting and professional enhancement or self-actualization. Improved management training that refines human relations skills is a must for such managers [4]. Even though a managerial job has been described as 30 to 70 percent face-to-face communication, interpersonal communication skills seem to be less well developed among managers in the scientific and technical community than in other employment communities [18]. These supervisors and managers should be encouraged to look to the technical communicators within their companies as resources for improving their interpersonal communication skills.

TECHNICAL COMMUNICATORS AS FACILITATORS

Although job descriptions for technical communicators and publications managers rarely, if ever, include formulating and implementing improvements in managerial-employee communication, clearly new opportunities exist along these lines. When one of the authors of this chapter began as a technical writer (euphemistically called a "senior documentation engineer") in the aerospace industry, writers and editors were not invited to strategy sessions before and during proposal preparation. Management has since discovered that the professional skills of writers and editors go beyond the clichéd insertion of commas and checking of spelling: developing document strategy has become a new, challenging aspect of the writer's job.

Today, when management's quest for continuous improvement has spread from the manufacturing process to such concerns as the quality of documents and presentations, technical communicators must be ready to make their unique contributions to another area in which improvement is needed: managerial-employee communication.

REFERENCES

1. R. D'Aprix, *Communicating for Productivity*, Harper and Row, New York, 1982.
2. R. D'Aprix, The Communication Gap, *IABC Communication World, 9*:1, pp. 30-31, 1992.
3. B. R. Schlender, Yet Another Strategy for Apple, *Fortune, 122*:10, pp. 81-85, 1990.
4. J. D. Sherman, Technical Supervision and Turnover among Engineers and Technicians, *Group & Organizational Studies, 14*:4, pp. 411-421, 1989.
5. J. Foehrenbach and S. Goldfarb, Employee Communication in the '90s: Great(er) Expectations, *IABC Communication World, 7*:5-6, pp. 101-106, 1990.
6. B. Whitworth, Proof at Last, *IABC Communication World, 7*:12, pp. 28-31, 1990.
7. G. S. Odiorne, An Application of the Communications Audit, *Personnel Psychology, 7*, pp. 235-243, Summer 1954.
8. P. V. Lewis, Auditing Organizational Communication, in *Organizational Communication: The Essence of Effective Management*, John Wiley and Sons, New York, pp. 261-288, 1987.
9. D. Jacobs, Maintaining Morale during and after Downsizing, *Management Solutions, 30*, pp. 5-13, 1985.
10. A. L. Smith, Getting Managers off Their Butts and into the Communication Game, *IABC Communication World, 9*:1, pp. 32-37, 1992.
11. M. S. Sashkin and R. L. Williams, Does Fairness Make a Difference? *Organizational Dynamics, 19*:2, pp. 56-71, 1990.
12. E. A. Herda and D. S. Messerschmitt, From Words to Actions: Communication for Business Management, *Leadership & Organization Development Journal, 12*:1, pp. 23-27, 1991.
13. G. S. Russ, R. L. Daft, and R. H. Lengel, Media Selection and Managerial Characteristics in Organization Communications, *Management Communication Quarterly, 4*:2, pp. 151-175, 1990.
14. A. B. Fisher, CEOs Think That Morale Is Dandy, *Fortune, 124*:12, pp. 83-96, 1991.
15. L. Rhodes, The Un-Manager, *Inc., 4*:8, pp. 34-43, 1982.
16. S. R. Axley, The Practical Qualities of Effective Leaders, *Industrial Management, 32*:5, pp. 29-30, 1990.
17. A. Shenhar, Improving Upward Communication Through Open-Door Policies, *Human Systems Management, 9*:2, pp. 77-88, 1990.
18. R. V. Rasmussen, A Communication Model Based on the Conduit Metaphor, *Management Communication Quarterly, 4*:3, pp. 363-374, 1991.

CHAPTER 3

Technical Communication Models That Ensure Productive Meetings

MARIAN G. BARCHILON

A growing trend in industry is more and longer meetings. As firms compete aggressively for markets and scarce resources, they place a premium on organizational adaptation and on obtaining fast, accurate information. Because modern organizations require more project teams and task forces to handle the constant change, meetings are necessary to coordinate and control organizational tasks [1, pp. 13-15]. Moreover, with the shift from an authoritarian to a participative style of management, managers are finding meetings essential to group analysis and decision making [2, p. 15].

At the same time that meetings are becoming increasingly essential in the business environment, business leaders complain that at least one-third of the time they spend in meetings is wasted [2, p. 22]. There is little doubt that companies must improve their meeting skills to compete in a global economy [3, p. 3].

Given these facts, publications managers and other professional communicators have a unique opportunity to become meeting communication experts. By using the agenda and meeting-minutes models described in this chapter, they can manage their own meetings and assist other managers in ensuring productive, cost-effective meetings.

WHY MEETINGS ARE UNPRODUCTIVE

Surveys conducted in 1982 and 1986 by R. K. Mosvick and R. B. Nelson revealed 1305 meeting problems, which they condensed into twenty-five specific categories. The top sixteen problems, listed in rank order, are not adhering to the agenda, not having goals or agenda, excessive length, poor or inadequate preparation, inconclusiveness, disorganization, ineffective leadership/lack of control, irrelevance of information discussed, wasting time during meetings, starting late, ineffectiveness for making decisions, interruptions from within and without, individuals dominating/aggrandizing discussion, rambling/redundant or digressive discussion, absence of published results or follow-up actions, and failure to provide premeeting orientation or cancelled or postponed meetings [1, p. 19].

W. A. Green and H. Lazarus report a direct relationship between productive meetings and preparatory elements used for those meetings. The most productive meetings are characterized by timely written agendas, previously understood outcomes, and well-prepared attendees [2, p. 18].

THE AGENDA AND
MEETING MINUTES MODELS

To prevent or overcome the meeting problems listed above, I propose the use of two structured models that assure greater meeting productivity. These models focus on the critical front-end (agenda) and back-end (meeting minutes) stages of the meeting process. Depending on the corporate climate, the models can launch publications managers and professional communicators into new roles as meeting communication experts.

The Agenda Model

The agenda model has three sections: objective, problem, and input. The objective section specifies the meeting's purpose and helps determine whether the meeting is needed. The problem section defines problems or issues to be discussed. The input section indicates what information the attendees should provide for the meeting. Of course, the model also includes all information commonly recommended by meeting experts: who will attend, where and when the meeting will take place, and how long it will be held (start and end times). To show how the model works, we need first to examine a typical meeting agenda that does not apply the model's elements (see Figure 1).

A. Jones, the Director of the ABC Museum and the meeting's facilitator, first drafted the agenda shown in Figure 1. In addition to minor omissions—the location and end time of the meeting—the agenda fails in three key areas:

- It does not establish a clear objective for the meeting.
- It does not raise problems or issues to be discussed.
- It does not specify whether any input or premeeting preparation is required of the attendees.

To understand why these areas are important, we must analyze the parts of the model in the context of meeting research.

MEETING AGENDA

To: Aaron, Abraham, Dill, Header, Jones, Lee, Maxim, Nath, Paul, Rose, Toolan, Turner, Williams, Yellow, Zell

From: A. Jones

Date: Thursday, August 26, 1993

Subject: Membership Problems meeting on August 31, 1993, at 9 a.m.

I look forward to seeing you at this important meeting.

Figure 1. A typical agenda.

The Meeting Objective

The 3M Meeting Management Team claims that one should never begin a meeting without a well-written agenda, the meeting's "blueprint" [4, p. 41]. To prepare for the meeting, the 3M Team recommends that the person responsible for arranging the meeting write a single sentence to state the meeting objective. That sentence, in turn, becomes the opening statement of the agenda [4, p. 43]. Likewise, C. W. Burleson suggests a "meeting mandate," a clear and defined notion of what to accomplish at the meeting [3, p. 3]. Such an objective statement not only helps focus the meeting, but also reflects a key communication principle: know your purpose.

The best objective statement uses action verbs such as "inform," "decide," or "solve." A clear objective statement defines the problems and the required input. Further, in writing the objective clearly, the person responsible for the meeting can determine whether another communication tool (e.g., a memo) might be more appropriate than the meeting.

For example, in Figure 1, Jones's memo has a subject, but not a stated objective. Jones does not indicate whether the meeting will be presentational (e.g., report, new product, information), involving one-way communication, or interactive (working) (e.g., problem-solving, decision-making, fact-finding), involving collaboration. If Jones envisions one-way communication, in which she will communicate the membership problems and/or direct action to correct them, then the action words in the objective should be "to communicate" and "to direct." The action words are the key that no attendee input is required, and they may signal to Jones that a memo would be a better communication vehicle than a meeting.

If, however, Jones wants to obtain information from the museum staff or wants to encourage them to discuss the membership problem, then she should rewrite the objective. Jones knows, after further review, that membership and revenue are not growing as quickly as anticipated. Therefore, she wants the meeting to focus on how to increase membership and revenues, and she needs information from the

---

MEETING AGENDA

To Attend: ——

From: ——

Today's Date: Thursday, August 26, 1993

Meeting Date: Tuesday, August 31, 1993

Time: 9-11 a.m.

Place: Board Room

Objective: To examine ways to increase Museum membership and revenue.

Figure 2. An agenda with a focused objective.

staff to help the museum solve its problem. This objective, which points to a problem-solving/fact-finding (working) meeting, requires two- or multiway communication with the staff. Given this situation, Figure 2 shows how the agenda can be revised to be more focused, well organized, and action oriented.

The Problem

The rewritten agenda is still incomplete, however, because it does not yet address the problem(s), or mention what premeeting input is required from the attendees. In this example, the problem is simple: each department must show how it can help meet the objective. It may be difficult, however, to state this as a single problem because it entails several smaller ones. In such a case, the 3M Team recommends developing a series of logically ordered steps to appear as separate problems in the agenda [4].

The Required Input

Now that the objective and problem are stated, the attendees also need to know what input is required of them. If they do not understand or have no indication of any required premeeting preparation, they will probably not contribute much and the meeting will be less productive. In this example, Jones wants specific information from the departments to help her achieve an objective. In particular, she wants new types of exhibits, new lectures and films, new tours and affiliations with other educational institutions, and the like. The revised agenda, which now incorporates all agenda model elements, appears in Figure 3.

Because this agenda now incorporates all the elements of the model, i.e., a clearly defined objective, a stated problem, and a request for input, it should produce an efficient and productive meeting.

The Meeting Minutes Model

The meeting minutes model, which should be used in advance as a template to keep the meeting on track, has five sections: issue, discussion, decision(s), follow-up, and postmeeting-action matrix. The issue section provides a proposed solution to the problem or an issue to be addressed. The discussion section highlights the attendees' discussion of the proposed solution or the issue. The decision(s) section states what decisions were reached and by whom, providing additional detail (e.g., dates, costs) when necessary. The follow-up section details what happens next. For example, if the attendees made a decision, this section specifies what steps must be taken to implement it. If, however, the attendees did not reach a decision, this section outlines what information is still required. Finally, the postmeeting-action matrix section summarizes the key information generated from the follow-up section.

MEETING AGENDA

To Attend: ——

From: ——

Today's Date ——

Meeting Date ——

Time: ——

Place: ——

Objective: ——

Problem: Let's determine how each department can contribute to the objective.

Input: **Director's Office**
-overall view of current status
Curatorial
-new types of exhibits
Communications
-new lectures, films, etc.
Education
-new tours, new affiliations with other educational institutions
Friends
-new mailing lists to local organizations, membership drives
Finance
-impact of more memberships, higher fees
Security
-concerns, if any

Figure 3. An agenda using the model.

ABC Museum's Membership and Revenue Meeting Minutes
Tuesday, August 31, 1993
9-11 a.m., Board Room

Attendees: Abraham, Dill, Header, Jones, Lee, Nath, Paul, Rose, Toolan, Turner, Yellow, Zell

Absentees: Aaron, Maxim, Williams

- Jones reviewed the annual budgets that showed the Museum needs to increase its revenue and the number of paying members.

- Jones turned the meeting over to the curatorial staff to recommend new exhibits that would attract more Museum visitors.

- Header suggested an exhibit on 19th Century German paintings since we have a large German population in our area. Many of the paintings are available in our collection and some are available from collectors in our area. He indicated our exhibition schedule is open from September 21 - November 9, 1994.

• • •

- Header also suggested a Contemporary Local Artists exhibit like the one held five years before, which attracted more than 500 new members. Header is collecting information about contemporary local artists.

- Header will collect and present information about contemporary local artists at the next meeting, on September 14, 1993

• • •

- Prints and Drawing is getting ready for the Styles Collection that opens September 9. Lee stated that if Publicity publicizes this show more, the Museum would enhance its revenues.

Figure 4. Typical meeting minutes.

- Nath and Paul agreed with Lee, but indicated there was no more room in this month's Magazine for information about the collection. Other departments also expressed similar concerns about lack of publicity for their exhibits.

- Jones recommended that priorities for publicity be discussed at the next Communications Department meeting on September 15, 1993. Jones suggested all curatorial staff be invited to attend.

- Header will provide Abraham with a list of attendees for the next Communications Department meeting on September 15, 1993, to discuss priorities in publicity.

- Rose discovered three new films are available from City University's collection: "Picasso's Blue Period," "An Interview with Andy Warhol," and "The Romanticism of Caspar David Friedrich." The films about Picasso and Warhol are available anytime during the next five weeks, but the Friedrich film is always available. All films can be borrowed at no cost to the Museum.

• • •

- Rose will arrange with City University to reserve the Friedrich film from September 21, 1994, to November 9, 1994.

- All attendees asked to see the complete list of available films.

- Rose will complete the list of available films (including those that are not free) and distribute the list to all departments prior to the next meeting on September 14, 1993.

Figure 4. (continued).

Again, like the agenda model, the meeting-minutes model includes all information commonly recommended by meeting experts: who attended, who was absent, where and when the meeting took place, and the start and end times. In addition, however, it classifies the attendees by department so the reader can see who represented the group. To show how the model works, we need to examine a typical meeting minutes document that does not apply the model's elements (see Figure 4).

While the meeting minutes shown in Figure 4 provide a step-by-step record of what transpired, their weak organization does not enable the attendees to retrieve important information quickly. In addition to unsuccessfully showing who represented what department, the minutes fail in three key areas:

- They do not highlight how each agenda issue was followed.
- They do not clearly identify what decisions were or were not reached.
- They do not easily delineate what follow-up was required, by whom, and by what date.

In fact, the meeting minutes simply serve as an unaltered transcript of what appears to be a series of discussions.

To understand the importance of these omissions, we must analyze the parts of the model.

The Issue Section

Because readers need to see how the meeting minutes tie to the agenda, an issue section is necessary. The issue section follows the agenda's established pattern of organization. In fact, the agenda's input section mirrors the meeting minutes' issue section, reflecting that each speaker proposes a solution to the problem or addresses the issue. Thus, the issue section establishes a clear relationship between the agenda and meeting minutes, and it helps readers find information quickly.

The Discussion Section

The discussion section, which appeared to be the entire meeting record in Figure 4, is only a small part of the meeting minutes. This section simply documents the attendees' discussion of the issue or proposed solution; it is a place where readers can find the attendees' contributions.

The Decision(s) Section

The decision(s) section is critical because it identifies what decisions were reached and by whom, providing additional detail only when necessary. Readers need to retrieve this information quickly because meeting decisions often result in additional work or responsibility.

The Follow-Up and Postmeeting-Action Matrix Sections

The follow-up and postmeeting-action matrix sections are related in that they specify what tasks are required after the meeting. As stated previously, if a decision was reached, the follow-up section mentions what steps are required to implement it. However, if no decision was reached, it highlights what information is still required to make the decision. The postmeeting-action matrix extracts key information from the follow-up section and summarizes it in a table. The meeting minutes in Figure 4, which did not contain either the follow-up or postmeeting-action matrix sections, veil any required follow-up actions. These minutes force readers to search the entire meeting record to uncover these postmeeting responsibilities. In contrast, the meeting minutes in Figure 5 illustrate how the minutes can be revised to include the follow-up and postmeeting-action matrix sections.

As we can see, the text used in the meeting notes without the model (Figure 4) and with the model (Figure 5) is similar. Yet the two function as very different documents because of their structures. Figure 4 appears to provide only discussion material; if the readers need particular information, they must read the entire meeting record. In contrast, Figure 5 provides readers with a clear roadmap. It rearranges the information in well-labeled sections so readers can find information quickly.

Moreover, the meeting-minutes model can also help guide the person who manages the meeting, the attendees, and the meeting recorder if they know in advance that the format is the meeting-minutes template. Using the model in this way, meeting participants understand they must focus on specific issues, discuss only what is relevant, make decisions that apply to the objective, and accept responsibility for following up on tasks. Thus, the meeting-minutes model, like the agenda model, keeps the meeting on track and produces results.

Because meetings tend to imitate the state of management art, the pressure is on to make them more efficient [5, p. 37]. The agenda and meeting-minutes models described here help communicators achieve this goal by showing practical ways to apply communication skills to the critical front- and back-end of the meeting process. These structured, yet flexible, models work effectively because their designs intrinsically target and solve the major meeting problems: unclear objectives, inadequate preparation/premeeting orientation, lack of control, and absence of published results or follow-up actions. Use of these models can ensure more productive and cost-effective meetings.

ABC Museum's Membership and Revenue Meeting Minutes
Tuesday, August 31, 1993
9-11 a.m., Board Room

Attendees:	Director's Office: Jones
Finance: Turner
Friends: Toolan
Security: Zell
Curatorial Division:
Header, Lee
Communications Division:
Abraham, Dill, Nath, Paul, Rose
Education Division:
Yellow
Absentees:	——

Director's Office

Issue: Annual budgets-Jones
Reviewed the annual budgets that showed the Museum
needs to increase its revenue and the number of paying
members.

Turned the meeting over to the curatorial staff to
recommend new exhibits that would attract more
Museum visitors.

Curatorial Division

Issue: Painting exhibits-Header
Suggested we have an exhibit on 19th Century German
paintings since we have a large German population in
our area. Stated many of the paintings are available in
our collection and some are available from collectors in
our area. Indicated our exhibition schedule is open from
September 21 - November 9, 1994.

Suggested a Contemporary Local Artists exhibit like the
one held five years before, which attracted more than 500
new members. Header is collecting information about
contemporary local artists.

Discussion: Zell was concerned about possible crowd control and the
need for hiring more security guards.

Decision(s):   All attendees agreed the German exhibit would enhance
revenue, and that the Curatorial Division should prepare
for this exhibit, subject to Security's concerns.

Figure 5. Meeting minutes using the model.

Follow-up: Zell and Header will meet and project attendance, and decide whether the Museum needs additional security, and discuss the cost of additional staff. They will bring results to the next meeting, on September 14, 1993. Header will collect and present information about contemporary local artists at the next meeting, on September 14, 1993.

Issue: Prints and drawings exhibits - Lee
The Department is getting ready for the Styles Collection that opens September 9. Lee stated that if Publicity publicizes this show more, the Museum would enhance its revenues.

Discussion: Nath and Paul agreed with Lee, but indicated that there was no more room in this month's Magazine for information about the collection. Other departments also expressed similar concerns about lack of publicity for their exhibits.

Decision(s):   Jones recommended that priorities for publicity be discussed at the next Communications Department meeting on September 14, 1993. Jones suggested all curatorial staff be invited to attend.

[Note: Because this issue did not pertain directly to the agenda's objective, the facilitator was able to use the agenda as a control tool to curtail the discussion.]

Follow-up: Header will provide Abraham with a list of attendees for the next Communication meeting on September 14, 1993, to discuss priorities in publicity.

Communications

Issue: Lectures/Films - Rose
Rose discovered three new films are available from City University's collection: "Picasso's Blue Period," "An Interview with Andy Warhol," and "The Romanticism of Caspar David Friedrich." These films about Picasso and Warhol are available anytime during the next five weeks, but the Friedrich film is always available. All films can be borrowed at no cost to the Museum.

Rose is also compiling a more complete list of films available from City University and other nearby educational institutions.

Discussion: All agreed that our Museum members enjoy films about artists. Yellow pointed out that the lecture hall is booked for the next two months; therefore, the Picasso and

Figure 5. (continued).

Warhol films cannot be shown when they are available. Header, Dill, Abraham, and Rose indicated the Friedrich film would best be shown during the 19th Century German exhibit. Toolan indicated he would like to circulate the film list to current members and ask for their input on which to show. Turner pointed out the current budget permits expenditures of $10,000 for films during the current year, and last year's budgeted amount was not spent. Turner also suggested compiling a list of other films that may be more expensive but more attractive to Museum visitors.

All attendees asked to see the complete list of available films.

Decision(s):   All attendees decided that the Museum should not show the Picasso and Warhol films at this time. The Friedrich film should be reserved from September 21, 1994, through November 9, 1994.

Follow-up: Richard will arrange with City University to reserve the Friedrich film from September 21, 1994, through November 9, 1994.

Richard will complete the list of available films (including those that are not free) and distribute the list to all departments prior to the next meeting on September 14, 1993.

• • •

Postmeeting Action Matrix

Date	Action	Responsible Parties
9/14	Bring results of meeting on German exhibit and security staff needs to next meeting.	Zell, Header
9/14	Present information about local contemporary artists at next meeting.	Header
by 9/14	Provide Abraham with list of attendees for the Communications meeting on 9/14 (re: priorities for publicity).	Header
by 9/14	Distribute a completed list of available films to all departments.	Rose
ASAP	Reserve the Friedrich film (9/21/94 to 11/9/94) from City University.	Rose

Figure 5. (continued).

REFERENCES

1. R. K. Mosvick and R. B. Nelson, *We've Got to Start Meeting Like This! A Guide to Successful Meeting Management,* Scott, Foresman and Company, Glenview, Illinois, 1987.
2. W. A. Green and H. Lazarus, Are Today's Executives Meeting with Success? *Journal of Management Development, 10*:1, pp. 14-25, 1991.
3. C. W. Burleson, *Effective Meetings: The Complete Guide,* John Wiley and Sons, Inc., New York, 1990.
4. 3M Meeting Management Team, *How to Run Better Business Meetings: A Reference Guide for Managers,* M. Jewett and R. Margolies (eds.), McGraw-Hill Book Company, New York, 1987.
5. P. M. Tobia and M. C. Becker, Making the Most of Meeting Time, *Training and Development Journal, 44*:8, pp. 34-38, 1990.

SELECTED READING

Haggerty, A. G., Ineffective Meetings Waste Time and Money, *National Underwriter, 88,* pp. 8-9, 1984.

Katz, S. N., Power Skills for Effective Meetings, *Training and Development, 45*:7, pp. 53-56, 1991.

Kirkpatrick, D., Here Comes the Payoff from PCs, *Fortune, 125*:6, pp. 93-102, 1992.

Lant, J., Effective Meetings, *Business and Economic Review, 37*:4, pp. 22-24, 1991.

Maher, T. M., Who Says Meetings Are Time Wasters? *National Underwriter, 93*, pp. 9-11, 1989.

Schabacker, K., A Short Snappy Guide to Meaningful Meetings, *Working Woman, 16*:6, pp. 70-73, 1991.

Slezak, J. M., How to Conduct and Enjoy Effective Meetings, *The National Educational Secretary, 56*:4, pp. 8-10, 1991.

Volkema, R. J., and M. Avery, Power Behind the Pen: Developing the Role of an Active Meeting Recorder, *SAM Advanced Management Journal, 53*:3, pp. 45-48, 1988.

PART II

Management and Supervision

The four chapters in this section offer practical information for publications managers faced with the responsibility of hiring and training publications staff. In addition, for students and entry-level communication specialists, particularly upwardly mobile writers and editors, the essays offer insights into both what supervisors may expect from them and their responsibilities should they become supervisors.

The first essay, "Comprehending and Aligning Professionals and Publications Organizations" by Daniel L. Plung, a manager with the Westinghouse Savannah River Company, is about hiring publications professionals. Plung analyzes the personalities of three types of publications organizations and provides information useful to managers for recruiting and aligning publications staff within each type of organization.

John G. Bryan's essay, "Culture and Anarchy: What Publications Managers Should Know about *Us* and *Them*," turns from the responsibilities of staffing to those of training. Bryan, who teaches in the Professional Writing Program at the University of Cincinnati, brings his experience as a writer, editor, and manager to a discussion of the fallacies of popular texts on organizational culture. He acknowledges the publications manager's responsibility for assisting publications staff in adapting to corporate culture, and he offers advice to help managers recruit, train, and sustain new employees so they can function harmoniously and effectively within an organization's culture.

David L. Armbruster's "Hiring and Managing Editorial Freelancers" describes the advantages and disadvantages of hiring freelancers. Armbruster, who is head of scientific publications in the Department of Health Informatics at the University of Tennessee, Memphis, offers suggestions for finding and negotiating with freelancers and discusses some specific management issues associated with employing them.

"Managing Internships" by Jody Heiken, a publications professional at Los Alamos National Laboratory, describes ways that industry sponsors, academic technical communication programs, and students can benefit from a well-run internship program. The industry environment augments classroom theory and experience to the student's benefit, while the intersection of classroom and workplace makes for better-qualified workers and balanced up-to-date academic programs.

CHAPTER 4

Comprehending and Aligning Professionals and Publications Organizations

DANIEL L. PLUNG

Let me begin with a simple truth learned through fifteen years of establishing and managing publications departments: Not all publications organizations are alike. Yet, the principal differences are not those of expanding work volumes commonly cited as our rationalizations to upper management to justify our continued vitality. Neither are they the dazzling array of quaint acronyms and initialisms we trade with colleagues to attest to our burgeoning armory of hardware and software. Nor are they the intricately woven depictions of our intellectual fencing with technical staff, depictions that we use to capture the imaginations of young recruits eager to demonstrate their newly acquired talents. Rather, the principal differences are those of organizational personality.

ORGANIZATIONAL PERSONALITY:
AN EXECUTIVE TOUR

Personality, both individual and organizational, is a balance of who we are, what we intend ourselves to be, how we fit in and interact with the rest of the community, and how we portray ourselves to that community. To appreciate the concept of organizational personality, let's assume we have a large department that is currently administered by three publications managers, equally personable and each with the same educational credentials, comparable experience and paygrade, and similar scope of managerial responsibility. We're wandering the publications building, acquainting ourselves with the department—either because we are currently interviewing for a position in publications or because there's been a corporate realignment and this organization now reports to us.

All three managers are off to a meeting, but we decide to take a quick look at their offices anyway. The first manager's office offers us bookshelves of communication, grammar, and style manuals. Prominently displayed on the walls are an impressive collection of STC, IABC, and other publications awards.

As we enter the second manager's office we find a different landscape: books on computers, software, new technologies, and applications. Awards recognize the manager's singular contributions to advancing the communications field.

Entering the third manager's office we are greeted by an eclectic, seemingly unrelated host of literature and awards. In the places where the first manager had books on style and the second had computer literature, this manager has a strewn-about collection of technical manuscripts, aging reports, and books that, because of their ostensible failure to obey any essential integrational pattern, appear vaguely reminiscent of a college student's library. The awards he posts do not speak to excellence in established product categories or for advancing the discipline, but to participation in societies and endeavors not overtly applicable to publications activities.

Extrapolating from this portrait, we recognize the inherent organizational personality questions we share, whether corporate officer or prospective recruit: Which organization is the best? Which one do I want to associate with? The answers depend on which organizational personality is most effectively aligned with the corporation's and the recruit's personality. Or, to reiterate our stipulated definition of personality, which personality constitutes the best match of assumptions, expectations, and objectives?

ORGANIZATIONAL IDENTITIES: A DEFINITION

Evidently, we need to make the delineation among the three organizations—traditional, resource, and progressive—more transparent if we are to comprehend where our talents and ambitions are best applied.

Traditional Organization

The first of the three types of publications organizations is the one with which people are most familiar. This organization, which I refer to as the traditional organization, has as its major focus the production of a finite set of communication products such as reports and manuals. At the core of its philosophy is a belief that authors, for their own good, must be made to adhere to an established set of communication quality criteria and product specifications. To promote this mission, tools generated include style guides and basic reference materials—including glossaries and product templates. Yet, the successful introduction of these tools into the corporate culture is sometimes limited by the department's working relationship and interaction with management and customers.

Historically, the traditional organization has a distant working relationship with both the senior management that authorizes its budget and the customer base that sustains it: senior management staffs these publications offices not from a keen expectation of high payback but from a nebulous, visceral appreciation that an undefinable discrepancy exists between accepted communication norms (whatever they might be!) and the writing capability of the technical staff. This visceral sense of something potentially lacking in product quality has been reinforced and anecdotally validated to management in criticisms received consequent to their young engineers' presenting unintelligible papers at national conferences.

Therefore, the conservative stance becomes one of default sponsorship: "Might as well have one; everyone else does and it can't do us any harm, anyway." This conciliatory management endorsement is then directly captured and reflected in the tenuous, if not adversarial, relationship the publications group often maintains with its customer base: the sense that the department represents, at best, an administrative hurdle on the course to publication in the open or corporate literature, and, at worst, an enclave of dilettantish sophists who have no real comprehension of the precise nature of the company's mission or its technical communications.

And, were this uneasy balance not demeaning enough, traditional organizations in their fervor to improve external relations, often elicit further deprecation by diminishing the significance of their own standards. In practices such as Levels of Edit, where efforts are made to define tangible measures for the group's proper status in the corporate universe, what is advocated instead are arbitrary editorial hierarchies, hierarchies that implicitly mortgage professional standards against the technical organization's willingness to accede to the publications department's schedules and cost structures. This arbitrariness reinforces the doubting customer's belief that rather than having a corporate-mandated charter to establish, uphold, and enhance the company's standards, the publications unit actually has no firm position in the operating pantheon.

The jeopardy resulting is evident. If the charter is undefined and sponsorship minimal, continued vitality is predicated on maintaining a volume and scope of work the continued existence of which does not operationally or monetarily challenge any of the better-connected aspects of the operating world. For if that balance is upset, this group—as with other loosely sponsored support services—is perceived as immediately expendable without great consequence to the company. The ill-defined heritage is also what contributes to the moveability of the group, as the group regularly finds itself buffeted about with each major corporate reorganization.

Further, given the limited expectations the company has of the traditional organization, as might be expected, the majority of the staff is assigned to accomplish standard noninvasive editorial activities—editing text from within the anonymous confines of the publications building and coordinating work through the labyrinth of other publication services (e.g., printing, document control, records, and patent and security reviews). And, with this restricted environment, an understanding evolves, even if tacit, that the organizational opportunities are generally confined to those existing within the jurisdictional responsibility of the publications manager. These include 1) continued individual editorial assignments, 2) project leadership for technical communication assignments that may entail more than one editor or teams from the editing and document-composition areas, 3) resident technical-expert responsibilities that entail ownership of certain product categories or production methodologies, and 4) limited supervisory opportunity within the publications network.

Resource Organization

The second type of publications organization is what might best be characterized as a resource organization. Here the focus of publications work is conceptually different, largely in recognition that publications capabilities are now distributed throughout the corporation. In the current office configuration almost every professional and clerical person alike has access to what five or ten years ago was an enviable cadre of desktop-publishing tools. Therefore, having leveled the accessibility of publications capabilities among all operating departments, the contemporary publications department must look to its innate inner strength: the unique expertise resulting from the educational preparation of its staff and from being the only organization that exclusively dedicates its professional time and energies to the discipline of communication.

Accordingly, whereas the product templates and the basic job specification have long been in existence, the predominant change from traditional to resource organization is in the spectrum of information management. Rather than a focus on discrete product taxonomies, the resource organization formulates operational strategies based on a multivariate concept of information—the concept that information can be gathered, manipulated, packaged, and transmitted innumerable ways.

In what might be considered a reversal of the exhaustive, though misconceived, attempt in years gone by to differentiate technical communicators from the technical community based on their acumen with audience analysis, the resource organization traces the question of information design, use, and transmission back to its sources. Thus technical communicators arrive at the conclusion that the technical community may have understood the question better than they did all along but rather than take advantage of the inherent opportunities, technical communicators offered tired diatribes instead of participative assistance.

This realization necessitates two forthright changes in operational strategy: first, technical communicators must rely on expertise and not on tradition or templates; and second, they have to forge an interactive alliance with information users, information generators, and many of the organizations—such as word processing and graphics—that they have disparaged as their intellectual inferiors in the publications pecking order.

This modification also implies a different set of expectations customers come to place on the publications group. Foremost, the publications office is no longer defined by the physical boundaries of the building. The first act of faith on the part of the publications professionals is mentally dissolving the protections afforded by their self-proclaimed territorial boundaries. Personnel are expected to move, mentally and physically, into the world outside, to cultivate customer relationships by proving worth and sharing project accountability.

Matrix Assignments and Team Membership

Moving into the world outside the publications shop often entails the equivalent of temporary reassignments in which publications personnel become part of the group they are supporting, but with a very significant caveat. The publications professional becomes an equal participant on the task team, not merely a satellite editing station, scribe, or administrative aide to the technical members of the group. The arrangement is one of teaming—responsibility, involvement, contribution, and accountability as an equal partner.

Establishing this relationship is the responsibility of publications management. At least for the first few interactive team assignments, forceful negotiation among management is needed to formalize the professional's involvement, and this must be complemented by regular assessments to ensure original contractual agreements are maintained. Publications management must also force technical and senior management to momentarily suspend their disbelief, overcoming the mythical borders that separate technical and administrative personnel.

Even with these firm agreements, numerous concerns and drawbacks must be anticipated. Most notable is the need to continually redefine the department—both in the customer's eyes and in the eyes of the publications staff. Just as people have an immutable conception that word processing remains nothing more than the high end of the clerical spectrum, so technical people will not easily relinquish their opinions that publications people are there to "pretty things up," to "wordsmith," and to find the appropriate spaces in which to insert missing punctuation.

Furthermore, publications professionals, despite their enthusiasm, will initially be reluctant to put themselves in controversial situations unless management has instituted a change in the performance evaluation process, a change that illustrates that rewards are no longer based on production volumes but on initiative, integrity, and perspicacity. Without all these elements firmly entrenched, publications professionals cannot evidence the strong professional ego that must complement technical knowledge if the resource organization's message is to be communicated consistently throughout the workforce.

Outcome: Organizational Enrichment

Once the transition is effected, most of the benefits resulting from having a resource orientation are evident. Perhaps the most important benefit is the professional satisfaction that arises from external confirmation that publications personnel are indeed the intellectual and contributing equals to the technical community. Second is the increased diversity of activity, which will both attract and retain a talented, capable staff. Related to the increased diversity is enhanced visibility for the organization and its personnel. The publications department will experience a sense of renewed vigor, enthusiasm, and energy. The professionals' broadened operational perspective invariably translates into energy and creativity. Projects are no longer one dimensional; offices become stopovers rather than hiding places; and people find an increased sense of corporate community. Not surprisingly, the range of promotion opportunities expands.

Horizons are stretched to allow for what might be referred to as resource experts. These individuals are cousins to the resident technical experts, differing in that their expertise is sought and applied in arenas other than those defined by publications boundaries. These individuals are sought by outside agencies and organizations to support various technical assignments.

And were the inherent benefits enumerated above not sufficient reason to proceed, the change also introduces another benefit, the measure most apparently lacking in the traditional organization: sponsorship. Whether operating in a world of overhead costs, chargeback, or some variation thereof, the resource organization is, in its own small way, a demonstration of free-trade economics, creating customers willing to procure and defend services because the value of the services is tangible—and can only be provided by experts who have the unique skills base represented by publications professionals.

Progressive Organization

The third type of organization is one that I have termed progressive because it is the natural progression and evolution from the resource organization. In this publications environment, the goal is to gain full appreciation for and utilization of the analytical, logical, and rhetorical skills generally attributable to many senior publications personnel. Once the resource organization has expanded publications activities throughout the available spectrum of communications opportunities, growth—both for the publications organization and its staff—is contingent on continually amplifying the same types of benefits that accrue from the transition from a traditional to a resource organization.

Once traditional barriers have been surmounted in the transition to resource orientation, technical communicators come to see that developing communications is merely one of a number of contributions they can make to an organization.

As a very basic illustration of the evolution through the three phases from traditional to progressive, we might consider the publications unit's role in supporting technical presentations: at the traditional level, the publications group prepares technical presentations from draft materials submitted by the technical groups; these materials are edited, brought into line with existing publication and presentations standards, produced using the best available hardware and software, and walked through the approval and clearance cycles. After a period of time, publications professionals maneuver to conspire with the technical groups in the development of a new product line. The teaming arrangement commits publications to determine the best use of technical information in designing appropriate communication packages, to develop an information management program that supports information flow among affected organizations, and to establish the migration of information into the various communication packages.

Extending the Workscope

After having gained credit for the capability to capture and comprehend information appropriately, the final challenge is to foster nonpublications applications for these same analytical skills. One apparent opportunity might be whenever another product line or piece of equipment is to be introduced. This time, in addition to having personnel supporting the information design element of the project, the teaming arrangement might include usability evaluation of the design as well as the manuals, assessment of the new system's compatibility with other systems with which publications may have gained extensive knowledge consequent to its editorial involvement with all operating organizations, and identification of additional applications for the new systems and equipment.

Each of these added work dimensions relies only on those same skills expected of senior publications personnel, not on the assumption that publications personnel must pass themselves off as surrogate engineers or scientists. In addition, as our example suggests, the structure is one of building on successes, of adding to the scope of work—not dismissing or diminishing elements associated with the traditional or resource organizations. The drive to add scope of work, increase credibility, and gain intellectual sophistication is predicated on a cumulative process, not on challenging the functional foundations.

Curiously, while, as one might expect, there is heightened reluctance among technical groups to allow publications personnel to institute this dramatic change in work scope, the greater reluctance is evidenced in the publications personnel themselves. Changing their image of themselves is often more difficult than changing the image others have of them. Experience shows that it is largely a matter of their faith in themselves that determines whether a publications group ever successfully reaches the progressive stage.

Personnel are more comfortable in recognizable terrain, and they disdain the sensation of flying without benefit of a harness or safety net. However, what must be understood is that the absolute scales that applied to traditional publication assignments no longer apply. Rather, on the playing field—where ethos and competency have already secured professional recognition—performance is gauged by degree of success, with outcomes characterized as reasonable success when within anticipated values and as significant success when exceeding anticipated values.

Outcome: Manifold Career Opportunities

As with the transition from traditional to resource organization, benefits accruing in the evolution to progressive organization result largely from enhanced opportunities and visibility. Further, these are complemented by two features: 1) the ability to ascend the career ladder is accelerated, allowing personnel to progress more swiftly through the publications ranks; and 2) the ladder has an attractive added dimension—greater opportunity for advancement to upper management.

Whereas restricted experience exclusively within a publications framework makes advancement beyond a certain management level improbable, nontraditional experience and involvement, when seen as a demonstration of decision-making competence and managerial potential, often lead to new job assignments outside the expected career ladder. And, in many scientific firms, this lateral pathway is often the only avenue to senior management. Similarly, whether the publications group reports to a technical or an administrative function, renewed recognition of one's analytical competencies often results in advancement beyond the traditional publications ladder. (Figure 1 depicts the career opportunities resulting from implementation of the three different publications organizations. Table 1 summarizes the differences among the organization options.)

ALIGNING STAFFING WITH ORGANIZATION PERSONALITY

As Table 1 delineates, the staffing ratios for the three organizational personalities are reflective of the organizations' different scopes of work, customer bases, and customer interactions. Yet, something else should also be apparent from this table and the preceding organizational descriptions: each of the staffing configurations is predicated on attracting and cultivating professionals with different dispositions and skill mixes.

The personality of the staff, as noted above, must be effectively aligned with the personality of the organization. The first step is to establish a firm direction in which to drive the organization. The second step is to determine how to foster alignment between that organizational personality and the personality of the staff. Because much of the technical communication industry is firmly in place, one would be remiss in suggesting that attitudes can be reformed unilaterally by sheer will power or the imposing presence of a few committed managers. The staff, like management, has to be led to believe and made capable of supporting the revised charter. This is achieved by 1) developing existing staff to support the transition, and 2) hiring new staff to fulfill the proposed charter.

Training Staff for Transition

Job descriptions for technical communicators have always been a mixture of self-effacing portraits and bravado. At various facilities, I have seen job descriptions

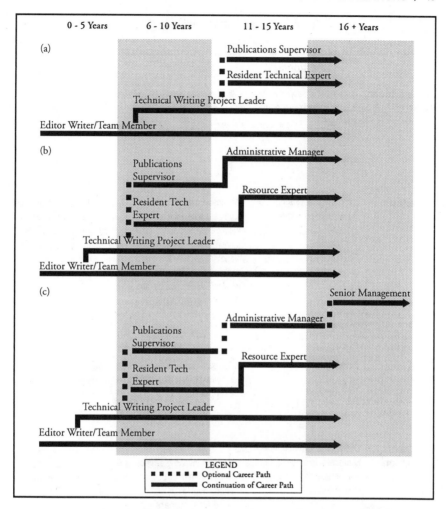

Figure 1. Career development opportunities: (a)traditional organization, (b) resource organization, (c) progressive organization.

that would challenge the likes of an E. B. White to fulfill, whereas at other locations, anyone vaguely conversant with the rudiments of the English language might consider applying. Such discrepancy occurs largely because managers have not concentrated on what the organizational profile approach would indicate as the proper path: defining job requirements based on skills not craft.

In contrast, current job descriptions catalogue the products one is expected to help produce. Computer companies list the hardware one is expected to support. Government facilities focus on preparation of technical reports and procedures. Entrepreneurial enterprises highlight marketing communications. And service

Table 1. Organizational Identity Chart

	Traditional	Resource	Progressive
Assumptions/ Charter	Role of publication is writing, editing, and publications management	Role of publications is to provide technical expertise to assist customers in using distributed tools and capabilities more effectively	Role of publications is to apply analytical, rhetorical, and data-synthesizing expertise to nontraditional environments and products
Products	Information packaged as discrete products— Reports Procedures Technical Papers	Information management and technical assistance basis of multiattribute support: information/product design and development, consulting on hardware and software utilization; technical leadership on specific customer problems	Information assessment and analysis, with rhetorical expertise applied in complete spectrum of operational activities, including technical and system design reviews, root cause analyses, readiness reviews, audits, investigations
Customer Base	Authors	Product owners; hardware/software owners/operators; technical support staff	Management task teams; project, facility, and system managers
Customer Interaction	Customer is external to process: interaction is intermittent through mail or phone	Interaction is direct with customer, often involving temporary reassignment of publications personnel to customer to perform discrete scope of work	Interaction is participatory, typified as team leader or contributing member of task force, assessment team, or project management responsibility
Staffing Ratios	60% writers/editors 20% writing project leaders 10% resident technical experts 10% coordinators, managers	35% writers/editors 15% writing project leaders 20% resident technical experts 25% resource experts 5% coordinators, managers	35% writers/editors; team leaders 15% resident technical experts 45% resource experts 5% coordinators/ managers (does not reflect personnel promoted to nonpublications management positions)

organizations typically forecast their need in terms of the size and volume of proposals to be produced. In other words, these job descriptions demonstrate the linear trappings of the traditional organizational personality, further dissected into subsets of particular product types.

Even if these organizations truly have a projected one-dimensional lifetime purpose for their publications units—which is highly improbable—the enthymeme on which they base their hiring construct is flawed:

> My department is chartered with producing a particular product. Only people experienced with this product can produce it. Therefore, I must hire only people experienced with this product.

The flaw is inherent in the assumption that each product is so distinct that no skills required for other products, or even other disciplines, are transferable from one product to another. Rather, what is true is that this situation, without intending to make the pun, is the traditional fallacy at work in the publications world. The assumptions are invalid: product lines change and evolve; lines between contributing disciplines are blurred; and abject specialization in the face of corporate fluidity is inviting obsolescence. Protection lies in developing, maintaining, and honing skills, not defending a craft.

So what are the skills publications staff need? A simple matrix of skills delineated by organizational personalities, charted against the educational emphases afforded by those undergraduate majors most typically hired into the publications organization, illustrates available skills. This matrix, as shown in Table 2, allows two advantages: 1) the abscissa affords a basis for writing skill-based rather than product-based job descriptions; and 2) the overall matrix affords both a hiring grid that suggests which undergraduate disciplines might best suit the organizational personality, and, for those already hired, makes more overt the types of skills and training warranted to bring an employee into better alignment with the department's orientation.

For example, let's assume that the technical communication staff is composed of a blend of technical communication and English majors, and that management is committed to moving to the resource orientation. Table 2 shows three areas in which the English major's skills most likely would need to be strengthened: publications management and control, computer skills, and technical expertise.

As regards the technical communication major, Table 2 indicates the major improvement focus would be on developing technical knowledge, with such areas as graphics being the most likely to support opportunities for resident technical expert or resource expert status.

Table 2 is also effective for assessing the probability of success and depth of commitment needed to make a transition from one organizational personality to another. For example, were the group staffed exclusively with liberal arts and business majors, a longer implementation phasing would be required to establish

Table 2. Alignment of Educational and Organizational Attributes

	Writing/Editing	Graphics	Printing	Pub Mgmt & Control	Interview/Data gathering	Internal Communication	Leadership	Subtotal	Computer Skills	Technical Experience	Subtotal	Organizational Concepts	Task Analysis	Problem Solving/Analysis	Independent Thinking	Subtotal	Total
English Major	A	B	B	C	A	A	B	16	C	C	2	A	A	A	A	12	30
Technical Comm Major	A	A	B	B	B	A	B	17	B	C	3	B	B	B	B	8	28
Technical Major (e.g., engineering)	B	C	C	C	B	C	B	10	A	A	6	B	B	B	B	8	24
Liberal Arts Major	B	C	C	C	B	B	B	11	C	C	2	B	B	B	B	8	21
Business Major	B	C	C	C	B	C	B	10	C	C	2	B	B	B	C	7	19
Enhanced Technical Comm	A	A	B	B	B	B	B	16	B	B	4	A	A	A	A	12	32

Traditional Organization   Resource Organization   Progressive Organization

A=Total alignment (3 points assigned)
B=Acceptable alignment (2 points assigned)
C=Minimal alignment (1 point assigned)

a resource organization than generally would be necessary for a department comprising English majors and technical majors. Of course, the chart also allows the manager to think more practically in terms of hiring new staff to complement the proposed organizational profile.

Hiring Staff to Fulfill the Charter

Many managers will argue against the veracity of the matrix presented in Table 2. The issue, however, needs to stay focused on the skills, not on the question of whether each of the depictions of educational disciplines is entirely accurate. I say this because the chart must be calibrated by each hiring manager: reviews of local programs, visits with faculty, and numerous student interviews must be conducted to determine precisely which majors should be listed on the ordinate to more accurately reflect the local availability of required skills.

Yet, beyond the hiring of those with majors that are best aligned with the unit's organizational vision, managers might be looking to our universities to be more responsive to trends in technical communication. As the bottom line of Table 2 shows, I see the possibility of an enhanced technical communication program that would provide writing and editing skills, document design and production skills, background in a technical discipline and the social sciences, and strong analytical and problem-solving skills.

MEETING THE CHALLENGE

Combining the concept of a planned organizational vision with a structured approach to staffing and staff development affords the kind of alignment that furthers the goals of the corporation, the publications department, and the publications professional. Without this alignment, friction remains that—whether articulated as job dissatisfaction, frequency of turnover, poor customer relations, or poor quality of work—always underlies the operational veneer.

But, to conclude this discussion, let's return to our three publications managers and to our original question of for and with whom we want to work. Had we made the decision at the onset of our evaluation, we would have subscribed to the tenet that the evident differences in managerial temperament or orientation might have been sufficient to support what is one of the most important career decisions we shall ever make. Assuming, even before we had stipulated terminology for these management personalities, that we had intuited that manager one is a practitioner of the traditional, manager two of the resource, and manager three of the progressive organizational personality, we still could not have made an efficacious decision. Now, however, owing to the preceding overview of organizational and personality alignments, we are better prepared to ask the right questions and comprehend the answers.

Namely, in addition to understanding management's inclination, the corporate manager who oversees the publications department and the new recruit must calculate the decision based on responses to at least four additional questions:

- What probability of continued success exists for the organization based on preparations and commitments made by both the company and the publications manager to sustain the selected profile?
- What is the strength and the appropriateness of the existing staffing configuration?
- What educational and training contingencies have been effected to support the staff's transition?

- Given the existing personal and departmental positioning, what personal advancement is predictable, and on what timeframe?

Only when we have ascertained answers to all these elements do we have enough information on which to base a judicious decision of how and where to align ourselves. While I recognize that this discussion cannot escape my personal bias to the progressive structure, there is something more fundamentally important about having publications managers and professionals comprehending the nuances of organizational and personal identities: Most vital to our continued professional integrity and survival is the confidence that derives only from the primal knowledge that what we do as managers is dedicated to making informed decisions that further the goals of our employers and better the lives of our employees.

CHAPTER 5

Culture and Anarchy: What Publications Managers Should Know about *Us* and *Them*

JOHN G. BRYAN

The hot topic among management theorists during the early and mid-1980s was the influence of organizational culture on organizational success. Following the lead of some careful researchers, pop-management writers such as Ouchi [1], Peters and Waterman [2], and Deal and Kennedy [3] made several claims that provoked the interest of business managers nationwide:

- Organizational cultures—like the cultures described by anthropologists—are marked by distinctive shared values, heroes, rites, rituals, communication and power structures, and goal orientations.
- "Excellent companies" (mostly evaluated according to financial criteria) share certain dominant values.
- Strong cultures promote success more than do fragmented cultures.
- Cultures can be changed to enhance corporate performance.

Based on those claims, many American business managers for the first time examined the cultures of their own organizations, and some undertook efforts to change those cultures with the hope that productivity and quality would improve, turnover would drop, harmony would reign, and profits would rise. The methods that managers used—and continue to use—in attempting cultural change vary widely, from the CEO's notification to senior managers that the door is always open to them, to the initiation of an internal newsletter intended to chronicle the employees' rites and heroics, to massive training programs that attempt to change employees' attitudes toward work, management, each other, the company, its products, and its customers. Most of the literature focuses on deciphering and altering existing organizational cultures, but some theorists suggest that, given the enormity of the task, a more feasible approach to change is through the recruitment and socialization of employees who fit the desired culture.

The issues of cultural change, socialization, and communication should interest publications managers and the members of publications departments because publications departments usually attract people whose education, skills, and personalities deviate from the prevailing corporate culture more than those of any other department's members. To work harmoniously and effectively in the corporate culture, publications staff need to be socialized.

The following pages characterize some of the research regarding organizational culture and offer guidelines for socializing new publications department employees.

CULTURE AND THE NEW RELIGION

Like most theories, the cultural perspective offers some modestly useful insights and methods. To know what constitutes healthy, successful, and productive cultures is useful for several reasons:

- Such knowledge forces us to recognize that an organization's complexity far exceeds that of statistical analyses and mathematical models.
- It forces us to include human resources among other resource calculations in determining the orientation and future of our organization.
- It gives us the opportunity to be introspective and to examine our behavior in the context of values that transcend our professional roles.
- It gives us the means of helping our new colleagues adjust to their new environment.

The cultural perspective also presents serious problems that need to be recognized. In 1981 and 1982, the best-selling books by Ouchi, Peters and Waterman, and Deal and Kennedy made a splash among business managers for three reasons.

First, the writers' breezy anecdotal styles, feel-good optimism, and focus on the human face of the corporation proved far more digestible than statistical analyses, mathematical models, and painful self-examination.

Second, they offered to many practitioners what seemed to be quick business salvation in the midst of a deep recession, absolving them of a host of sins: being in the wrong market, struggling on the down side of the business cycle, operating in a heterogeneous culture, making an inferior product, and incompetently managing resources. One pair of researchers report knowing a converted CEO who "pounded the desk and ordered: 'I want one of those cultures, and I want it on Monday!'" [4, p. 266].

Third, the notion of "shared vision" as a source of inspiration and organizational cohesion appealed to the egos of top managers, many of whom already had messianic delusions.

By the mid-1980s, scores of articles on the subject had filled the popular business press as well as academic business journals. Managers having opened their arms to embrace the new religion, consultants rushed to fill them with multiphase training programs, retreats, posters, banners, and three-ring binders filled with step-by-step instructions for deciphering existing cultures, closing culture gaps, team-building, chronicling the corporation's heroes, constructing the right symbols, modifying behavior, promoting the work ethic, improving interpersonal communication, establishing appropriate rituals, and articulating and inculcating values. Not only did the consultants make the culture-change process seem straightforward, the books had already identified for the managers which values they *should* have. They need not submit to introspection and self-examination when they could plainly see from the published tables that the proper values consisted of high-quality products, professionalism, and ethics.

As quickly as the practitioners seized the consultants' totems, however, some academic theorists cautioned the expropriation of their cultural perspective, and some consultants warned that changing organizational cultures involves far more work and is profoundly more difficult than rearranging an organizational chart, publishing a mission statement in the company newsletter and annual report, or completing an eight-step training program. More importantly, some companies seemed so absorbed in tending the organizational culture that they neglected business strategy. (For some examples of these diverse dissenting voices, see Carroll's withering critique of Peters and Waterman [5], McManis and Leibman's amusing pot-shot at Allen Kennedy [6], Georges' attack on "softskills training" [7], Wilkins and Patterson's smart reining-in of the runaway theory [4], and Beer, Eisenstat, and Spector's critical analysis of the theoretical foundations of change programs [8].)

Culture-change theory involves other problems as well.

All the literature concedes the difficulty of changing cultures, and many of the cases chronicling attempts emphasize the futility of programs directed by leaders who are not themselves committed to the task. The result is not only failure and confusion but also greater cynicism among employees. (See, for example, Mironoff [9], Kanter and Mirvis [10], and Beer, Eisenstat, and Spector [8].)

Many executives, seeing anarchy in the business environment and chaos throughout their organizations, decide that their problems originate in their culture, not in the business nor in the company's existing alignment and exercise of power, the incentives they offer their employees, the high ratio of management-to-worker wages, and certainly not in their own character or behavior.

The argument that "strong cultures" are better than weak cultures is true only when the culture is moving in a productive direction; otherwise the culture's strength makes it resistant to redirection [11, pp. 15-27; 12, p. 111].

Much of the literature assumes a single culture within an organization and argues that cultural change must originate and be led by a strong, high-level executive [13, p. 162; 11, p. 101; 14]. Some later work in the field argues the opposite: that most organizations have complex subcultures, even countercultures [4, p. 273; 15, p. 132], and that true cultural change can begin only outside the bureaucracy at the periphery of the organization [8].

Much of the literature concentrates on identifying which values lead to success and, therefore, which values corporate executives should inculcate in their employees; but recent research suggests that far more important is the congruity of values among individuals and units within an organization [12, p. 58]. Thus, when a particular department exhibits values that match those of the executives (even if corrupt), that department gains power—often disproportionate to its strategic role in the organization.

While many practitioners claim they want a change in culture, what they truly want—and what they often mistake for cultural change—is a change in behavior. Programs that use behavioral incentives to reinforce change may find that, once the incentives disappear, the old culture and behavior reemerge [16, p. 253]. In this regard, adapting the cultural psyche resembles psychotherapy and suggests the argument used by behavioral psychologists: rather than spend years in understanding and treating the origins of dysfunction, why not change the behavior and let the change in psyche follow?

Culture-change programs often claim the purpose of improving performance but instead become means of justifying the status quo [12, p. 112]. In describing such situations, Mironoff compares the corporation to Stalinist regimes: "See the gray, uninspired masses going through habitual motions while company slogans, exhortations and training programs rain down upon them. 'Do it right the first time!' 'Commit to excellence!'" In some instances the urge to control people makes change extremely difficult, and management's response may be merely a "superficial fix within the framework of totalitarian organizational design" [9, pp. 31-32].

Despite these problems with the construction and implementation of the culture-change theory, to ignore the existence of organizational culture is to surrender the inevitable socialization process to chance or to change agents from our organization's countercultures—often with undesirable effects. Publications managers have an important responsibility to those they hire and supervise.

HELPING PUBLICATIONS STAFF ADAPT TO CORPORATE CULTURE

On the first day of my job as a writer for a large international consulting firm in 1979, my boss led me to the company archives and, with a sweep of his arm, introduced me to hundreds of bound reports, proposals, and brochures prepared over the company's twenty-five year history. That introduction, plus long Friday lunches with colleagues and martinis, constituted my training program. Of course, I also had the tedious corporate policy manual on my shelf, a handshake and a handful of forms from the personnel director, and the editing of my work by typists who explained, "That's the way we've always done it around here."

Like most members of publications departments, I came from a background in the humanities rather than the sciences, engineering, or business. Nonetheless, I succeeded because of my adaptability and my willingness to bridge the gap between the culture of my department and the cultures of the dominant organizational units. Finding adaptable, willing employees and socializing them to succeed in such an environment are among the publications manager's most important responsibilities. I offer the following observations, which I hope will be useful in that process.

Recruitment and Hiring

Socialization begins before the candidate joins your department.

Don't Hire the Best Writer, Editor, or Designer: Hire the Best Potential Employee who can Write, Edit, or Design

During the recession of 1982, I hired an acquaintance who I knew to be an excellent writer and who desperately needed a job. Unfortunately, she could not disguise her contempt for the company; her failure to "fit" affected the quality of her work, her reliability, and her relationships with other employees. When the deepening recession forced staff cutbacks, I fired her first. Despite her impending financial hardship, she expressed relief that her tenure with the company was over.

Certainly, the job candidate should be competent. He or she should also "fit" the culture of the larger organization and of your department. Recruiting employees whose values and orientation approximate those of the organizational culture makes more sense than attempting to convert employees to an alien vision of themselves and their places in the organization. For example, many writers see themselves as "creative types" who are proudly unconventional and who disdain the worlds of commerce and technology. While you want your employees to be creative, they must also be able to adapt to the character and purpose of your organization. The "creative type" may fit well in a small advertising agency but not in an engineering firm. Other prospects may be technophobes or may feel uncomfortable writing promotional material. Trying to force a fit with such people usually damages productivity, encourages countercultures, creates management headaches, and makes no one happy—least of all the ill-fitting employee. (Kotter and Heskett deal with this issue on an organizational level, discussing the nature of good fits between cultures and markets [11].)

Preview the Culture—Warts and All—for the Candidate

The recruitment and hiring process is competitive, and just as job candidates present their best faces in resumes and interviews, so most interviewers tend to present the best corporate face. They hand the candidate glossy brochures and newsletters that present idealized versions of the corporate reality. While such publications may reinforce management's vision of the company and its values, once the new hire discovers the discrepancy between that vision and reality, cynicism will likely follow.

Some aspects of the culture will be apparent to the candidate from the physical environment, publications, and personnel. The candidate should receive a preview of the less apparent aspects of the organizational culture and the departmental subculture. For example, what attitudes and behavior does management value? Loyalty, obedience, and conformity? Creativity, innovation, independence? Does management fragment the organizational culture by pitting internal units against each other (such as through the establishment of small profit-centers)? What do you as a department manager value? Are interdepartmental relations cooperative and respectful? Or does the dominant culture regard publications employees as secretaries, as overhead, as a drag on profits?

The preview should be candid, neither unrealistically positive nor unreasonably harsh. If you, your department, and your organization are working in good faith to overcome the problems that exist, outline the problems, your solutions, your commitment to that process, and top management's support of your efforts. If you have a vision of what the department should become, share that vision but also indicate the distance between reality and the goal. And, by all means, emphasize the role you expect the employee to play in achieving that vision. This preview, as Kanter and Mirvis suggest, "inoculates" incoming employees with "realistic idealism" [10, p. 239].

Negotiations, Orientation, and Training

The intensive socialization process begins once you have chosen your top candidate and begun negotiating terms. It continues through the first several months after the hiring.

Immediately and Explicitly Establish your Standards and Expectations and Provide the Authority Needed to Meet those Expectations

Of course you expect consistently professional work, but what are the limits of the employee's responsibilities? The division of labor—especially in technical environments—encourages individual workers to assume responsibility only for that portion of a project they control. When an editor finds that other members of the project staff have fallen behind schedule or are producing inferior work on a collaborative project, must the editor compensate for the others' shortcomings or is it enough to shrug and explain, "I did my part"? If a writer suspects the engineering department of supplying fraudulent data, what should the writer do?

Once employees have joined your department, they deserve to know exactly what you expect from them. If you expect them to accept some responsibility for the project's total quality and timeliness, you must tell them so. If you expect them to uphold certain values of the department or the organization, you must explicitly tell them and must specify the methods of dealing with violation of those values.

Prepare Them for the Cynics

Those long Friday lunches with colleagues and martinis socialized me as no training program could. My colleagues, both vice presidents, gossiped expansively about the corporation at a high level—most of it not flattering to the company. At a later company, my traveling companions furnished the same kind of informal socialization. Unfortunately, gossip outside the office almost always conveys the most negative aspects of an organization. And invariably, the people most free with gossip are those most frustrated with their own situations and most resentful of other people's success. The values they convey may indeed reflect the subculture to which they belong, but their values may not match those you are struggling to uphold in your department.

Prepare the new employee for the cynics, not by denying the problems and inequities they describe, but by describing what you and others are doing to solve them and—more importantly—by describing how the new employee can contribute to that effort. (Kanter and Mirvis provide an interesting discussion of our growing social cynicism and of the need to create cultures that fight that cynicism [10].)

Define the Compact between Company and Employee, between Department and Employee

By establishing your standards and expectations, you give responsibility to employees for upholding the values of the organization and your department. What can they expect in return? Most expectations have reciprocals, and many socialization and culture-change programs fail because the managers who espouse production-enhancing values fail to fulfill the reciprocal side of those values. They claim that quality is their highest value and try to induce employee loyalty, but at the end of the next bad quarter, they lay off some of those employees, perhaps proving that profit ranks higher than quality and that the company is loyal to its employees only when it can afford to be. Companies need not prove their loyalty into bankruptcy, but they should candidly explain the realistic limits of their values and should admit the self-interested motivation of their actions.

As publications manager, you should explain what your employees can expect from you: the extent of your loyalty, support, respect, and partisanship. You should also explain what they can expect from the company. Sometimes, that isn't much more than a paycheck. One senior editor at a mid-sized company recently told me that the company president had warned a large gathering of professional staff that they should all remember: they could be replaced by anyone he pulled off the street and trained. In such an unhealthy corporate culture, the publications manager must struggle to grow a healthy subculture.

Encourage the New Employee to "Invest" in the Organization and the Department

Some culture-change programs do enjoy limited success by getting employees to "invest" in the organization; that is, the employees commit their own professional, emotional, and financial capital to the organization. In doing so, they see their own success tied to the organization's success and work harder to fulfill their own vision of the organization.

The means of investment vary. The most common, of course, is financial through profit-sharing and stock ownership plans. Those plans rarely succeed in altering employee behavior, however, because most employees fail to see a direct relationship between their own work and financial performance. (A fascinating exception resulted from the extraordinary efforts of Springfield Remanufacturing Corporation to educate its employee-owners at every level in the intricacies of the company's financial reports [17].)

Another means of encouraging investment is through formal initiation, especially rites of passage that mark the employee's transition from outside cultures to the inside culture [18, p. 370]. As in military boot camps and fraternity hazings, rites of passage usually require the initiate to pass through one or more challenging physical or mental trials. The trials separate the initiate from those who have not joined the exclusive club and bond him or her with other survivors of the rites. Of course, the initiate is responding not only to the sense of accomplishment, but also to the desire not to seem foolish for having devoted so much time and toil to the tests. (Robert Cialdini describes this desire for psychological consistency as one of the principal allies of con artists [19].)

Of course you aren't going to haze new employees, but a variety of reasonable techniques do lend themselves to this initiation process. The technique should employ some challenge and should be met collaboratively by the new hire and one or more other employees. (The new hire's receipt of a desk, office, computer, and other tangible evidence of belonging to the organization entails no trial and no bonding with fellow initiates and so evokes no sense of accomplishment.) For example, a retreat or off-site orientation gives you an opportunity to provide a lot of information about the company and department, to symbolically separate the employee from past employment or educational affiliations, to undergo trial by imposing a grueling schedule, and to bond with others in the group through collaborative learning and through social contact (what Trice and Beyer call "rites of integration" [18, pp. 385-387]).

Another, less formal, method consists of assigning the initiate to join a challenging collaborative project that will tax his or her abilities, will require some surrender of independence for the good of the group, will require a heavy investment of time and energy, and will demonstrate your department's work methods; of course, the project should also be one that will succeed and should be headed by a person who models the values and behavior you favor. No symbols, stories, or other rewards will socialize the new employee more quickly than that employee's own investment in the success of the organization.

Assign a Mentor

As much of this advice suggests, the new employee needs a steady source of socialization, a source to convey values, expectations, and stories, and to model behavior. As publications manager, you may not have time to fill all those roles, but someone must. Indeed someone will. And if you don't make the choice, the department cynic may elect himself to the task.

Define and Create an Effective Us

The *Us-Them* polarity seems to exist in every social structure and is part of the fabric of a competitive, free-market economy. Much of the success of Japanese industry is attributed to that homogeneous culture's clear definition of itself, the workers' clear understanding of who Us is and, therefore, who Them is. By contrast, at least some of the weakness of American industry is attributed to our heterogeneous culture's unclear definition of itself, our workers' perception of Us as a small local group, and therefore their perception of Them as a large array of self-interested opponents who are the enemies of Us.

Publications departments—usually small, culturally unlike, and subordinated to the larger, more powerful departments in an organization—often see themselves as a small local Us. Nurturing a strong subculture in the publications department can be very good, but if the members of that subculture fail to see themselves as members of the larger organizational culture, their work will suffer. As publications manager, you must send your employees beyond the boundaries of your department to work with people in other departments, to learn and appreciate the larger culture, to understand "the business" of the larger organization, to demonstrate the competence and usefulness of your department, and to identify an Us that incorporates the entire organization.

Creating an effective Us proves especially difficult when your department members view the rest of the organization antipathetically, a likely view if they feel unappreciated by the dominant culture, besieged with staff cuts in hard times, the last to get new resources in good times, underpaid and overworked by organizational standards. Under those conditions, management and the dominant departments become the Them. And worse: No enemy is more reviled than one on whom we are dependent—as is the case in organizations that classify the publications department as an overhead expense, or, as one of my employer's accounting departments classified our work, "unproductive."

One means of creating an effective Us under those circumstances is to identify a Them that doesn't include management or other departments. The Them you identify may be the company's competitors, a market challenge, or a research challenge—any entity that provides a common enemy or challenge for the organization as a whole. Keith Denton and Barry Wisdom quote Jack Stack, the CEO of

Springfield Remanufacturing Company, as saying, "Everyone has to have an enemy. We keep our enemies outside of our operation. We focus the innate anger in people. If you can focus it outside your operation they (employees) won't turn on you internally" [20, p. 67].

One caveat: Don't vilify your organization's competitors in order to create a Them. Doing so demeans your profession and the process of market competition. Remember, too, that you may wish to work for the competitor some day.

Establish Professional Goals for your Employees

While accountants and engineers studied and trained for the work they are doing, many writers, editors, and designers who find themselves in publications departments studied literature or art and only lately turned toward the industrial environment. They have come to work in a company that offers a paycheck and, depending on the values of the organizational culture, perhaps not much else: few opportunities for promotion, sometimes little respect or recognition from outside your department. You, as a publications manager, may create a strong subculture that rewards its members, but if your employees are to grow and excel professionally, they need more than the support you can offer.

Encourage contact with the world beyond your organization by bringing in consultants for on-site training and by promoting participation in the local and national professional societies pertinent to their fields. Support their attending meetings and entering professional competitions, insofar as you can, by supplying materials, entry fees, and time off, and by sending them out for additional education and training. When they succeed, recognize them publicly in the department and fight for organizational recognition of them.

Some managers fear their employees' contact with professional societies because the societies offer contacts for finding jobs elsewhere. Employees are not indentured servants, however, and if they find the satisfactions of your department lacking, they will either leave or their work will not be what you wish it to be. Supporting their professional growth offers them one source of greater satisfaction with your department.

Beware Heavy-handed Socialization

The secretaries who edited my work and the engineers who ignored the composing heuristic I proposed—all explaining *That's the way we've always done it around here*—showed that they had been well socialized and showed the danger of strong cultures: they resist change, whether it is for better or worse. Naturally, I believe that I brought better practices and publications to my employer, fulfilling their stated purpose in hiring me. Nonetheless, their need to maintain the status quo proved almost irresistible.

As the publications manager, you likely will see the new employee as a high-quality lump of clay that is to be shaped according to the organizational culture's mold. As much of this essay suggests, some of that perception is true. We also need to remember, however, that outsiders may bring fresh perspectives, may challenge the status quo, may actually be able to help the veterans.

Rather than telling the new employee, *That's the way we do it around here,* explore what the employee knows. If the alternatives the employee suggests make sense, try them. If they seem not to make sense, ask the employee to try your methods and set specific measurements and duration for either trial. In other words, negotiate with an open mind and with the focus on results (what we hope to accomplish), not on methods.

Your open-mindedness will encourage what P. M. Senge calls "generative learning," that is, an organization's ability not only to adapt to its changing environment but also to anticipate the future needs of the environment [21].

Maintenance

Socialization is a continuous responsibility of the publications manager and pertains to veterans as well as newcomers.

Bridge Cultures for your Department

Corporate battles put managers in the awkward position of choosing sides, thus breaking down the larger organizational Us and creating a Them that consists either of your department, another department, or management. The bloodiness of such battles increases as corporate resources become more scarce. Overhead departments often become the first targets of cutbacks because top management sees them as the fastest way to reduce costs without impeding production. Targeting such departments can be short-sighted if those reductions diminish the quality of the services or products delivered or impede the ability to secure new work.

Most publications managers' first impulse is to defend the department against such targeting, and that may be necessary if the strategy seems short-sighted or disproportionate to the benefits to be gained by the organization. But other motives for departmental partisanship—such as ego and power protection—should be suppressed for the benefit of the larger organization. Indeed, supporting top management's decisions will likely yield greater power as the result of value congruity (the exhibition of values consistent with those held by top managers) [12, pp. 47-94].

Some managers, savvy to the influence of value congruity and confident that milking the assets of their departments will yield little damage before they move on, give in too easily. Under such circumstances, the employees of the department probably already see the manager as a toady of management, as one of Them; if not, such an alignment will ensure such a view and can create departmental anarchy.

If the publications manager has bridged cultures and has created an inclusive Us by integrating the departmental subculture with the larger organizational culture, and if the members of the subculture continue to receive candid information about the values and performance of the larger organization and about the department's role in that performance, they may agree with top management's decisions or may propose alternatives that promote organizational interests while limiting departmental pain. For example, the department may propose to take an across-the-board pay cut rather than lose a member; or members may ease their demands for the high-end equipment they want and accept the hand-me-down computers from another department.

Convey Values with More than Abstractions

Two years after joining one company, I attended the retirement party for one of the company's founders, a passing that seemed to portend few changes. Ironically, the retirement party itself became an agent of change because it resulted in a series of impromptu stories about the company's early days. For example, another founder recalled a long marketing trip the two of them had taken during a bitter winter storm. After a full day of driving across the hills of the Ozarks, they shared a grubby motel room. The scene he described seemed quite remote from my own very comfortable travels "on the company." The story did not create any heroes of the stature described by the culture-change chroniclers, but it did change my own attitude toward my expense account.

Gossip's power derives in part from its narrative form and its familiar characters. The same power is available for conveying values, and most companies have hundreds of small success stories that reflect the past implementation of the values you wish to reinforce: the weekend that everyone gave up to get a brochure out, the night the president stayed to help proofread a report, the contract we lost—despite the client's saying the proposal was the best written he had ever read—the lunch that lasted all afternoon after we learned we won a contract that everybody said was beyond hope. Such stories, far more than abstract statements, are memorable and effective in conveying values and in creating ties to the company or corporation.

Concrete rewards also reinforce what you say you value, but give the employees a voice in choosing their rewards. Lunch out with the boss is more torture than reward for many people. A certificate that the cynical employee knows cost a dollar to produce can do more harm than no reward at all. A profile in the company newsletter may make a cynical employee feel complicitous in what he or she sees as a self-serving corporate propaganda campaign. Ask the department members for suggestions and then give individuals choices acceptable to your budget: perhaps an afternoon off or a display of the work being rewarded.

These guidelines are neither absolute nor exhaustive. As publications manager, you will want to become familiar with the theories on corporate culture and socialization, keeping in mind that they are not religion but are useful in guiding your human resources to fulfill a shared vision of your profession and your department's future in the organization.

REFERENCES

1. W. G. Ouchi, *Theory Z*, Addison-Wesley Publishing Company, New York, 1981.
2. T. J. Peters and R. H. Waterman, Jr., *In Search of Excellence: Lessons from America's Best-Run Companies*, Harper & Row, New York, 1982.
3. T. E. Deal and A. A. Kennedy, *Corporate Cultures: The Rites and Rituals of Corporate Life*, Addison-Wesley Publishing Company, Redding, Massachusetts, 1982.
4. A. L. Wilkins and K. J. Patterson, You Can't Get There from Here: What Will Make Culture-Change Projects Fail, in *Gaining Control of the Corporate Culture*, R. H. Kilmann, M. J. Saxton, and R. Serpa (eds.), Jossey-Bass Publishers, San Francisco, pp. 262-291, 1985.
5. D. T. Carroll, A Disappointing Search for Excellence, *Harvard Business Review, 61*:6, pp. 78-88, 1983.
6. G. L. McManis and M. S. Leibman, Corporate Culture: What It Can and Cannot Do, *Personnel Administrator, 33*:12, pp. 24-26, 1988.
7. J. C. Georges, Why Soft-Skills Training Doesn't Take, *Training, 25*:4, pp. 42-47, 1988.
8. M. Beer, R. A. Eisenstat, and B. Spector, Why Change Programs Don't Produce Change, *Harvard Business Review, 68*:6, pp. 158-166, 1990.
9. A. Mironoff, De-Stalinizing the Corporation, *Training, 27*:8, pp. 30-33, 1990.
10. D. Kanter and P. Mirvis, *The Cynical Americans: Living and Working in an Age of Discontent and Disillusion*, Jossey-Bass Publishers, San Francisco, 1989.
11. J. P. Kotter and J. L. Heskett, *Corporate Culture and Performance,* Free Press, New York, 1992.
12. C. A. Enz, *Power and Shared Values in the Corporate Culture*, UMI Research Press, Ann Arbor, Michigan, 1986.
13. L. A. Miller, *American Spirit: Visions of a New Corporate Culture*, William Morrow and Company, Inc., New York, 1984.
14. R. S. Ruch and R. Goodman, *Image at the Top,* Free Press, New York, 1983.
15. M. R. Louis, Sourcing Workplace Cultures: Why, When, and How, in *Gaining Control of the Corporate Culture,* R. H. Kilmann, M. J. Saxton, and R. Serpa (eds.), Jossey-Bass Publishers, San Francisco, pp. 126-136, 1985.
16. V. Sathe, How to Decipher and Change Corporate Culture, in *Gaining Control of the Corporate Culture*, R. H. Kilmann, M. J. Saxton, and R. Serpa (eds.), Jossey-Bass Publishers, San Francisco, pp. 230-261, 1985.
17. B. L. Wisdom and D. K. Denton, Compensation Management in Practice: Using the Numbers to Communicate Corporate Vision, *Compensation and Benefits Review, 21*:4, pp. 15-19, 1989.
18. H. M. Trice and J. M. Beyer, Using Six Organizational Rites to Change Corporate Culture, in *Gaining Control of the Corporate Culture*, R. H. Kilmann, M. J. Saxton, and R. Serpa (eds.), Jossey-Bass Publishers, San Francisco, pp. 370-399, 1985.
19. R. M. Cialdini, *Influence: Science and Practice,* Scott, Foresman and Company, Glenview, Illinois, 1987.
20. D. K. Denton and B. L. Wisdom, Shared Vision, *Business Horizons, 32*:4, pp. 67-69, 1989.
21. P. M. Senge, The Leader's New Work: Building Learning Organizations, *Sloan Management Review, 32*:1, pp. 7-23, 1990.

CHAPTER 6

Hiring and Managing Editorial Freelancers

DAVID L. ARMBRUSTER

The decision to employ editorial freelancers depends upon an organization's needs, structure, and philosophy. Both advantages and disadvantages attend the use of freelancers. In discussing these and suggesting ways to minimize potential disadvantages, I focus on the following:

- The organization's perspective
- The manager's perspective
- Finding the right freelancer
- Negotiating with a freelancer
- Planning work with a freelancer
- Management techniques for working with a freelancer

THE ORGANIZATION'S PERSPECTIVE

Editorial freelancers have long been employed on occasion for special projects. Increasingly, however, organizations are maintaining a small, professional in-house staff and relying on expert freelancers for a variety of tasks. In either case, freelancers can help achieve the organization's goals by augmenting existing resources in a number of ways.

For example, a small editorial staff in an organization that publishes in several disparate disciplines might lack a particular content expertise that a freelancer could provide.

Similarly, freelancers can provide specialized publication services (e.g., indexing and abstracting, translating, or rewriting) and other expertise. An organization whose editorial staff normally prepares technical monographs with many tables, figures, and references might hire a freelancer who specializes in user manuals to produce a user manual for its new accounting system. Or a publications staff that normally prepares twenty-page reports might lack the organizational skills needed to edit a 500-page book manuscript. A freelancer with the expertise to handle this volume of material within the time available, to prepare an index, and to mark the manuscript appropriately for production can save the publications office time and money.

And finally, freelancers can help an organization handle an erratic publishing workload, one with a series of peaks and valleys. Because staffing for peaks is rarely feasible, freelancers can help an organization surmount the peaks in a cost-effective, efficient manner. To cover their own overhead, freelancers generally charge an hourly rate higher than that paid to in-house staff, but freelancers are not paid during slack periods. In addition, organizations save on the cost of benefits (e.g., vacation, sick leave, health insurance, and workers' compensation) and save the stress of layoffs. Freelancers can also be more cost-effective than in-house editors who must spend time on organizational and administrative chores. An hour's pay buys an hour's work, and the organization doesn't have to pay for staff meetings, phone calls, and other interruptions.

The primary disadvantage of hiring freelancers, from both the organization's and the manager's perspective, is that a certain degree of control is lost. A freelancer might not meet organizational deadlines or produce work that accords with institutional editorial policy. It is among the manager's tasks, however, to select and supervise freelancers in such a way as to minimize this disadvantage.

THE MANAGER'S PERSPECTIVE

For the editorial manager, employing freelancers can provide (or force) significant advantages in the form of effective planning and organization. Before explaining project goals and procedures to the freelancer, the manager must determine those goals and procedures, develop style specifications, and resolve (or at least anticipate) departmental and organizational jealousies or antipathies. Organizations with a sizable editorial staff generally will have done these things, but such planning and organization can be a formidable task for a small editorial department.

Moreover, because they represent areas of expertise, freelancers can increase a manager's flexibility by providing valuable training for the editorial staff. For example, a freelancer might teach scientific or technical editors to prepare more effective newsletters and press releases. A freelancer might provide editors of manuals with the appropriate forms and checklists to organize, edit, and produce a conference proceedings. A freelancer might conduct writing or proofreading workshops for others in the organization, thereby relieving the manager of an important, but time-consuming, task.

A freelancer can actually boost staff morale by reducing work overloads and interacting effectively with the staff in a well-managed setting. On the other hand, the manager must guard against the possibility that employees will view the freelancer as someone trying to usurp their jobs.

Freelancers are often solo operators who have chosen this path because they do not enjoy working within an organizational structure. This attitude can pose a problem for managers, especially those in a highly structured setting.

When a large project is involved or the deadline is tight, a manager might want to consider soliciting bids from an editorial firm or consortium (more on this later). The editorial firm can provide depth in staffing, thereby guaranteeing project completion, even if the original editor breaks an arm and is unable to complete the work.

FINDING THE RIGHT FREELANCER

A manager who has decided to hire a freelancer must then figure out where to find one. Unfortunately, anyone who has a degree in English or journalism or who edited a high school newspaper twenty years ago can—and often does—call himself or herself an editor. While such a person might prove to be an excellent technical editor after extensive training, the manager seeking a freelancer generally needs a professional, not a tyro.

Preparing for the Search

Before searching, a manager must consider carefully the traits needed in a freelancer. Obviously, such attributes as love of words and language, sense of relative importance of stylistic issues, humor, skepticism, humility combined with self-confidence, and an eye for detail are probably innate to most good editors. Does the freelancer need to be on site or able to work with nonnative speakers of English? How much autonomy will the freelancer have? How much and what kind of experience does the freelancer need?

A good way to begin searching is by contacting local editors and colleagues in similar disciplines or organizations. University presses normally use freelancers and are quite helpful. Membership directories of editorial, publishing, and communication societies are also important sources (e.g., Society for Technical Communication, American Medical Writers Association, Council of Biology Editors, and Association of Editorial Freelancers). If such organizations have local or regional chapters, membership lists often include members' consulting specialties or areas of interest. Editorial firms and individual freelancers advertise in professional trade journals. *The Literary Market Place* (R. R. Bowker Company), *Directory of Editorial Resources* (Editorial Experts, Inc.), and professional meetings are other sources. Finally, freelancers are often able to provide referrals if they are too busy to accept a project.

Evaluating Candidates

After a list of names has been prepared, a manager should screen it. A number of tools can be used here, depending on the manager's particular style and needs: tests, interviews, reference checks, telephone interviews with candidates and others of the freelancer's clients, and the grapevine, for example.

A surprising number of candidates submit resumes and cover letters containing typographical or grammatical errors, helping to narrow the list. If a candidate offers a portfolio, the manager should ask for actual edited samples, not just completed publications.

Checking references and asking specific questions about a candidate are important if a manager is to find a satisfactory freelancer. A candidate described as "personable and knowledgeable" might never have met a deadline. Such information is often more easily obtained over the telephone than in a letter.

An editorial exercise is one of the most successful tools for evaluating promising candidates (for permanent as well as freelancing positions). I have found success with a portion (four to five pages) of an unedited manuscript that contains both stylistic and substantive problems and that typifies the organization's work and editorial problems. If properly used, the exercise can provide important indications of a candidate's skill and "style." For example, does the candidate

- Resolve inconsistencies (e.g., "percent" and "per cent")?
- Understand generally accepted technical style conventions (e.g., comma before the final conjunction in a series)?
- Tend to rewrite or revise in a way that changes the author's style or meaning?
- Query the author in a helpful or an argumentative manner?
- Identify weaknesses in logic and organization?

In organizations with personnel policies that require the use of standardized, validated tests, use of the editorial exercise might pose a problem. Calling it an "exercise" rather than a "test" and making it optional are possible solutions. Another approach is to compensate candidates for editing a short trial manuscript. The goal is to determine how a candidate edits *before* signing a contract.

Additional Considerations

Managers seeking a freelancer would be advised to look for an established, independent editor. Some editors who call themselves freelancers are really looking for a full-time job. A manager can ill afford to invest training time on freelancers who then use such skills and experience to find permanent jobs elsewhere. Managers should also consider whether an editor who consults in addition to holding a full-time job has the necessary time or energy to devote to a project with strict deadlines.

On the other hand, many managers hire freelancers with the goal of working them into a permanent position with the publication group when an opening occurs.

Another consideration is the motivation of the freelancer. A retired editor might see freelance editing as a source of supplemental rather than primary income. Such freelancers might have more time to spend on a project, editing more for the personal rather than monetary reward. On the other hand, a freelancer whose sole income is generated by editorial work wants continuing clients and will work hard to please a manager who can provide additional projects.

What about contracting with an editorial or publication services company? By hiring a company, managers can often find expertise in several areas (e.g., writing, editing, proofreading, and indexing) with just one contract. A disadvantage of this approach is that a contractor company usually has higher overhead than does the solo freelancer, so costs can be greater for the former. Another consideration might be a lack of consistency from job to job if the company were to shift the assignments of its employees.

Some large cities now have publications consortia—informal groups of professionals with various skills and areas of content expertise who network effectively for themselves as well as for clients.

NEGOTIATING WITH A FREELANCER

A manager will have difficulty negotiating with freelancers without some idea of what levels of work to expect from them, how much to pay them, and how much time they will need for a specific job.

Level of Work Expected

The manager must describe to the freelancer in broad terms the manuscript and what is expected: for example, style specifications; level of edit or rewriting; responsibility for such tasks as creating art work, retyping, and verifying references; level of complexity of the manuscript; proofreading responsibilities; responsibility for resolving queries with the author; and time available in which to complete the work.

Payment Considerations

The matter of pay rates should be discussed briefly at an early point to screen out those whose minimum rate exceeds the organization's ability or willingness to pay. In addition to charging varying rates based on experience and on location (i.e., area of the country), freelancers charge in various ways: by the hour, page, project, and so on. Experienced freelancers can readily translate rates from one system to another; a manager should be able to do this as well.

The manager should ask how much and in what manner the freelancer expects to charge. If they decide on an hourly rate, they must reach an agreement about a minimum amount of work per hour, and the freelancer's progress should be monitored carefully.

The negotiation process should be exactly that—a negotiation, not a monologue. Both the manager and freelancer should ask many clarifying questions, some of which one or the other might be unable to answer immediately. The process of finding answers and communicating more clearly what is needed by both parties will help ensure a more successful effort.

Many organizations use a bid process to contract with freelancers. The problem of the low bid—you get what you pay for—holds for both the bid process and negotiating with an individual freelancer. A very low bid or hourly rate can mean desperation or inexperience. Likewise, a very high bid or rate can mean little interest or, again, inexperience. Neither case promises to produce high-quality editing.

If the editorial group works on a cost-recovery basis, the data for estimating project costs are available. If not, the best approach is for the manager to track the time necessary for the group to complete several publications and then to develop general cost estimates.

Regardless of the method used to estimate the cost of a particular editing job, the manager must consider many variables when determining rates and total cost for the job. How experienced is the freelancer? What amount of editing is normally needed for manuscripts from this particular author? Are there problems with the manuscript that warrant including a contingency?

Finally, while managers are responsible for the appropriate use of organizational funds, they can gain a great deal of good will by paying a bit more than might be required by prevailing rates and freelancer experience. Those freelancers who have been given a favor will most probably return the favor when a manager is in a bind.

The Contract

A contract protects the manager and the organization as much as the freelancer. Contracts can take several forms (e.g., letter agreements and purchase orders), but some basic information should be included in every one: description of the publication and the job to be done, rate of pay, maximum cost, and deadlines. Some form of contract should be prepared for every job, even those being done by freelancers who have worked with the manager for many years.

Having decided to employ freelancers and found the right candidates, a manager can maximize chances for success through proper planning and managing.

PLANNING WORK WITH A FREELANCER

Planning really begins when a manager starts looking for the right freelancer, but *detailed* planning is what is important at this point. For example, if the organization requires strict adherence to certain style specifications, these must be provided to the freelancer with instructions that the editing must be done accordingly. My preference is to sacrifice some organizational consistency for the freelancer's own consistency.

Managers of editorial freelancers must accept the fact that many editorial problems (e.g., usage, hyphenation, use of numbers, and format) have more than one correct solution. A competent freelancer will provide a professional solution; while it might not be the *manager's* solution, it will be a legitimate one.

A small editorial office probably has little need for its own all-inclusive style manual, but a freelancer must be given at least general guidelines. One solution is to keep the guidelines as generic as possible: Use a standard style manual (listing those preferred or not, as necessary); use a standard dictionary to verify spellings and hyphenations (when spelling variants exist, use the first form found in the dictionary); and prepare a style sheet indicating additions to, and deviations from, these guidelines. The manager should also make available a list of the common abbreviations and unique terminology of the organization.

Time is, obviously, a critical component of planning. Because the freelancer generally is not working on site, the manager must have a clear sense that meetings, telephone calls, fax transmissions, and similar activities must be planned more carefully than if the work were being done in-house.

Planning by a manager should include the author and the effect of a freelancer on the author-editor relationship. A successful manager of freelancers learns to determine which authors can easily work with freelancers and which ones need in-house attention. The freelancer and author both need to know the extent of the other's responsibilities and authority. Informing everyone involved, especially an author who is working with a freelancer for the first time, of policies and procedures at the beginning of a project will enhance a manager's credibility with both freelancer and author and will improve the manager's ability to use freelancers effectively in the future.

MANAGEMENT TECHNIQUES FOR
WORKING WITH FREELANCERS

Good management practices are just as essential with freelancers as they are with in-house staff.

The Basics

Managers must provide the necessary background information: intended audience, purpose of the publication, deadlines, and political and organizational sensitivities. The manager must also provide all appropriate information about work flow, production procedures, approvals, and signatures required. Introductions to in-house staff, the author, and others with whom the freelancer might have contact will provide a more open and comfortable work situation for everyone. If the freelancer is in a distant location, a conference call for introductions and general discussion might be helpful.

A manager should maintain contact with the freelancer throughout the project so that neither will be surprised. Especially for large projects, it is prudent to ask a freelancer to submit portions of the project when presenting periodic bills so that review of work as well as production can proceed smoothly. (Many experienced freelancers will do this as a matter of course.) The manager must remember to schedule the freelancer's work with all other projects in progress.

Feedback

Throughout the project if possible, but especially at completion, a manager must provide feedback to a freelancer: the approaches and techniques that worked or didn't work, the organization's stylistic peculiarities that the freelancer missed (or perhaps were omitted from the style specifications), political sensitivities that arose during the project, and production problems caused unwittingly by the freelancer. Freelancers who do not receive this information will continue making the same mistakes. Feedback to the freelancer should begin with the manager but might be delegated later.

While work review and feedback are essential between any manager and staff, they are especially critical for the first few manuscripts. But competent, experienced freelancers should quickly be given autonomy to perform the job they were hired to do.

Feedback, like the negotiation process, should be a give-and-take situation; the manager should encourage feedback from the freelancer. How can communication between the manager and freelancer or between the author and freelancer be improved? What problems were encountered that might have an easy solution? How can the organization make the freelancer's job easier?

The Extras

A copy of the publication and a letter of thanks are certainly appropriate for a job well done. Acknowledging in the publication the freelancer's contribution is an effective way to give recognition, but the freelancer should always approve the acknowledgment.

To obtain special expertise, a manager may find it necessary to hire a freelancer from outside the local area. The management problem here is similar to dealing with a manuscript from a distant author or organizational unit. The telephone and overnight delivery services, while somtimes expensive, are often worth the cost. The manager must maintain greater control and initially take more time with a distant freelancer. But a qualified distant freelancer can quickly become an asset for the manager and organization.

The process for paying freelancers, whether periodically or at the end of a job, should have been discussed during the negotiation process. A manager can maintain the good will of a freelancer if payment is prompt. A manager can suggest that if the freelancer has not received payment within a month (or other appropriate period), the freelancer should call the manager, who should immediately determine the problem, resolve it, and tell the freelancer the status of the check.

The ending point is the beginning point: The same good management practices used with in-house staff should be used (or adapted appropriately) with freelancers. The appropriate investment of the organization's time and resources in freelancers should yield professional and financial rewards for both parties.

With planning and flexibility, an editorial manager can use freelancers to augment an organization's capabilities and expertise. Being as specific as possible about organizational needs, time and cost restrictions, style specifications, and anticipated problems is crucial to a successful job. While employing freelancers does not come without a price, this approach can be productive in achieving the manager's and organization's goals: well-edited publications.

SELECTED READING

Bentsen, M., Working Successfully with Editorial Freelancers, *The Editorial Eye, 13*:4, pp. 1-2, 1990.

Caernarven-Smith, P., Computers and Communication: Getting the Most Out of Contracting, *Technical Communication, 36*:1, pp. 67-71, 1989.

Darrow, T. L., Temporary Expertise Develops into a Permanent Solution, *Management Review, 78*:11, pp. 50-52, 1989.

Feinberg, K., Help for Freelancers Who Can't Collect, *The Editorial Eye, 15*:6, pp. 10-11, 1992.

Firman, A. H., Improving Vendor-Client Relations, *Technical Communication, 34*:2, pp. 79-83, 1987.

Hackos, J. T., Managing Creative People, *Technical Communication, 37*:4, pp. 375-380, 1990.

Rodriguez, G., A Degree of Opportunity: University Presses Rely on Free-Lance Copy Editors, *Righting Words, 3*:1, pp. 15-23, 1989.

Simons, J. L., The "Retired" Freelancer, in The Business of Technical Communication, Dart G. Peterson, Jr. (ed.), *Technical Communication, 37*:2, pp. 182-183, 1990.

Taylor, P. S., Do You Have the Personality Traits That Make a Good Editor? *The Editorial Eye, 12*:5, pp. 1-3, 1989.

Upton, C. R., Independent Contractors and Cottage Labor (report of a conference session), *CBE Views, 15*:1, pp. 11-13, 1992.

Whalen, E., Keys to Success on Copyediting Tests, *CBE Views, 15*:3, pp. 51-55, 1992.

CHAPTER 7

Managing Internships

JODY H. HEIKEN

intern (n): an advanced student or recent graduate undergoing practical
training
intern (v-tr.): to detain or confine (especially in wartime)
—*American Heritage Dictionary of the English Language (1981)*

The definitions quoted above lend themselves to some obvious humorous comments, but in fact, the principle of internships is heartily endorsed by industry sponsors, academic institutions, and students, all of whom have benefited from existing internship programs.

A technical communication internship is a period during which a student works as a technical communicator under supervision in a professional environment to gain practical experience. Internships usually are arranged to fulfill technical writing curriculum requirements, but occasionally they are apprenticeships independently undertaken to provide an individual some specific training.

Because internships generally involve agreement among the industrial sponsor, the academic program adviser, and the student, they can be tailored to meet the needs of each. Internships are legitimately promoted as a great bargain for all three sides of the triangle: the industry sponsor gains a well-educated temporary employee, the student gains practical experience, and the academic institution gains an industrial partner who not only provides an aspect of training unavailable in the classroom but also helps assess the usefulness of the technical communication program.

Internships may be a component of undergraduate coursework, may fall between graduation and graduate school, may be required in a graduate program, or may be an intermediate step before a permanent job. They may even take the form of part-time jobs at any of these stages. The large number of reentry students in both undergraduate and graduate technical communication programs means that student interns run the gamut from young adults who haven't yet held a full-time job to seasoned employees who are beginning a second or even a third career.

Whatever the timing or the student's age and experience, internships are an important supplement to academic coursework and provide the vital transition between classroom theory and professional practice. Thus internships represent added value for everyone because they result in an individual who is better prepared to take on responsibilities in the workplace, is more able to appreciate an employer's "bottom line," and functions at a higher level of competence and confidence.

HOW INTERNSHIPS WORK

The success of any technical writing internship program is dependent on a well-planned effort that takes into account the expectations and requirements of the industrial sponsor, the student, and the academic program. Therefore, it is helpful to examine the process from all three perspectives.

For the Industrial Sponsor

The industrial sponsor enters into an internship agreement for a variety of reasons. Usually the sponsor's primary goal is to hire an individual to accomplish specific tasks, and the secondary purpose is to offer experience to the intern.

The company gains a limited-term employee with a technical writing education—almost always at entry-level (or slightly lower) salary. In many cases, the job assigned to the intern involves a project that otherwise might not be undertaken because of staffing or budget constraints. In addition, industry sponsors may view the internship as an opportunity to "try out" an individual they might wish to hire at a later date; this is especially the case with a postgraduate internship when the student is already beginning to look for full-time employment.

Increasingly, industry sponsors recognize that internships offer a forum through which they can help shape the training of the technical writers they will need in the future; by providing feedback to academic advisers, they are able to influence the content of technical writing programs in colleges and universities. As a *pro bono* initiative, the internship program is an excellent way for the company to integrate with the community, invest in the education of potential future employees, and extend regular employees' professional experience in mentoring and supervision.

Having embraced the principle of internships, first-time industry sponsors should assign an individual to research the process. The initial step is to examine various university or college technical writing curricula to find several programs that emphasize the skills, background, and approach the company requires of its regular technical writers. For example, programs differ in their requirements for science, mathematics, computer, and language courses; some schools offer greater opportunities for computer training; some departments may approach technical writing through a journalism or rhetoric point of view. Although some companies are able to look for interns from colleges or universities close to home, others must look outside the local community or even out of state.

After establishing a relationship with likely technical writing programs and, usually, with an individual faculty member within those programs, the company may want and need advice from the academic adviser to establish a framework for the company's intern program. Especially if the supervisor or mentor chosen by the company to work with the student has had no direct experience with internships, the academic adviser can help by suggesting appropriate types of projects, helping to structure the intern's responsibilities, judging the level of expertise that can be expected of the intern, planning for the best use of the intern's time, writing the job description for a suitable level of experience, and helping screen and select the candidate.

For the Academic Institution

Most departments that offer technical communication programs are fully aware of the benefits of internship programs and subscribe to the concept. From that point on, however, the approach seems to vary a great deal [1-3]. Some universities and colleges feel it is in the best interest of the students and the program to investigate potential employers fully, play a role in structuring the content of the intern's responsibilities, provide written contracts, negotiate salaries, suggest appropriate students for interviews, and continually review the process.

At the other end of the spectrum, some academic departments favor the idea that students should find their own internship opportunities and that the program adviser's only contact with the sponsor should be to request a final evaluation of the student's performance—an approach they feel reflects more closely the "real-world" experience and permits the usual employee/employer relationship to develop. Most academic programs fall somewhere along the line between these two extremes, and many academic advisers are willing to work with the industrial partners to find a mutually agreeable version tailored to the circumstances.

It is obviously much easier for most companies to deal with a single academic adviser than with a flood of applications from individual students. For instance, the academic program director, knowing the sponsor's needs as well as the students' capabilities and interests, can suggest appropriate partnerships between students and potential employers. This prematching can eliminate a great deal of wasted effort in screening resumes, testing, and interviewing.

If such an approach is to be used, sponsors and internship program directors should frankly discuss the sponsor's requirements, the intern project, the salary, supervisory details, and the type of individual needed. By discussing the students' strengths and backgrounds, the program director and industry sponsor can be sure that the students being considered are appropriate for the job.

Once the sponsor and the program director agree on the basics, it is good practice for the director to suggest as large a selection of potential candidates as is practical for the company to interview. If the industry sponsor prefers to do all the screening, the academic adviser might only need to discuss with the sponsor the nature of the internship opening, the job description, and the tasks to be accomplished, and then merely post the company's advertisement in the department.

If the company is contacted directly by a student who requests an internship, there may be limited opportunity for interaction between the industry sponsor and the academic adviser. Some companies appreciate this approach because there is no "academic barrier" between the intern and the company and because the student has used initiative in contacting the company independently. The role of the intern then is much like that of any other employee, except that the length of employment is finite. However, even in such independently arranged internships, if the student is earning course credit for the internship, the academic adviser usually requests a telephone interview with the intern's supervisor or, at the least, a final evaluation.

For the Student

The practical experience gained in a technical writing internship is immensely valuable to students, although the advantages are most substantial for younger undergraduates with little or no experience. Reentry students who have spent years working in other fields still benefit from on-the-job technical writing experience that augments their previous experience and academic coursework. The value of professional contacts and on-the-job experience is more likely to be immediately important for senior and graduate-level interns than for those who still have several years before they enter the job market. In addition to the expected day-to-day nuts-and-bolts information, interns gain a more realistic view of employers' expectations, the complexities of the work environment, working within a team framework, the scope of activities related to a typical project, and their own personal skills.

Students express a variety of opinions about the advantages of faculty-arranged internships versus finding their own. Some students feel confident enough to approach companies on their own, while others want the additional assurance of stepping into an established position. Again, there is the expected difference in the confidence level of younger undergraduates and that of more experienced reentry students. Many students who have a specific career path in mind prefer to seek their own opportunities because they can tailor the search to their own specific future needs and interests. In addition, many students prefer the freedom to select their own potential industry sponsors because they realize that an internship might open the door to future permanent employment.

Paid internships are obviously more attractive to students than those where experience alone is the reward—a well-paid internship could fund an entire academic year for a student. In addition, many industry sponsors, academic institutions, and students feel not only that the concept of value for money is important to both student and company, but also that a salaried position maintains the professional status of technical communication [2, 4]. Another comment is that "volunteer" status does not provide a valid workplace experience because it sets the intern apart from regular employees in terms of professionalism, job responsibilities, commitment, and expectations. However, it must be noted that salary is not always the best criterion by which to judge the value of the potential position. A low-paying or even nonpaying job with some employers could be worth a great deal in terms of the experience, portfolio material, significance on the student's resume, professional contacts, and letters of recommendation.

SELECTING AN INTERN

The selection process should take place after the industry sponsor has defined the job responsibilities of the intern to be hired and, as appropriate, discussed the company's needs with the academic adviser.

The procedures of requesting resumes, transcripts, and portfolios for screening applicants differ little from those followed for regular employees. Although many students have limited portfolios, they usually can provide at least classwork examples of writing, editing, and document production. Students on strained budgets frequently do not have multiple copies, so the portfolios should be returned as quickly as possible in case they are needed for other interviews. If the industry sponsor intends to use a writing/editing test as a part of the selection process, this should be made clear in the job advertisement.

Although students seeking internships are usually close to obtaining their undergraduate or graduate degree, it is obvious that their transcripts, gradepoint, major and minor emphases, previous job experience, life experience, and goals will vary widely.

It is also quite likely that the company will interview a broad range of applicants—from students in their early twenties to mid-life reentry students. Companies would benefit from either the freshness and energy of the first group or the maturity and work experience of the second group. The choice can be more difficult because the natural computer skills of younger students must be weighed against the depth of knowledge older students bring with them. The job content of the particular internship may be a deciding factor.

Matching the individual to the project should be based on the company's needs, faculty adviser's assistance, and the student's interview, portfolio, and resume.

GREAT EXPECTATIONS

The industry sponsor, academic institution, and intern may differ in their chief reasons for participating in the internship program and in the details of their arrangements, but there should be total agreement in what they expect the program to accomplish and how they expect the internship to function. An effective relationship among the three parties depends on each understanding the expectations of the other two.

The Industry Sponsor's Expectations

Industry sponsors want interns who are productive and capable employees.

A Product

Very few companies that hire interns are nonprofit; most are in the business of selling a product—whether it is a widget, science and technology, or their own expertise. For this reason, industry sponsors must approach the intern experience as an investment in their company's productivity rather than as a purely altruistic effort. Companies are gambling by hiring an individual who may or may not yet have the skills they require of a more experienced professional, and in return they pay this intern at a lower rate than they would a regular employee.

Usually the industry sponsor wants an intern for a specific short-term project such as a technical document, a script, or a research project that can be completed within the internship period. Sometimes, however, an intern is needed simply as another team member during a period of peak activity.

It is important to be realistic about how much an intern can accomplish during an internship period, what types of tasks can be delegated to an intern, and how much time a supervisor will be able to spend with an intern. In addition, assignments should be sharply focused so that interns are aware of the boundaries and can plan their effort effectively. Projects should not require a great deal of background information that is available only to regular employees.

A clear channel of authority should be agreed upon so that other employees do not ask the intern to take on additional tasks (however interesting or important) at the expense of the original project. The intern's written job description should, at the very least, outline the scope of the project, name the supervisor, state deadlines, list evaluation criteria to be used in the performance appraisal, and specify the period of employment [5].

The supervisor must understand the scope of the intern's assignment, be informed about all deadlines, know what types of assistance the intern will need, be aware of the student's expectations, and be able to keep the project moving toward completion. This is a time-consuming responsibility; both the company and the supervisor should be aware of just how much time it will involve [6].

The supervisor will need to teach the intern about the company's culture, standards, and style preferences as well as the actual subject matter of the project.

Meetings, progress reports, training sessions, and performance evaluations all require an investment of effort and time. For this reason, it is helpful to assign additional employees as mentors and subject-matter resources.

Presumably, everyone involved—the supervisor, mentors, and coworkers—is interested in the intern's professional experience as well, but the supervisor and intern must focus primarily on the end-product. Common experience tells us that time passes more and more quickly as a deadline approaches. If the inevitable learning period, unavoidable delays, and changing priorities are complicated by procrastination, unrealistic estimates of time required, or inadequate planning, an intern can reach the end of the allotted time without completing the project. Therefore, it is imperative that the intern and supervisor discuss schedules and milestones early in the internship, chart progress by memos or calendars, and continually reevaluate the project.

An internship should provide as full an experience as possible: it should include elements that will challenge without intimidating, use the intern's skills without exploitation, and enhance the intern's confidence without instilling a false sense of accomplishment.

A Capable and Professional Employee

The company expects an intern to display the skills and knowledge reflected in the application, resume, interview, and portfolio—those are the bases upon which the student was hired. The company usually is paying the intern and anticipates a certain amount of value for the money. Professional demeanor is certainly a reasonable expectation as well. Because the internship is of limited duration, the company understandably does not want to spend a great deal of time settling, briefing, and training an intern. Like any new employee, an intern is expected to move quickly from novice to "old hand" and to take up an assigned project equally swiftly. Unfortunately, sometimes the company has unrealistic expectations or fond hopes that an intern will bring to the job a degree of professionalism, experience, and wisdom beyond the intern's years. A frank discussion during the interview should clarify any ambiguity about what the company requires in computer skills, product knowledge, and professional writing ability.

The Academic Adviser's Expectations

Among other things, academic advisers want their students to have "real-world" experience and professional evaluation.

Effective Management of the Intern and Placement of Future Interns

Most academic institutions strive to ensure that the intern's experience is as profitable as possible—after all, the institution's students are its product and they must be marketable following graduation. One of the best methods for improving the quality of internship experiences is to require from interns regular reports that outline the tasks required, the working relationship with others in the project, the challenges, and the overall impression of learning opportunities. By keeping in touch with previous interns now working at regular jobs, faculty obtain further information about the long-term value of internships.

Companies that are interested in a continuing source of interns find it extremely helpful to establish a close relationship with technical communication programs. For instance, if the department is aware of the specific needs of a company, faculty can help students prepare themselves as candidates for those internships.

Of course, industry sponsors who have a history of hiring former interns into permanent positions will be highly recommended as potential internship opportunities by both former students and the academic adviser. Industry sponsors find that the investment made in training an intern is well spent when that intern may become part of the permanent staff.

Industrial Partners for Planning the Technical Writing Curriculum

Interns and their industry supervisors also help faculty assess how well the technical communication program has prepared students for their future profession. Through interns' reports and supervisors' evaluations, faculty are able to track the continually evolving jobs of technical writers in industry. Feedback from internships provides a window on the job market and helps technical writing programs determine what changes should be made in the department's curriculum.

Although the basic principles of writing, rhetoric, and grammar may not have changed a great deal in the last ten years, the day-to-day scope of a technical writer's job has expanded substantially. For example, in the last decade, subject matter expertise, computer skills, audience analysis techniques, and familiarity with multimedia have become common requirements for even entry-level positions.

On-the-Job Education for the Student

Faculty realize that there is no way to provide students with all the skills and practical experience needed on the job in the limited hours and courses available through a regular curriculum. The entire purpose of the internship is to broaden the students' experience and introduce them to the work environment in a fairly controlled situation. As mentioned earlier, internships also substantially enhance students' marketability to future employers.

It is impossible always to place students in internships that reflect their long-term interests and goals. In some cases, the only available options are far afield from the type of work students plan to do; in other instances, students simply have not decided what they want to do.

However, no work-related experience is ever wasted. The breadth of technical communication today offers graduates a bewildering array of possible career paths. At the very least, an internship will appear on the intern's resume, provide practical experience, and allow the intern to evaluate interests and skill in some aspects of technical communication.

The internship may very well stimulate a lasting interest in a particular area of technical communication and provide valuable professional contacts for the future.

Promotion for the Technical Writing Program

Documents or other products created for the industry sponsor by interns not only are needed for the interns' portfolios, but also are valuable in the institution's collection of student work. These products are concrete evidence of the program's success and its benefit to participating community sponsors. Institutions use these portfolios to show the range of student capabilities and to demonstrate the value added by communication professionals. Technical writing programs strive to produce well-trained, highly skilled communicators for today's extremely competitive business world; one of the best measures of a program's effectiveness is the intern's success in real-world situations. Through the interns' reports, their supervisors' appraisals, and the products from internship projects, the institution is able to evaluate the strengths and weaknesses of its program.

The Student's Expectations

Students enter an internship with a host of expectations.

Responsibilities that Reflect the Intern's Qualifications and Training

Occasionally industry sponsors hire well-qualified interns, but do not match them to appropriate projects. Although it is unrealistic to expect interns to have the expertise and judgment of professionals with several years of on-the-job experience, it is just as inappropriate to assign interns to jobs that do not use their abilities.

The caliber of students graduating in technical communication programs today is extremely high. Many have a second degree in a technical field, and almost all have experience with a variety of computers. Because many students are beginning their second or even third career, they bring with them years of experience in the workforce. It is a loss for both the company and the intern if this knowledge and experience is wasted.

Appropriate Level of Supervision

A student entering the business world usually expects and welcomes supervision in the form of clear assignments, discussion of approaches to the project, delegation of suitable tasks, appropriate support in the case of conflicts, and so forth. However, if the opportunity to learn is diminished by either too much or too little supervision, the intern, like any other employee, has grounds for complaint.

Whether the intern and supervisor work closely and a team relationship evolves or the intern does not even see the supervisor on a regular basis, a written description of the tasks to be completed during the internship and a frank discussion of the employer's expectations is needed. The supervisor should define the intern's part in the project for everyone involved and provide a strong foundation for future discussion of work progress. The intern is then left in no doubt as to what is expected and is able to judge more easily when to ask for more assistance.

In addition, regular written reports from students to supervisors serve several purposes. Students learn the value of documenting progress as well as how to analyze their work in relation to an entire project. Supervisors are able to judge immediately whether work is proceeding at an appropriate pace and if there are problems. Copies of the job description and reports to a supervisor show an academic adviser the scope of an intern's responsibilities, the stages of a project, and a student's adaptation to the workplace.

Although many interns want to strike out on their own, there is reassurance in knowing that a supervisor/mentor is there to assist if a problem simply outstrips an intern's knowledge, skills, or experience. If nothing else, the supervisor serves as a sounding board off which an intern can bounce ideas—a process that helps articulate the issues and provides an atmosphere in which to discuss possible solutions. One of the supervisor/mentor's most important roles in an internship is to demonstrate methods of resolving disagreements and reaching compromises without having to sacrifice deadlines, quality, or personal dignity.

Product for the Intern's Portfolio

One of the most easily achieved goals of an internship is material for the intern's portfolio. Obviously, any document the intern produces should be included—but only with the permission of the supervisor. In some cases, the intern's assignment involves proprietary or sensitive material that the company does not wish to disseminate; however, it may be possible to include portions or to show the document at a later date. The supervisor and intern should discuss this issue early in the internship so there are no misunderstandings. If proprietary information is involved, it is sensible to put into writing the industry sponsor's policy regarding products of the intern's efforts.

Even if the project assigned is not one that will produce a suitable publication by the end of the internship, the intern's work could be displayed through marked up drafts, design layouts, illustrations, interview notes, outlines, or document plans. A portfolio can effectively demonstrate project management through a paper trail that reveals the steps taken to bring a project to completion.

Professional-Level Experience

The internship is often the student's first professional-level experience in technical publication, and the move from the controlled classroom environment to the high-pressure business world can be bewildering. Emerging from a culture in which the focus is on the intellectual growth of the student into a culture in which the individual no longer is the central concern can be a rude awakening for some interns. Some thrive on the challenge; they seem to expand to fill the position immediately and require only occasional guidance on professional conduct and attitudes. Others are intimidated and need more direction and structure before assuming full responsibility for their role.

If an intern is part of a publications department or is supervised by a mentor in the same field, there should be some natural opportunities to attend seminars, share source material, or at least get involved in discussions that deal with technical communication issues. However, if an intern is located outside such a department, it may be necessary to make opportunities for contact with other technical communicators on the job.

If deadlines and workload permit, supervisors should encourage interns to attend local professional meetings, read journals, or spend time with other technical communicators within the company. These contacts are part of the professional experience and could be valuable when an intern needs help in solving a communication problem or begins looking for a permanent job.

Access to Latest Equipment

For some students, an internship is the first opportunity to develop skill on computer platforms with a variety of software. Many industry sponsors encourage exploration in the interest of increased familiarity with a product or system— provided the intern completes assignments, meets deadlines, and doesn't incur additional expenses in the process. However, it is reasonable to ask the intern to experiment on his/her own time. In addition, obviously, the supervisor must give permission and set any necessary restrictions. This last is particularly important if, for example, the industry sponsor is a computer company where proprietary information may be involved.

Letter of Recommendation and Credit on Resume

Students are well aware that potential employers examine a resume for practical experience as well as for the college or university degree, and therefore internships are highly valued. Familiarity with "the culture" of different work environments lends credibility to a student's resume and assures the prospective employer that the student will make the transition from classroom to workplace more quickly and completely.

Interns hope to gain a strong letter of recommendation for their portfolio from their industry supervisor. In addition, potential employers frequently request information directly from the industry supervisor. If for some reason the internship has not been a success, the supervisor should discuss that matter frankly with the intern. It may be possible to arrive at an agreement about some positive elements of the experience that can be emphasized instead of merely mentioning the negative aspects.

WRAPPING IT UP

At the end of an internship, it is important to evaluate both the intern's performance and the internship's success—two components that must be considered separately. The first depends primarily on the intern; the second depends for the most part on 1) the industry sponsor's ability to structure a job that is appropriate to an intern and to assign a supervisor who works effectively with an intern, and 2) the academic program's ability to produce a properly trained student for today's job market.

The intern's supervisor usually writes a formal evaluation for the intern's academic adviser and provides a copy for the intern. If the internship is considered part of the program coursework, the academic adviser may use this evaluation, with the student's reports, to determine a grade [7]. The intern also may wish to use the evaluation in a portfolio or as part of the background material required for acceptance to graduate school.

The industry sponsor, the intern, and the academic adviser should each evaluate the success of the internship and recommend changes, if necessary, for future internships. Interns generally are responsible for a final report to their adviser, but unfortunately, that report and the work accomplished for the industry sponsor frequently stand in lieu of an actual evaluation of the internship process from the intern's point of view.

The intern should also examine the outcome of the internship because only the intern can know how much he or she profited from the process [1, 8]. Some intern supervisors and academic advisers recommend that the intern's evaluation be written in two parts: the first portion immediately, while facts and impressions are still fresh, and the second part after several months, when the intern is able to see the entire period more objectively.

Supervisors can also use the exit interview to elicit information and opinions from departing interns. Unfortunately, however, this interview often takes place during the last days of an internship when neither intern nor supervisor has time to consider the matter properly.

Through internships, the industrial sponsor, academic adviser, and student have an opportunity to contribute to the profession of technical communication. The results are seen in superbly trained employees, strong technical communication programs, and industrial support for the value our professionals add in the workplace. The time and effort required of industry and academic departments to establish and maintain high-quality internship programs is well spent.

REFERENCES

1. W. O. Coggin (ed.), *Establishing and Supervising Internships,* Teaching Technical Writing Series No. 9, Association of Teachers of Technical Writing, Lubbock, Texas, 1989.

2. B. K. Bowers and C. Nelson (eds.), *Internships in Technical Communication: Guide for Students, Faculty Supervisors, and Internship Sponsors,* Society for Technical Communication, Arlington, Virginia, 1991.
3. R. Femmel, Why Not Make Internships Mandatory for Everybody, *Journalism Educator, 33*:3, pp. 17-19, 1978.
4. D. K. Farkas, Payment for Undergraduate Interns: Benefits, Problems, and Solutions, in *Establishing and Supervising Internships,* W. O. Coggin (ed.), Teaching Technical Writing Series No. 9, Association of Teachers of Technical Writing, Lubbock, Texas, pp. 115-122, 1989.
5. L. B. Applewhite, D. L. Armbruster, R. A. Grice, M. L. Keene, V. W. Mikelonis, C. Soderston, and F. F. Storer, Internships in Technical Communication: Their Creation, Maintenance, and Rewards, in *Establishing and Supervising Internships,* W. O. Coggin (ed.), Teaching Technical Writing Series No. 9, Association of Teachers of Technical Writing, Lubbock, Texas, pp. 1-19, 1989.
6. L. A. Sharon, How to Organize and Manage a Technical Communication Internship, *Proceedings of the 37th ITCC,* Society for Technical Communication, Washington, DC, ET82-ET85, 1990.
7. F. F. Stohrer and R. L. Norman, Current Internships in Technical Communication: A Descriptive Survey, *Proceedings of the 36th ITCC,* Society for Technical Communication, Washington, DC, ET11-ET14, 1989.
8. J. Corey and M. J. Killingsworth, The Internship Report, *Technical Writing Teacher, 14*:2, pp. 133-141, 1987.

PART III

Project Management and the Information Development Cycle

Most technical communicators, whether they are called managers or not, find themselves managing projects and collaborating with others to develop documents. The six essays in this section consider some of the issues involved in project management.

In the first chapter of this book James Souther, "Managing Technical Publications: A Growing and Changing Responsibility," points to the need for publications staff to integrate document development at critical points in the information development cycle. Christopher Forbes opens this section with practical advice about how writers and editors can participate in the information development cycle. In "The Role of the Technical Communicator within Organizational Development Cycles," Forbes, a publications specialist with Boeing Computer Services, brings both academic and workplace experience to an analysis of the varying levels of responsibility publications staff can assume throughout the cycle. These levels range from the use of basic editing skills to full management participation in the development of organizational publications.

The second essay in this section is by Barbara Weber, manager of Documentation and Methods Analysis for El Paso Natural Gas Company. In "Project Management: The Art of Managing Deadlines" Weber offers suggestions for meeting deadlines, handling missed deadlines, and avoiding future misses by developing standards, guidelines, and templates.

The next two essays, by John S. Harris, professor of English at Brigham Young University, and Lynn H. Deming, associate professor in the technical communication program at New Mexico Institute of Mining and Technology, recommend worksheets and templates to guide publications staff in streamlining document production.

Harris' "The Project Worksheet for Efficient Writing Management" encourages the use of a project worksheet to help managers and writers determine documentation specifications before a project begins. These specifications include definition of purpose, scope, form, length, graphic aids to be used, and sources of information.

In "Document Standardization: Maintaining Project Harmony" Deming considers some of the finer issues of design and terminology that require standardization to maintain uniformity, quality, and efficiency throughout a documentation project. In addition, she provides sample format and terminology specification sheets and useful pointers to guide in their preparation.

One of the challenges of managing a documentation project is determining document costs. David L. Smith's "Estimating Costs for Documentation Projects" reflects his experience as publications section chief for the Physical Science Laboratory at New Mexico State University. Smith estimates documentation costs based on an analysis of the size and content of the document, the complexity of the subject matter, and the level of quality required.

Finally, Robert M. Brown, director of the technical writing program at Oklahoma State University, offers an alternative to the time-consuming and morale-shattering document cycling that takes place in many organizations. Brown's "Team Conferences: Full Collaboration in the Report Writing Process" describes a procedure for using team conferences—including managers at all levels, the principal investigator for a project, and writers and editors—in a collaborative effort to plan, write, and review lengthy reports.

CHAPTER 8

The Role of the Technical Communicator Within Organizational Information Development Cycles

CHRISTOPHER J. FORBES

Information development cycles in professional organizations vary according to an organization's size, resources, mission, and/or products. But regardless of variations, all organizations work with an information development cycle that can be generically defined as the process an organization relies upon to generate, organize, refine, produce, and distribute information for use in a specific manner (to complete an analysis, obtain funding, establish a database, and so on). In different capacities and at different levels of visibility virtually all members of an organization contribute to its information development cycle, including top-level administrators; middle and line management; and professional, technical, and clerical personnel. The basic mechanics of an information development cycle are illustrated in Figure 1.

It is important to emphasize that the information cycle depicted in Figure 1 is very general. In a small organization with few employees, for example, the cycle can move quickly and close as early as stage 5. In a larger organization, each stage in Figure 1 usually entails a complex iterative process drawing in resources from the organization's divisions, departments, and department sections. An organization that is very small often employs an information cycle without *any* input from technical writers/editors, simply because the small organization cannot afford the expense of specific technical communication employees. Larger organizations, on

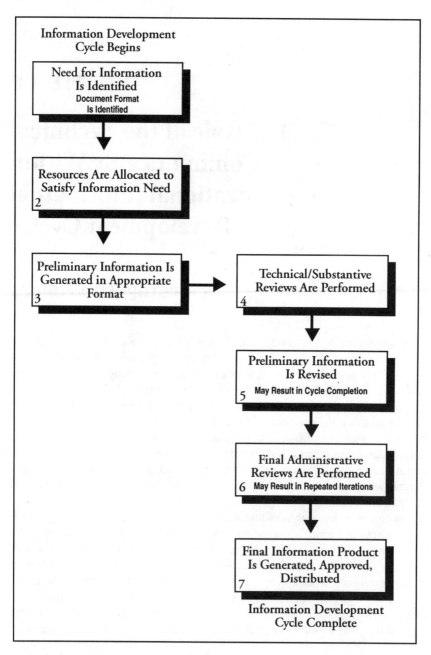

Figure 1. Basic stages of an organizational information development cycle.

the other hand, employ distinct publications groups (writers; word processors; technical illustrators; reproduction, distribution, and clerical personnel) that exist specifically for the purpose of supporting an information development cycle.

The primary focus of this chapter is on the varying ways that writers/editors (and, by extension, the publications groups they represent) draw upon different levels of project management skills to support the demands of an organization's information development cycle.

INTEGRATING PROJECT MANAGEMENT SKILLS INTO AN INFORMATION DEVELOPMENT CYCLE

Any meaningful discussion of the contributions of technical communicators to an organization's information development cycle begins with a recognition of the support role that is assigned to technical communicators and their publications departments. *Support,* in this context, means that the technical communicator's primary responsibility is to provide and coordinate a standard array of technical communication resources (writing, editing, word processing, technical illustrations, document production and distribution) to a technical group that requires such services. In a typical organization there is little debate whether a support group *will* accommodate a request for services. The questions that can be asked are, basically, to what *extent* and how *quickly* can the support services be provided.

Inevitably, certain inherent antagonisms develop between technical and support groups, especially since support personnel tend to be viewed as subordinate to engineers, scientists, and other technical professionals. As a result, technical writers/editors frequently encounter extraordinary support-service expectations. For example, a request for a one-day turnaround of a 200-page document (including both editing and word processing) occurs so often as to be stereotypical.

Yet, despite the occurrence of such unrealistic requests on (practically) a daily basis, it is a mistake to think writers/editors and their publications groups must always react to these demands, especially when the demands render them unable to effectively use their project management skills within an information development cycle. Between the two impossible extremes of always doing everything exactly as requested or outright rejection of requests for support exists a range of options that can be negotiated.

The dimensions of the negotiations greatly depend on the level at which a writer, editor, or publications group participates as a support entity in an organization's information development cycle. Often this participation depends upon the project management skills that the writer, editor, or publications group commands.

Level One: Basic Contributions to the Information Development Cycle

Providing basic contributions to an organization's information development cycle requires skills that are specific to the mechanical aspects of the cycle. These contributions usually occur in the last few stages identified in Figure 1. A typical scenario could unfold as follows:

- A technical group determines the need for a 100-page topical report.
- The technical group determines the appropriate format for the report and identifies the technical personnel with the expertise to develop the report.
- The technical personnel generate a report draft, guide it through a series of reviews and revisions, and then generate an interim draft that is finally ready for technical editing.
- At this point, support services from a technical writer/editor or publications group are requested.

In this case a technical writer/editor or publications group is asked to enter the information development cycle at stage 5, where preliminary information is revised. Essentially at this stage all that is left for the writer/editor to do—in terms of project management—is clean up the report. This could include a light text edit to prepare the draft so that final administrative reviews can be performed (stage 6). The report is then revised into its final format. Approvals are obtained, and the technical writer's project management responsibilities devolve to production activities (stage 7) that support distribution of the report to the intended audience.

Contributing to the information development cycle in this basic way can be demanding, especially since the time constraints in a cycle's last stages are usually very tight. But *complex* project management skills are not required. This mode of support includes few project management challenges beyond light editing and basic document coordination capabilities. At level one, then, the technical communicator's primary obligation is to ensure that the information cycle moves efficiently in its latter stages so that the final document is distributed on schedule.

Contributing project management skills to the information development cycle in this way, the technical writer/editor is basically reactive, with a comparatively low degree of visibility or accountability. There is an excellent opportunity for success in this case, but not much potential for the writer/editor to participate in or be perceived as an integral part of the information development cycle. This is because the writer/editor enters the cycle at its concluding stages and does not contribute substantially to the important information-generating early stages of the cycle.

The shortcomings of a basic contribution to an information cycle are fairly evident, but they should not obscure several clear benefits of level one project management skills. After all, providing basic support for an organization's information development cycle is *exactly* what an entry-level writer/editor needs to do, as the writer/editor learns ways to function effectively in a new working environment and, gradually, acquires more sophisticated project management skills. For such personnel, exposure to and involvement in limited parts of the information development cycle constitutes valuable experience that will provide a good foundation for more challenging future activities.

At the same time writers, editors, and publications groups need to remain aware of the dangers of exclusively supporting an information cycle with basic project management skills. In doing so, writers/editors limit their challenges and workplace visibility to a fairly repetitive and predictable series of production-oriented activities. For people (or groups) who thrive on activities measured through metrics, such as page counts, a level one approach to project management skills is fine. However, consistent relegation to those activities that always support the final stages of an information development cycle also positions support personnel into a niche where their efforts are commonly perceived as minimal.

Finally, a publications group that aims to provide only basic contributions to an information development cycle will inevitably force its employees to operate in a reactive mode. As such, technical communicators will be unable to effectively control the time elements that often become critical in the last stages of an organization's information development cycle.

Level Two: Substantive Contributions to the Information Development Cycle

The technical writer, editor, or publications group providing substantive contributions to an organization's information development cycle enters the cycle in its early stages and remains part of the cycle until closure. In this case the project management responsibilities of the writer/editor are considerably larger and more challenging than in level one.

The writer/editor who makes substantive support contributions to the information cycle can still be (and usually is) responsible for the same end-of-the-cycle, production-oriented project management activities that characterize level one. However, the stage 5, 6, and 7 activities that define level one project management skills represent only a part (and usually a small part) of the level two writer/editor's overall involvement within an information development cycle.

The writer/editor who makes substantive (that is, content-generating) contributions to an information development cycle is acknowledged as one of the main resources needed to make the cycle work efficiently. Consequently, at level two the writer/editor enters the cycle no later than stage 2 and is expected to begin applying a wide array of project management skills at that stage. A typical scenario could involve the following steps:

- A technical organization requests the support services of a writer, editor, or publications group immediately after that organization determines its need for a specific document type (for example, a policy manual containing 12 administrative procedures). This occurs in stage 2.
- The writer/editor is given whatever rudimentary materials the organization has available and is tasked with the responsibility to take this preliminary information, "go away," and come back with draft procedures that are suitable for reviews.
- The writer/editor contacts the main specialists (scientists, engineers, technicians), obtains information from them, and then shapes the input into a review document (stage 3).
- The writer/editor then oversees and coordinates the document as it flows through various iterations, ensuring (among other things) that 1) all contributors work on the same version of the procedures; and 2) each successive draft reflects the latest information (stage 4). NOTE: In stages 3 and 4 the writer/editor *also* contributes information to the document through substantive technical writing, organizing, and reviewing capacities.
- During the final stages of the document, the writer/editor produces a final document (stage 5), obtains administrative approvals (stage 6), and closes the cycle by ensuring appropriate reproduction and distribution functions (stage 7).

Contributing to the information cycle in these ways involves project management capabilities far beyond those needed at level one, especially as there are many variations in the ways a technical writer/editor can make substantive contributions to an information cycle. For example, in addition to standard technical writing/editing functions (coordinating writing, word processing, technical illustrations, and so forth), a writer/editor may be asked to schedule, track, and report on the progress of a document through the stages of the information development cycle. In another capacity, the writer/editor may be required to act as the technical organization's focal point for certain stages, or *all* stages, of an information development cycle.

Perhaps the most important difference between the project management skills needed to make basic and substantive contributions is that, at level two, the writer, editor, or publications group exercises specific project management skills that control the *timing* of stages of the information development cycle. While the "pace" of activities in specific stages of the information development cycle is seldom relaxed, at level two the writer, editor, or publications group manages the final production stages for a document in a more controlled fashion than at level one, thereby minimizing the potential for a rushed and consequently error-prone final product.

Despite the obvious benefits of a writer's substantive contributions to an information development cycle, almost paradoxically level two project management activities have more potential shortcomings than those at level one. At level two, for example, the technical writer, editor, or publications group naturally interacts with many people within several technical departments, and this results in a higher degree of workplace visibility than at level one. This added visibility can be beneficial, as long as the information development cycle works well (since an efficient cycle will reflect positively on its members). If, however, an information development cycle falters, more of the responsibility for its failure will (legitimately) be assigned to level two support personnel than is true at level one.

Level two project management skills also require more creativity, risk, and energy than do level one skills. At level two the technical writer/editor is usually called upon to manage a wide variety of tasks during each successive stage of the information development cycle. During this process, almost certainly at some stage, if not all stages, the writer/editor will encounter a set of options to choose from and *no* guidance will be available beyond the writer/editor's expertise. Level two participation demands the willingness and capacity of the technical writer/editor to make independent decisions based on working experience and authority.

In addition, because of an almost endless menu of tasks to be managed during an information development cycle, the technical writer/editor cannot expect that all the project management decisions that are made will be recognized or appreciated. In fact, because substantive contributions to the information cycle are largely made in stages 2 through 4, the nuts-and-bolts work that is part of stages 5 and 6 (which the editor also performs) often is taken for granted at level two.

For some technical writers, editors, and publications groups, the level two visibility, pressure, risks, and pronounced emphasis on decision making are problematic. For others these elements are challenges, goals, or just parts of the job that are counterbalanced by the freedom, autonomy, and expanded project-management opportunities that level two participation allows.

As with level one, the down side to level two participation should not obscure its benefits. The capacity to contribute in a significant manner to the information-generating stages of an information development cycle results in an increased ability to *manage* and *control* that cycle. In terms of workplace development, the challenges involved with level two activities clearly offer desirable developmental goals for communciation professionals seeking increased levels of responsibility. In fact, the ultimate workplace needs of most technical writers and editors are usually met by level two responsibilities and activities, because of the wide spectrum of project management activities this level of participation allows.

Clearly, it is in a publications group's long-term interest to be able to contribute substantively to an information development cycle. The publications group that can *manage* instead of just *react* to the main stages of an information cycle has a much better chance to minimize "technical" versus "support" group distinctions. This, in turn, further empowers a publications group, often to the extent that the group can negotiate its contributions to specific projects. With these kinds of options, level two participation can offer employees enhanced professional growth opportunities, thereby improving the publications group's chances to attract high-achieving personnel.

Level Three: The Technical Communicator as Authoritative Resource for the Information Development Cycle

Level three participation in an organization's information development cycle is somewhat more difficult to define than level one and level two participation because level three contributions are oriented more towards overall information management responsibilities and less towards actual performance of the specific tasks involved at the other levels. Level three contributions to an information development cycle are made by senior technical communicators—including managers of publications groups—who often create the boundaries of an organization's information cycle. At level three, technical writers, editors, or publications groups act primarily as architects of or arbitrators within the information development cycle. Task-specific contributions to the cycle are secondary responsibilities that may be assigned to or coordinated with less senior personnel.

As an authoritative resource to an organization's information development cycle, the technical writer, editor, or publications group establishes the basic rules of the information development cycle by creating standards, guidelines, and requirements in such forms as information/document hierarchies, documentation plans, writer's guides, and top-tier administrative procedures. An organization's departments are required to follow these rules in order to achieve such goals as uniformity, standardization, efficient resource utilization, quality control, and so on. Consequently, the organization's departments begin working with a level three documentation manager at the very first stage of the information cycle, which identifies the specific type of information product that is needed.

Level three project management skills are also more difficult to define than the communication skills required at levels one and two. A level three contributor to an information development cycle might:

- be asked to develop an entire set of administrative standards for an organization's departments to follow when they become involved in any stage of an information development cycle
- be given the responsibility to lead an effort to design and implement upgrades to the technical documentation (policies, procedures, specifications, reports, and the like) generated within one specific department of the organization
- be the focal point for a formal audit of an organization's entire technical documentation system
- be responsible for ensuring that mandated changes are made in the mechanics of an organization's information development cycle.

In these and other instances, the level three technical communicator brings a systems awareness to the overall information development cycle, typically creating the boundaries of an organization's information development cycle, defining the formal integrity of the cycle, or resolving disputes between participants within the cycle.

The positive and potentially negative aspects of level three participation are fairly clear. On the positive side, the ability to design and the power to enforce an organization's information development cycle command far more influence than the comparatively limited capacity to complete specific tasks within distinct stages of the information development cycle. Possessing the ability to establish the parameters of an organization's information development cycle, the level three contributor also is empowered to initiate and complete significant modifications to the cycle.

Another positive factor is that technical communicators or communication groups recognized as authoritative resources for an overall information development cycle routinely are asked to provide project management expertise in terms of guidance, advice, and recommendations to technical departments at every stage of the information development cycle. This obviously allows level three contributors a significant amount of influence and control over specific stages in the information cycle for distinct projects.

There are, of course, some potential pitfalls to level three participation. One difficulty stems from escalating a support person or group to an authoritative position (which technical personnel might resent) for matters of conflict resolution during stages of an information development cycle. Another drawback is that the writer, editor, or publications group's *direct* involvement in specific stages of the information cycle becomes much less important than overall administrative activities. These administrative activities translate into project management responsibilities that draw more upon supervisory skills than actual writing, editing, and related coordination tasks, and this can be frustrating to some technical communication professionals who prefer to exercise specific editing and writing skills rather than overall administrative actions.

The pressures and politics of exercising level three skills can also be negative factors. Many technical communicators either do not enjoy or are not prepared for the spotlight that is regularly trained on level three personnel. Others do not work easily with the political brokering that occurs when level three contributors mediate alterations to information development cycle mechanics between support and technical groups, especially when *both* technical and support groups expect allegiance from the level three contributor.

Finally, the ability to provide level three contributions to an information development cycle requires extensive time, training, and experience. It is a serious mistake to rush a technical writer, editor, or publications group into level three participation before that person or group has sufficient knowledge and experience to cope with project management responsibilities that extend far beyond those of levels one and two.

IMPLICATIONS

The levels of participation discussed here do not point to many prescriptive conclusions or recommendations about which project management skills technical writers, editors, or publications groups may develop and pursue. For example, level three project management capabilities do not necessarily represent an upper-end ideal that technical communicators or publications groups should *always* strive for. However, the spectrum of different project management skills that characterize levels one, two, and three do lead to some overall generalizations about different levels of workplace abilities that are expected of technical communicators and their respective support organizations. These generalizations are summarized in Table 1, along with other factors that influence the development of project management skills in the technical communication workplace.

In terms of developing and applying different levels of project management skills, it must be emphasized that different organizations establish very different expectations and procedures for technical communicators to follow. In some organizations the specific charter for a technical writer, editor, or publications group is strictly limited to the basic activities that characterize level one. Here there simply are no project management alternatives, opportunities, or options beyond level one parameters. Another organization, however, may routinely expect technical communicators to exercise project management skills at levels one and two. Yet another organization will require the authoritative administration of level three participation, *or* expect to be able to choose combinations of skills deriving from all three levels. These varying expectations make it quite arbitrary to argue that the project management skills characteristic of one level are inherently "worse" or "better" than others.

At the same time it is important to recognize that—in terms of professional growth or future opportunities—the project management capabilities needed for level one activities are extremely limiting. Fundamentally, level one project management skills are, for technical writers, editors, or publications groups, most valuable insofar as they establish a sound basis for developing subsequent level two and—possibly—level three project management capabilities. Given the wide spectrum of project management opportunities available to technical writers, editors, and publications groups, there is no good reason to prevent technical communicators or publications groups from acquiring the highest level of project management skills as quickly as possible, as long as an organization's institutional makeup will support this workplace development.

In the 1990s and beyond, the workplace for technical communication professionals will undergo many changes. Despite the uncertainty of predicting these changes, those technical communication professionals or groups equipped with a wide and flexible array of project management skills will fare considerably better than those possessing a comparatively limited range of skills. The workplace of the future will be much more secure, and challenging, for the

Table 1. Workplace Abilities of Technical Communicators at Different Levels of the Information Development Cycle

Element	Basic Level 1	Substantive Level 2	Authoritative Level 3
Project Management Skills	Limited project management skills required to support production activities	Advanced project management skills required to support technical groups	Comprehensive project management knowledge required for maintenance of information cycle
Primary Abilities	Primary reliance on writing/editing skills	Primary reliance on acquired working knowledge of organization	Primary reliance on administrative skills
Assignments	Assigned to varied projects within overall organization	Assignments may be varied or dedicated to technical group	No assignment beyond support organization
Interfaces	Limited organizational/project interfaces	Regular interfaces with all contributors to information project	Comprehensive organizational interfaces
Knowledge	Emphasis on learning organization's information cycle requirements	Emphasis on applying information cycle requirements	Emphasis on creating and enforcing information cycle requirements
Accountability	Accountability limited to narrow editing and production activities	Accountability on equal level with technical counterparts	Full accountability for information development cycle
Autonomy	Little autonomy	High degree of autonomy	Full autonomy
Production Activities	Production activities comprise major part of workloads	Production activities are secondary to coordination tasks	Rarely involved in production activities
Productivity Measures	Focus on individual productivity goals	Focus on synergistic team productivity	Focus on overall organizational productivity
Editing	Requires light editing skills	Requires major editing/revision skills	Requires full editing and writing skills
Visibility	Limited visibility opportunities	Visibility equal to technical personnel	Full visibility
Years of Experience	1 - 3	2 - 5	3+
Position in Information Cycle	Not perceived as primary contributor to information cycle	Perceived as equal to technical personnel, or as main contributor to information cycle	Perceived as expert/creator of information cycle requirements

technical communicator with a full array of project management skills. This is especially true since these *combined* skills will need to be continually applied in a creative and supportive manner that suits the evolving needs of an organization's information development cycle.

In a related context, managers of publications groups (in order to be successful in the future) will need to find ways to train and *retain* more individuals who can contribute project management skills at level three. But these managers will also need to take advantage of other individuals who prefer to exercise level one and level two skills within an information development cycle.

Similarly, while technical writers and editors who wish to solidify and further professional development opportunities should aim at acquiring (at minimum) level two and (possibly) level three capabilities, level one project management skills cannot be forgotten or neglected. The need to refine and apply these skills will never be eliminated. At the same time, by developing basic technical communication skills into sophisticated project management capabilities, technical writers, editors, and publications groups will do much to ensure for themselves a more certain future workplace position as integral resources within an organization's information development cycle.

SELECTED READING

Grice, R. A., Verifying Technical Information: Issues in Information Development Collaboration, in *Collaborative Writing in Industry: Investigations In Theory and Practice,* M. M. Lay and W. M. Karis (eds.), Baywood Publishing Company, Amityville, New York, pp. 224-241, 1991.

Kirsch, J., Trends in the Emerging Profession of Technical Communication, in *The Society of Text: Hypertext, Hypermedia, and the Social Construction of Information,* E. Barrett (ed.), MIT Press, Cambridge, Massachusetts, pp. 209-234, 1989.

Prekeges, J., Planning and Tracking a Project, in *Techniques for Technical Communicators,* C. M. Barnum and S. Carliner (eds.), Macmillan Publishing Company, New York, pp. 79-106, 1993.

CHAPTER 9

Project Management:
The Art of Managing Deadlines

BARBARA WEBER

Managing a publications project is, in some ways, like managing a scuba diving expedition. When you manage a dive, you determine a destination, develop a plan, and then implement it. In developing your plan, you must ensure you have enough air to reach your destination. When you implement your plan, you must reach the targeted destination or the boat will not be waiting for you. Similarly, when you manage a publications project, you develop a plan and then implement that plan. If all the members of your project team have a common destination toward which they are striving and if they work together according to a common plan to reach that destination, you should be able to successfully complete the project.

However, in publications management, as with dive plans, the critical factor is time. When you dive, if you take longer to reach your destination than you planned, you could potentially run out of air and a crisis would develop. When you manage a publications project, if you take longer to complete your project than you planned, you could miss your deadline. Again, a crisis would develop. Although a missed deadline is not life-threatening in the publications business, your career could be at stake. Learning to manage deadlines effectively, then, is an essential skill for the publications manager.

Following are some practical suggestions to help you, the publications manager, manage deadlines. These suggestions include information about how to meet deadlines, how to handle missed deadlines, and how to avoid missing deadlines in the future.

MEETING DEADLINES

Long after most scuba students receive their certification, they can still hear their instructor's voice echoing in their memories the often repeated phrase: Plan the dive; then dive the plan. If you are serious about meeting your deadlines, you must learn to develop successful plans and implement those plans successfully.

Develop Successful Plans

So what does it take to develop a successful plan? Any publications product, whether it is a reference manual, a handbook, or a quick-reference card, is produced in phases. To develop a successful plan, you will need to identify the phases and determine how much time each phase will take. Phases include research, writing, reviews, revision, and printing. You will also need to consider purpose, style, audience, and deadlines. Once you have established these basic parameters, you are ready to plan your project.

You can begin to plan your project by dividing the project into tasks and determining intermediate deadlines for each task. These deadlines then become collective goals for your project team. For example, if you have a month to produce a handbook of approximately eight chapters, you might assume you need to produce about two chapters a week (inclusive of all the phases it takes to produce two chapters). The reality is that you need to produce about three chapters a week.

Consider for a moment the scuba diver who is planning a cave dive. The rule for cave diving is to turn around when your air supply is three-quarters full. In other words, you spend one-quarter of your air supply going into the cave and reserve three-quarters to find your way out of the cave. The publications manager, like the cave diver, must learn to plan for unexpected detours.

Potentially, you could encounter delays during any phase of a publications project. In making your plans, therefore, you will need to anticipate what can go wrong in each phase and plan ways to avoid these traps.

During the Research Phase

First of all, your team will need to conduct the research for your project. If you are interviewing subject-matter experts, your experts may be unavailable when you need them. If they do not perceive that giving you information is a significant part of their job, they may put you off while they try to meet their own deadlines. Even if they have been assigned the responsibility of giving you information or if they are actually part of your project team, you still may have delays caused by an unexpected illness, a death in the family, or another unplanned event.

Therefore, you will need to communicate with your subject-matter experts while you are planning your project. At this time, let them know what information you will be needing, what your deadlines are, and what significance the project will have to the organization as a whole. At the same time, find out from them about their current workload and seek ways to coordinate your project with their schedules. Also, it is always a good idea to find alternate sources you can use if your key source is unexpectedly unavailable.

During the Writing Phase

The writing phase is generally the phase least susceptible to disaster because, of all the phases, it is the one that is most within your control. However, even in this phase, you may be left shorthanded unexpectedly when a team member encounters a sudden illness or emergency. You may also experience delays (and a lot of frustration) if your equipment malfunctions. A printer that refuses to print can be very frustrating, especially if the malfunction occurs simultaneously with an impending deadline. Still more frustrating is having the entire mainframe fail when you are just on the verge of meeting a critical deadline. Most frustrating of all, though, is having that same mainframe come back up only to discover that while it was down, it managed to delete all your documents.

To guard against these delays, always have back-up plans for your staff, your documents, and your equipment. It is a good idea to include general back-up plans in your routine department procedures. However, in addition to those plans, you may need to develop specific back-up plans for individual projects. For example, you may want to consider how you could realign personnel if a key member of your team were to become unavailable. If you are dealing with a very tight deadline, you could keep additional back-up copies of all diskettes during the critical phases of the project.

You will probably also want to consider where you can obtain alternative equipment or services in the event your own equipment fails. For example, if your printer broke down at a critical point in your project, you could take a diskette of your draft to a Service Bureau to have a master copy printed. You should become familiar with the service warranties of all your critical equipment and find out what arrangements can be made for borrowing or renting additional equipment. If you know your options in advance, you can react more quickly when a crisis develops. In any case, always ensure that you have an adequate system for backing up all work performed on computers.

During the Review Phase

If the writing phase is the least vulnerable phase, the review phase is the most vulnerable. Writers sometimes resort to pleas, threats, bribery, and just about everything short of murder in their attempts to coax reviews out of subject-matter experts. One effective approach in dealing with this problem is to notify the reviewers (in writing) that you need the draft reviewed by a specific date. Tell them that, in the event it is not returned, you will assume the information is correct and print it as is. Although this approach helps eliminate the bottleneck caused by reviewers, it does not necessarily contribute to the integrity of the work. Therefore, you will probably want to use this approach only as a last resort.

During the Revision Phase

Revisions always seem to take more time than you allow for them. Even if you plan your project so well that you allow sufficient time for revisions, you can still get caught in a crunch due to last minute changes in the product you are documenting. For example, if you are writing a software instruction manual, changes are common right up to the minute the software is released. Every time the software is changed, you will need to make corresponding changes to your manual. This can be devastating to a carefully planned project with rigid deadlines. The best safeguard, then, is to build in as much of a cushion as possible for the entire revision process.

During the Printing Phase

You have managed to get your material researched, written, reviewed, and revised. Now you must get it printed and bound. How much time should you allow? The time your product spends in the print shop will probably vary greatly from project to project. At this point in the project, you are at the mercy of the workload and the priorities of your print shop. For this reason, you will want to have a good rapport with the print shop, to be as considerate of them as possible, and to establish as much good will as possible between crises. Then when you must go to them with yet another request for the impossible, they may bail you out.

Once you have developed a plan that takes into consideration all the special needs of each phase of your project, you are ready to implement your plan.

Implement Plans Successfully

When you manage a publications project, you will actually be managing two distinct components: the product and the people. In planning the project, you are primarily concerned about the product. In implementing the plan, you must focus on the people.

Your project team may consist of any combination of writers, editors, graphics artists, technicians, and layout artists. Once you have identified project goals, you will need to communicate these goals to the entire team. As you adjust deadlines throughout the project, you will need to formalize a means for communicating these changes to your team. Too often, informal communication is used because the project manager is too busy to write a memo or the members of the project team do not have time to attend a meeting. Just as often, projects encounter unnecessary delays because someone on the team was overlooked and did not hear about a change in the plan.

As you implement your plan, you also need to anticipate the various working styles of the individual team members. Are some of your writers detail-oriented while others are big-picture people? Are some of the team members self-motivated while others need direct supervision to keep them focused? In her article "Managing Creative People," JoAnn Hackos describes two types of technical communicators: those with high-growth needs and those with low-growth needs [1]. Writers with high-growth needs are self-motivating and easy to manage, except when they exceed their budget, as they tend to do. Writers with low-growth needs, on the other hand, require more effort on the part of management to keep them growing professionally.

In implementing your plan, you need to consider the individual work styles of your team members and plan ways to meet their needs. In so doing, you will be ensuring that each of them will be able to perform at his or her best level. For example, in delegating responsibilities, you can try as much as possible to give your team members opportunities to do the things they enjoy doing and the things they do well. This will keep your entire team motivated and enthusiastic toward the project. Of course, you will also want to provide your staff with opportunities to develop new skills to keep them growing professionally and help guard against burnout.

Regardless of how well you plan and how successfully you implement that plan, you will sometimes encounter situations where missing a deadline seems inevitable. Think about what would happen to your carefully planned project if, for example, the deadline was moved up. Recall the previous illustration. You have one month to write eight chapters. You plan carefully, knowing that to meet your deadline you must produce three chapters a week. Then, a week into the project, you are told that the handbook must be available by the end of the third week. You look with disbelief at your calendar and realize you now have two weeks to finish. A difficult assignment has just become impossible.

HANDLING MISSED DEADLINES

So, what *can* you do when you realize you cannot meet your deadline? There are no easy answers to this question, but if you want to be a successful publications manager, you will have to find some workable solutions, because it will happen.

Miss the Deadline

The most obvious solution is simply to miss your deadline. Whether or not this is feasible in your organization is a decision only you can make. However, if you rely on this solution once too often, you will probably find your career in as much trouble as the cave diver who waited until her tank was half empty before she turned around.

Of course, rather than miss your deadline, you could ask to have the deadline extended. This is probably a safer option, but it may be just as deadly for your career. Again, only you can know whether this is a viable option. If you eliminate missing or extending the deadline as options, or at least save them until all else fails, what are you left with?

Work Overtime

The next most obvious option is to work overtime. It is rare these days to see a publications group that does not work large amounts of overtime. In today's highly competitive business environments, overtime is probably unavoidable to some extent. However, there are pros and cons to this solution that you, as project manager, need to consider.

According to recent studies, working overtime actually decreases productivity. When people become tired, they do not perform well, their creativity diminishes, and they lose their perspective on how things interrelate [2]. To make matters worse, if overtime is mandatory rather than voluntary, people generally resent the intrusion into their personal lives. This resentment can quickly escalate into a severe morale problem that, in turn, may lead to further decreases in productivity.

Overtime is a much more effective solution when it is voluntary, when it is relatively short term, and when the motivation is based on professional reputation. In other words, to make sure your group is behind you when crunch time comes, you need to make sure they are behind you the rest of the time. If they believe in you, in the work you are doing, and in the organization, you will not even have to ask them to work overtime. They will know when it is necessary, and they will feel that making the deadline is as much their responsibility as you feel it is yours.

Get Help

On the other hand, if you are already working considerable amounts of overtime, this may not be a solution at all. Besides, your team needs time off, and so do you. So what else can you do?

One solution might be to ask for additional help. Whether or not this is a feasible solution depends on what kind of budget constraints you have, as well as whether you have the time and/or resources to train someone new. However, if the project is important and your reasons are good, this may be the most effective solution. It might be possible to transfer someone from another project team into yours, or you might request contract help for the duration of your project. Contract help is rapidly becoming a way of life in corporate America in the nineties. It is probably a good idea to keep a list of names and phone numbers of contracting firms in your area.

Even if you cannot increase the size of your project team, consider enlisting the help of clerical personnel. Publications projects generally include a variety of routine tasks, especially when materials are being prepared to go to print. If you can delegate some of this work to clerical personnel, you will free up valuable time for the members of your professional staff (and save your company money at the same time).

Shorten the Scope

Another technique that might save the day for you is to simply shorten the scope of the project. If you are being asked to deliver a publication in less than the amount of time that you could reasonably be expected to produce it, propose a compromise. Suggest eliminating nice-to-have features, such as a glossary. Offer to condense a four-volume set of manuals into two handbooks and a quick-reference card. Before you propose such a compromise, however, do your homework. Make sure you fully understand your client's essential needs. You want to compromise quantity, not quality. If it is feasible, you might suggest that you will produce some of the materials by the deadline, and the rest at a later, agreed-upon date. Sometimes, if your material is being used for in-house training, you can initially issue a draft of the material in place of the final printed copy.

Work More Efficiently

If none of these options is viable or if they are not enough in themselves to save your project, you will need to get creative. Look for ways to work more efficiently. If you are performing the role of editor-in-chief, is it possible that you are being too much of a perfectionist? Remember the law of diminishing returns. At some point, the extra quality that results from additional effort is not worth the time it costs.

What else can you do to work more efficiently? Can you borrow pieces of previous projects? Are your team members communicating with each other so that they are not duplicating each other's efforts? If you are in a crisis, you need your team to be as committed as you are. Are they? Do they feel that it is their project—or yours?

You might try getting the entire project team together for a brainstorming session. Explain the crisis and seek their ideas. However, you must listen to them with an open mind. If they sense you are trying to con them, you will not get the help you need.

You may also need to take a close look at how the work is getting done. Are any of your team members spinning their wheels? How can you get them back on track? Are you a bottleneck, perhaps in your editing cycle? Find out where time is being wasted and put a stop to it.

If none of these ideas work for you, work out your own solution. When you consistently find creative solutions that help meet deadlines, your management will learn that they can count on you—and so will your staff.

AVOIDING FUTURE MISSES

You cannot be an effective publications manager if you simply move from one crisis to the next. Although many managers will tell you that crunches are inevitable in this industry, you need to recognize that you do have options. Even if you cannot prevent the next crisis, you can do a number of things to diminish the impact.

Create Standards and Guidelines

For example, between crises, you can try to standardize as much of your publications process as possible. According to the *Xerox Publishing Standards,* when you standardize the processes your writers use, you not only increase their efficiency, you also reduce the risk of errors. The editors maintain that "the later a change is made the more it costs." An error found while a manuscript is being written is easily fixed. However, a serious error discovered after distribution can result in "major incremental costs" and "serious customer-relations problems. Standards won't solve all these problems, but they can prevent many of them" [3, pp. 1-5].

Frequently, creative people rebel against the imposition of standards. However, they will be less resistant if you allow them to help develop the standards. In the long run, you will find that it is better to standardize as many of the routine processes as possible so that your staff can use their creativity where it is needed, for the nonroutine, challenging aspects of their publications. At the same time, you can develop guidelines for formatting your publications, and you can collect examples of frequently used material that can easily be copied from one document to the next.

Develop Templates

Taking this concept one step further, you can save a lot of time by developing templates (that is, prototype documents that are already formatted and ready to go). Your writers then simply pour new text into shell documents. Much of the time that is traditionally spent formatting and laying out copy is saved. You can develop templates for all types of documents. You may even want to develop two or three formats for each document type, so your writers will have a choice. Depending on the nature of the material, one might be more suitable for a given publication than another. Many desktop publishing guides, such as *Desktop Publishing by Design* and *The Hammermill Guide to Desktop Publishing in Business,* provide useful templates to help you get started [4, 5].

Elicit Feedback

Finally, to seek additional ways to save time on future projects, call a postcrisis meeting of your staff and ask for feedback. Discuss candidly with your team what worked and what did not. Ask where time could have been saved if you had been more organized or if you had known then what you know now. Your staff will probably have seen things that you did not. If they know you will listen, they will probably want to share this information.

A cave diver turns around when her tank is three-quarters full because she cannot anticipate everything that might happen on the trip out of the cave. She survives because she has learned to manage deadlines. You, as a publications manager, cannot anticipate everything that will happen during the course of a project. However, you can master the art of managing deadlines by first finding ways to meet as many deadlines as possible, then finding ways to handle the deadlines you do miss, and finally finding ways to avoid missing similar deadlines in the future.

REFERENCES

1. J. T. Hackos, Managing Creative People, *Technical Communication, 37*:4, pp. 375-380, 1990.
2. Want to Be More Productive? Leave Your Office at Five, *Working Smart,* p. 3, Sept. 1, 1990.
3. S. Heinemann and V. Croft (eds.), *Xerox Publishing Standards: Manual of Style and Design,* Watson-Guptill Publications, New York, 1988.
4. R. Shushan and D. Wright, *Desktop Publishing Design,* Microsoft Press, Redmond, Washington, 1989.
5. B. McKenzie, *The Hammermill Guide to Desktop Publishing in Business,* Hammermill Papers, Memphis, Tennessee, 1989.

CHAPTER 10

The Project Worksheet for Efficient Writing Management

JOHN S. HARRIS

When employees produce poor quality documents, the fault may lie not with their incompetence or lack of devotion to the job, but with inadequate and unclear assignments from their project managers or publications managers. The Project Worksheet is designed to help managers give initial writing assignments, effectively manage documents during production, and evaluate finished products. The following pages describe the Worksheet and suggest ways publications managers can use it effectively.

THE PROJECT WORKSHEET

The Project Worksheet consists of a series of questions that help writers and managers consider the factors involved in planning a document. I developed the Worksheet years ago, and faculty in the technical writing program at Brigham Young University have successfully used it to teach technical writing for some years. After graduation, many of our students continue to use it in industry to plan documents and make document assignments.

What the Writer Must Consider

The manager and writer must determine the document's intended readers, its purpose, scope, form, length, graphic aids, and sources of information.[1] They must

---

[1]Although this chapter explains how managers can use the Project Worksheet for managing documents, the books listed under Selected Reading explain how writers can use the Worksheet and other methods to design technical documents for various audiences and purposes.

know such things before the writing begins. Failure to consider them results in inefficient document production and poor-quality documents.

Experienced writers in an organization usually answer these planning questions intuitively or subconsciously. Or they get the answers by direct conference, by study of past documents, or through the grapevine. They then efficiently plan and write good documents.

But less-experienced writers learn the answers to the questions only by the inefficient and expensive trial-and-error method of submitting draft documents and then repeatedly amending them as management requires.

Managers—whether of engineering projects, scientific studies, or computer software documentation—can reduce the trial-and-error writing cycle by providing complete answers for such planning questions during a writing assignment conference. But managers cannot provide the answers to the planning questions without first knowing the questions and their consequences. The Project Worksheet in Figure 1 guides both writers and managers in considering the important factors in planning documents. It can, of course, be adapted for special situations. Managers may want to reformat it to allow more space for answers, and some may wish to put it into a word processor as a template. Let us first examine the Worksheet questions and then consider procedures for using the Worksheet for document management.

Housekeeping Headings

Headings such as assignment date, due date, writer, and assignment authority are self-explanatory. Still, listing them together permits the use of the Worksheet as a tracking document for projects. The *document subject* is the file subject. The *document title* may be the same, or it may be something less prosaic—especially if the document is going out of house. Thus a document subject could be *Dental Hygiene,* and the document title could be *Your Teeth: An Owner's Manual.*

Primary Reader

No factor is more important for the writer than full understanding of the nature and needs of the document's primary reader. Experienced writers know this, of course. But even they do not always know everything that management knows and believes about the readers of the projected document. Too frequently both managers and writers assume they understand who the readers will be, but they may have two quite different audiences in mind. Using the Worksheet, managers and writers can reach an understanding of this and other questions.

Reader's Technical Level

By carefully considering the technical level of the reader, the manager and writer can decide the proper level of explanation needed. How much information does the reader already have? Are definitions of *photo-grammetry* or *perihelion* or

PROJECT WORKSHEET

Subject _____Title _____

Assigned by_____ Approved_____ Assignment date _____

Writer _____ Agreed to _____ Due date _____

Primary Reader:

      Technical level (education, experience, etc.):
      Position (title or organizational relationship):
      Attitude toward subject:
      Other factors:

Secondary Readers (others who may read the document):

      Technical level:
      Position:
      Attitude toward subject:
      Other factors:

Reader's Purpose:
      What should the reader know after reading?
      What should the reader be able to do after reading?
      What attitude should the reader have after reading?
      How will the reader access the material?

Writer's Purpose:

      Intellectual purpose:
      Career or monetary purpose:

Logistics:

      Sources (lab reports, library research, etc.):
      Physical size limits (if any):
      Form or medium prescribed or desirable:
      Available aids (graphics, etc.):
      Means of production:
      Outline (Preliminary):

Distribution and Disposition:

Figure 1. Project worksheet.

debentures needed? Considering such things can help avoid losing the reader in a maze of technical jargon, or alternatively avoid alienating a reader with overly simplistic explanations. In the trade-off between those two extremes, erring on the side of simplicity is nearly always better.

Reader's Organizational Relationship

The writer must also consider whether the document will go to the executive tower or to the shop floor. Since writers often prepare documents for someone else's signature, the manager—and the writer—must consider the organizational relationship of the reader *to the document's signer*. Thus, if the document will be signed by the boss, the writer must—for the task—carefully assume the persona of the boss. Is the signer addressing superiors, subordinates, or peers? Such situations raise delicate questions, and the manager must recognize the entailed problems and pass on an understanding of those problems to the writer.

Reader's Attitude

Similarly, the attitude of the reader must be considered. Is the reader hostile to the new manufacturing procedure because it will result in downsizing her department? Or is the reader skeptical about the efficacy of new cutting-edge technology because it has not yet been proved? Or is the reader torpid and apathetic and needing a stiff jolt to see the promise—or the threat—of the subject of the document?

Other Factors

Often even more subtle factors about the reader must be considered. Some of these may overlap the preceding questions, but they may also affect the kind of document needed. Is the reader a white, conservative Republican woman of sixty, raised on an Iowa farm, or a young Afro-American male from the South Bronx, or a highly educated but condescending academic? Is the reader an Ivy-League MBA obsessed with this year's bottom line, a high school dropout production-line worker who is fearful that increased automation will eliminate jobs, a displaced homemaker with an acute case of computer anxiety, or an immigrant with limited understanding of English? Such demographic factors may require delicate adjustments in the document.

Secondary Reader

Often a secondary reader must also be considered. The company annual report may be read by both stockholders and the CEO. An advertising brochure intended for customers may also be read by the competition. An environmental impact statement may be read by both the Douglas Fir Plywood Association and the Sierra Club. A report intended for Level 2 management may have to get past a Level 3 gatekeeper. Such situations require that the writer juggle the factors of two or more audiences at once, and this requires some skill. If the readers differ in attitude, the writer must watch out for red-flag statements that may cause a secondary reader to charge. If the differences are in technical level, the secondary reader's need for more elementary explanations or more technical information can often be taken care of in footnotes, glossaries, sidebars, or appendices.

The Reader's Purpose

Organizational documents have purposes as varied as securing approval for a new manufacturing process, justifying spending public funds for a reclamation project, instructing a software purchaser on how to use a spreadsheet, or easing the worries of environmentalists about the effect of a new highway near a prime trout-fishing stream. Four basic questions about the reader's purposes need consideration:

- What should the reader know after the reading?
- What should the reader be able to do after reading?
- What attitude should the reader have after reading?
- How will the reader access the information?

What Should the Reader Know after Reading?

What factual information does the reader need to obtain from the document? Does the reader need to know the percentage of radial keratotomy patients who can pass a 20/40 eye examination without glasses after the operation? The percentage of impurities remaining in palladium after the macrocycle solvent extraction process? The change in numbers of predator kills of sheep after reintroduction of wolves to the grazing range? Often the specific information the reader is to gain from the document can be presented in lists, outlines, tables, or graphs.

What Should the Reader Be Able to Do after Reading?

What the reader can *do* after reading may be quite different from what the reader *knows*. Knowing the names for the stages of mitosis is different from being able to recognize telophase through a microscope. Knowing the stoichiometric ratio for combustion of a gasoline/air mixture is different from being able to adjust a fuel-injection system to achieve the ideal mixture.

What a reader can do after reading may depend on technical skills. It may also depend on the reader's capability to make executive decisions based on the information contained in the document. Thus the reader's needs probably extend beyond gaining general information to applying specific knowledge. A reader may use the information on color changes in a chemical solution to perform titration in the assay laboratory. Or a reader may use the information on the size of natural gas reserves of the overthrust belt to decide the feasibility of building a 24-inch pipeline from Wyoming to California.

What Attitude Should the Reader Have after Reading?

Earlier the Worksheet asked about the reader's attitude before reading. Here the Worksheet asks about the attitude the writer and manager want the reader to have *after* reading the document. Do they want the reader to believe and feel that the proposed SDI weapons system is an effective deterrent to foreign aggression? Or do they want the reader to believe that it is a horrendously expensive and impractical pork-barrel boondoggle? Though such attitudes in technical documents may be based on hard data, they are nonetheless attitudes—sometimes emotionally charged attitudes—and the writer must realize that shaping those attitudes is sometimes part of the job, even a moral responsibility. The technical writer uses different tools for shaping attitudes than the politician or advertiser does, and may have a higher regard for truth, but like the politician or advertiser, the technical writer may be an attitude shaper.

And one other attitude deserves consideration: the attitude that the reader should have toward the preparer of the document. The writer wants the reader to think that the document was prepared by a credible and meticulous professional who cares about the subject, the needs of the reader, and the needs of his or her employer. Though this point may seem obvious, writers do not always automatically consider it.

How Will the Reader Access the Information?

We read novels, murder mysteries, and perhaps newspaper editorials beginning-to-end, but almost everything else, we read in some other fashion. We do not read dictionaries, phone books, repair manuals, computer documentation, or encyclopedias beginning-to-end. We often read textbooks and journal articles in a nonlinear fashion too. Sometimes the text is well designed to help us get the critical information quickly. Or, exasperatingly, the text may bury critical information in the middle of a full-page paragraph. Whatever way the text is designed, readers scan, or skip around trying to find what they want without reading every blessed word.

Realizing what information the reader wants, the writer or manager can design documents so that the information is easy to find. Information accessibility relies on such devices as

- Headings
- Outlines
- Indexes
- Graphics
- Underlining
- Sidebars
- Glosses
- Varied typefaces

- Cross references
- Bulleted lists (like this)

USA Today uses many of these devices. *The New York Times* uses fewer. *USA Today* lacks the substance of the *Times,* but it is easier to get the news from it quickly. A similar comparison could be made between *Popular Science* and *Scientific American.* The differences in format reflect how the writers and editors anticipate the publications will be read.

The writer and manager must carefully consider whether the reader will read beginning-to-end or access pieces of data individually. The basic consideration should be the importance of the information being conveyed. The more important the information, the more accessible it should be. The document manager must help the writer anticipate *all* the ways that *all the readers* will want to access the information and require the writer to provide the machinery that will allow that access. Most writers of technical and scientific documents should pay much more attention to accessibility. Few readers of technical documents read them beginning-to-end.

Writer's Purpose

The writer's and reader's purposes for a document differ just as the buyer's and seller's purposes differ. Both have their agendas. The writer—or the manager—may want to have a project approved. The target reader may want to know if the project is feasible.

The writer probably has potential salary, prestige, and promotion purposes for writing, but may also be writing because the task is challenging or intellectually interesting. The writer and manager should decide in advance whether the project is routine and can be done rather perfunctorily, or whether it will affect the safety of the user, the prosperity of the company, the security of the nation, the preservation of the environment—or the continued employment of the writer. These questions help the writer and manager determine the priorities of the task.

Logistics

The logistics are the nuts and bolts things—such as where the information comes from, the size of the projected document, and what form the document will take. These too must be considered in advance.

Sources of Information

Will the document be based on observation, personal opinion, government reports, a literature search, engineers' notes, customer interviews, public opinion polls, laboratory tests, compilations of vendors' brochures, or what? Frequently, lead time may be required, so early consideration of sources is wise to allow tests to be run, surveys to be conducted, or publications to be ordered.

Size of Document Expected

A two-page memo will not do if a twenty-page report is expected, and a twenty-page report will not do if a two-page memo is expected. Again, the question should be resolved between the writer and the manager before the writing begins.

Form or Medium Prescribed or Desirable

The form or medium of the eventual document should also be considered in advance. Should the document follow the company style sheet? Would a film, a wall chart, a wallet card, or a video be a more useful medium? *Such choices should be made according to subject, purpose, reader (user), and cost.*

Graphic Aids Available

Would photographs or art work be useful? Are facilities available to prepare them? Is there time? Are funds available? Again, these must be considered early.

Means of Document Production

The means of production of the document also need to be considered early. Will the document be laid out on a Macintosh with PageMaker software? Will it be photocopied, or multilithed? How will the means of production affect the legibility and credibility of the document, and how much will it cost?

Outline

Even at the early planning stages, the writer and manager should consider the topics to be treated, their order, and their proportion of the expected document. Such an outline can, of course, be revised during preparation.

Distribution and Disposition

How many copies will be needed? Where do they go? What happens to them? The manager and writer should consider these questions—and their many consequences—in advance. Will the document be read by the competition? Will it come back to haunt everybody ten years later? Will it be subpoenaed in court? The wise consider such things.

PROJECT PLANNING CONFERENCE

The manager and the writer must come to an agreement about a document's audience, purpose, and scope, and the logistics of its development, production, and distribution. Such negotiation is most efficient in a planning conference. Usually the manager calls the conference, but the negotiation can take a variety of forms, depending on the situation and the experience of the writers.

With an inexperienced writer, the manager may say, "Willoughby, I want you to write a proposal for my signature recommending adoption of the hyperbaric procedure. It should be addressed to Allardyce, the plant manager. He is a chemical engineer with twenty years' experience on the job. But it will also be read by Sung. She is the company comptroller and has ultimate approval power on expenditures. She is pretty conservative, but her attention to cash-flow probably saved the company during the last recession."

With a more experienced writer, the manager can more inductively and democratically ask, "Kim, we need a brochure about our prefabricated forms for concrete. What ways do you see to make a brochure that will meet the needs of all of its readers?" Obviously, here the manager respects the writer's knowledge and expects useful suggestions.

Whatever the method, the manager and writer should agree upon the answers, write them down—Yes, and *sign off—each keeping a copy.* Such a signed-off Worksheet is then a kind of contract agreed to by both parties, and both can feel more secure with it. The manager is now more secure knowing that the assignment is clearly understood, and the writer is more secure knowing what is expected.

POSTCONFERENCE MANAGEMENT

Obviously other factors may arise during the writing. The manager may receive new data, or the writer may see new ways to deal with the problems. Depending on their impact on the document, such things may require additional conferences and a renegotiating of the specifications.

As needed, the manager may discreetly ask about the progress of the document, or may even ask to see sections in draft. However, if the initial assignment has been done carefully, a responsible and skilled writer should be able to produce a sound document with little intermediate prodding.

The writer properly attaches the Project Worksheet to the draft form of the document when submitting it. Then the manager checks to see if it fulfills the assignment. If it does, the manager approves it for production.

Quite often, however, problems appear. Of these, failures to match the assignment are the most obvious, and the manager can ask for a rewrite to make the document match the specifications. The most common problem seems to be a failure to consider adequately the technical levels of all the readers.

Or it may become clear that the specifications need changing. If for good reasons they do need changing, the manager can change them and ask that the new specifications be followed, but the manager who has agreed to the original specifications is less likely to make such changes capriciously or arbitrarily. If lessening the power to make arbitrary changes seems to take the fun out of being boss, then the manager should recognize that the resultant empowerment of the writer is not only enlightened and trendy, but also pragmatically effective.

OTHER APPLICATIONS

If the writer's manager does not make such detailed assignments, the writer obviously can still use the Project Worksheet for planning. Or the writer can use the Worksheet to initiate a conference and negotiate with the manager. We have found that managers are often impressed when writers request such conferences and demonstrate through their questions—the Worksheet questions—that they have a clear understanding of the situation.

The Worksheet is also effective in negotiating contracts in freelance writing assignments, or as an assignment device between editor and writer. In the university, a professor can make writing assignments following the Worksheet questions. Or a sharp student can use the questions to clarify a vaguely given assignment. And many problems of master's theses and doctoral dissertations would be avoided if candidates and supervising professors negotiated the specifications for theses and dissertations through the Worksheet.

In much technical writing, the most important work is the planning done before the first words of the document are written. If managers will use the Project-Worksheet approach to document management, their writers will work more efficiently and produce better documents.

SELECTED READING

Anderson, P. V. (ed.), *Teachinq Technical Writing: Teaching Audience Analysis and Adaptation,* ATTW Anthology No. 1, Association of Teachers of Technical Writing, St. Paul, Minnesota, 1980.

Caernarven-Smith, P., *Audience Analysis and Response,* Firman Technical Publications, Pembroke, Massachusetts, 1983.

Mathes, J. C. and D. Stevenson, *Designing Technical Reports: Writing for Audiences in Organizations* (2nd Edition), Macmillan, New York, 1991.

Pearsall, T., *Audience Analysis for Technical Writing,* Glencoe Press, Beverly Hills, California, 1969.

Souther, J. W., and M. L. White, *Technical Report Writing* (2nd Edition), John Wiley & Sons, New York, 1977.

Spilka, R., Orality and Literacy in the Workplace: Process- and Text-Based Strategies for Multiple-Audience Adaptation, *Journal of Business and Technical Communication,* 4:1, pp. 44-67, 1990.

CHAPTER 11

Document Standardization: Maintaining Project Harmony

LYNN H. DEMING

> If writing must be a precise form of communication, it should be treated like a precision instrument. It should be sharpened, and it should not be used carelessly.—Theodore M. Bernstein [1]

Maintaining precision in a technical document is not always easy, particularly when the document is the product of a team—a collaborative effort. In such cases, for writing to be "a precision instrument" all team members must be well informed about the project and must work with as much uniformity as possible. For this to happen, the document manager must have a clear vision of the entire production process and foresee many of the needs of team members, be they authors, writers, editors, illustrators, text processors, or printers. To enable all team members to work as effectively and efficiently as they can, the manager must know the document strategy; determine the document design; and standardize, as much as possible, the terminology. Standardizing document design and terminology at the outset of document production, then updating those standards as necessary, allays anxiety among team members, saves time, minimizes duplicated effort, and streamlines document production. The end result is more effective documents produced with fewer problems and greater harmony.

SETTING AND MAINTAINING STANDARDS

Most businesses, companies, and laboratories that employ writers and editors have an in-house style guide, use the style manuals of their professions—e.g., the American Psychological Association (APA), the American Institute of Physics (AIP), the Council of Biology Editors (CBE), the Modern Language Association (MLA), or the Society of Petroleum Engineers (SPE)—or follow a trusted, generally well-accepted standard, such as *The Chicago Manual of Style*. Nonetheless, each large documentation project requires specific standards tailored to that project. With the help of specification sheets, the document manager should set the document standards and meet with team members to discuss the document and the specification sheets.

Specification sheets for format, typography, and terminology are particularly useful for initiating and maintaining standards. However, an important consideration is whether the document is already written and in need of revision and editing or is being written. A document manager can read through an already-written document, fill out the appropriate specification sheets, and then give sections of the document to team writers or editors along with the completed specification sheets and be fairly sure that the document will receive consistent rewriting or editing.

However, when a document is being written, the document manager must rely on the request for proposal (RFP), previous documents developed for the customer, similar documents developed for other customers, or customer specifications to create the *initial* specification sheets. Then the document manager should call a meeting of all project writers and editors, assign sections of the document, distribute the initial specification sheets, and request that writers and editors take note of additional standardization needs as they develop their sections. The document manager should call another meeting of all project writers and editors the following week to update the specification sheets and respond to questions and concerns. Indeed, such meetings may be necessary once a week for the first weeks of a project. After that, the document manager may need only to distribute updated specification sheets to the writers and editors each week or until most questions have been answered, inconsistencies corrected, and the document is well standardized.

DESIGNING THE DOCUMENT

The purpose of any technical document is a major factor in determining how to direct and design that document for success. Another major factor is meeting customer specifications or the requirements on an RFP or some other action item. The document manager, the project manager, and the customer need to agree on the aims of the document, and subsequently, the design of the document. Once they agree, the document manager needs to provide the writers and editors on the project with both hardcopy and electronic templates and guidelines for the format and typography of the document.

Format

Format is perhaps the most essential element in document design. It enables the reader to see immediately the structure, hierarchy, and major content sections of a document. Format includes headings, margins, indentation, justification, figure references, figure placement, figure captions, headers, footers, and pagination. If the document manager completes a format specification sheet (see Figure 1) tailored to meet project and organization needs, and, early in the document development process, distributes it, along with electronic templates, to all project writers, editors, and text processors, the document will have uniformity at least with regard to format.

FORMAT SHEET

TITLE	• of Document
PAGE	• 8-1/2" by 11"
HEADINGS (See box below)	• First-degree heads: all caps, boldface, and centered • Second-degree heads: upper/lower case, boldface, and side • Third-degree heads: upper/lower case, underlined, and side
SECTIONS	• Begin all main sections on the right-hand page.
MARGINS	• Top margins of main sections should be 2"; all other margins (top, side, bottom) should be 1".
INDENTATION	• None, except for long quotations–indent 10 spaces.
JUSTIFICATION	• Left only.
LINE SPACING	• Single space all text; double space before and after all headings.
FIGURE REFERENCES	• (See figure X.)
FIGURE PLACEMENT	• As soon after figure reference as possible. If a paragraph has only one figure reference, place the figure after the paragraph. If a paragraph has close, consecutive figure references, place all figures consecutively after the paragraph. If a paragraph has more than one figure reference but the paragraph is long and the references are several sentences apart, place each figure as soon as possible after the reference to it.
FIGURE CAPTIONS	• Place below figure, flush with left side of figure, downstyle, end with a period.
PAGINATION	• Upper right-hand corner on odd pages. Upper left-hand corner on even pages.
HEADERS	• Precede odd page numbers; follow even page numbers.
FOOTERS	• None.

FIRST DEGREE HEAD

Second Degree Head

Third Degree Head

Figure 1. Sample format specification sheet.

Typography

Typography is a primary, yet frequently slighted, element in document design. Although numerous typefaces are available, too many documents, as Jonathan Price remarked at a recent conference, still look as if they were produced on typewriters. Knowing the purpose, audience, content, and size of a document, the document manager should select an appropriate typeface. This sounds easy, but it takes knowledge and practice. Many good books are available for information and guidelines on using type effectively ([2-5], to name a few).

Some general considerations when selecting a typeface include size, classification (e.g., serif/sans serif), weight, and, most importantly, readability (not only of letters but of numerals, superscripts, punctuation marks, and special symbols). Point size, for example, can be very misleading: a 12 point is not a 12 point is not a 12 point (to corrupt Gertrude Stein) except in terms of vertical block. Take, for example, the following word presented first in Helvetica, second in Times Roman, and third in Courier:

Encyclopedia   Encyclopedia   Encyclopedia

X-height, cap (capital) height, kerning, leading, stress, and weight are all different in each typeface. Consequently, the typefaces are not actually the same size.

Once the document manager has selected an appropriate typeface for the document, he or she will find a typography specification sheet is a useful tool (see Figure 2). All writers, editors, and word processors on the document should have a copy.

Readability should determine typeface selection. Some typefaces can be interesting and eye-catching, but unreadable—at least some of the characters may be unreadable. For example, I once chose a typeface only to find out well into the document that the capital *i* was identical to the lower case 1. When put together in Illinois, the letters were indistinguishable. Another time, I chose a typeface without regard to the numerals and symbols. Superscript numerals were unreadable, quotation marks were right side only (and looked wrong on the left side), and some symbols were unavailable in that particular typeface. If the text has many lists, a proportional typeface is usually best because nonproportional numerals and letters do not align.

Before selecting an unfamiliar typeface, the document manager should print out all characters—letters (both upper and lower case), numerals, symbols, and all points of punctuation. Some typefaces, such as Hobo, have no descenders—the tails of *g, j, p, q,* and *y* do not descend; thus, g looks similar to 9. This can reduce readability, especially for international audiences and other nonnative speakers of English. Also, some typefaces are very limited, while others have many symbols, characters, dingbats, and the like. Every character can be important in the readability of a document.

Moreover, just because multiple typefaces are available, a document should not become a hodgepodge of typefaces. Professionals generally suggest one typeface

TYPOGRAPHY SPECIFICATION SHEET

TITLE	• of Document
TYPEFACE	• Times and Helvetica
CLASSIFICATION	• Serif for text (Times) Sans serif for headings (Helvetica)
SIZE	• 16 pt for title 12 pt for text and figure captions 14 pt for headings
WEIGHT	• Boldface first-degree headings Underline second-degree headings Italicize third-degree headings

Figure 2. Sample typography specification sheet.

family, perhaps serif for text, sans serif for headings, and varying weights (italics, boldface, underlining, and so forth) and point sizes for headings, text, captions, labels, and so forth. Handled judiciously, however, mixed typeface families can produce interesting results.

TERMINOLOGY

Selecting the right word is always important to a writer, but nowhere is it more important than in a technical document. Unlike the words of poems and fiction, the right words in a technical document are not the most powerful or most expansive or most expressive words; rather they are the correct words—the words that are the most accurate and most understood.

Standardizing terminology means determining the right words. This requires attending to meanings, usage, and mechanics. It means remembering that English is a dynamic language and knowing and having access to authorities on correctness and standardization in specialized areas (e.g., [6-10]). Here again, a specification sheet is useful (see Figure 3).

TERMINOLOGY SPECIFICATION SHEET

TITLE   • of Document

MEANINGS
Definitions   • use <u>clear</u> only to mean transparent
Jargon
Buzzwords to avoid
Acronyms/Initialisms
Nouns/verbs   • use <u>project</u> only as a noun
Synonyms   • avoid

USAGE
Nongender-bias   • instead of <u>man hours</u> use labor hours
Narrative perspective • use first person plural–we
Articles   • use <u>the</u> with EPA–the EPA

MECHANICS
Capitals
Abbreviations/
Units of measure   • use postal abbreviations for states
Plurals   • always use <u>data</u> as a plural
Spelling   • use American spellings
Hyphenation   • hyphenate <u>high power</u> when used as a
                          coordinate adjective, e.g., high-power
                          microwave antenna

Figure 3. Sample terminology specification sheet.

Meanings

Determining the right words requires knowing their definitions and correct and intended meanings in context, removing inappropriate jargon or translating it into standard English, ensuring (as much as possible) that each word has only one meaning in the document, and not using synonyms for technical terms.

Definitions

Defining words is a science (see [11]), as the plethora of dictionaries in any library attests. Technical dictionaries are especially plentiful, and with good reason: technical terms are specialized. Take, for example, *phosphorescence*.

According to *Chambers Science and Technology Dictionary* [7], *phosphorescence* means something different to a chemist, a physicist, and a zoologist. To the chemist, it is the "greenish glow observed during the slow oxidation of white phosphorus in the air." To the physicist, it is the glow or "fluorescence which persists" after a substance has been illuminated by visible or ultraviolet rays. To the zoologist, it is the "production of light" in animals such as glow-worms, usually "with little production of heat."

In addition to technical terminology, the English language itself is complex and often confounding. Few words in English have one meaning. Many words in English have similar spellings and pronunciations (material, materiel; ordinance, ordnance; discrete, discreet) and are easily confused. Technical documentation requires accurate technical terms and correct English.

Vogue Words

Because English is dynamic, words come into being, fade from disuse, and are rediscovered. Like clothes, words and expressions come in and go out of fashion. William Safire calls these vogue words [12]. *Empathy* was a vogue word in the 1960s and 1970s. *Segue* is a vogue word in the 1990s.

Not only can words be "trendy," they can also change meanings, add meanings, and lose meanings. Today, *cool* and *hot* can be interchangeable: "Those shoes are so cool." "Those shoes are so hot." *Gay*, on the other hand, is so singularly used to mean "homosexual" that college-textbook editors often gloss the word when it means "merry." Vogue words are not limited to conversational English. They are just as prevalent in the technical arena as in contemporary conversation and popular media; however, in the technical arena they become jargon.

Jargon

Technical writers are not usually at the forefront of popular culture, but they are often involved in the latest technological advances, and technology does affect culture. The computer, for example, has certainly had a global impact, and the personal computer has forever altered the way most people conduct their business and even their personal lives. Along with new technology comes new language (not always new words, but words used in a new way). *Interface, utilize, state-of-the-art* are particularly overused, and misused, words. Each is perfectly acceptable in correct and spare use. "Computer interface," "utilize an economic system," or "state-of-the-art instrumentation" are examples of correct usage. "Interface with a customer," "utilize a hammer," and "state-of-the-art memoranda" are not. They are examples of misused jargon.

Jargon abounds in all fields, but surely its proliferation and use is nowhere greater than in the government, especially the military, where buzzwords and acronyms are the rule rather than the exception. Because most high-tech industries and laboratories survive on research grants and contracts that come from the government, often from the military, technical documents are replete with jargon.

Much of the jargon either requires definition or removal; indeed, jargon is the jungle undergrowth that technical writers have to slash and remove so readers can find their way through a document.

Buzzwords — Buzzwords are so commonplace in technical documents that technical writers have to be careful not to overlook them. Buzzwords are not only inappropriate in most technical documents, they are obfuscating. Gerald Cohen's buzzword wheel (see Figure 4) cleverly exemplifies both the silliness of and, unfortunately, the dependence on buzzwords.

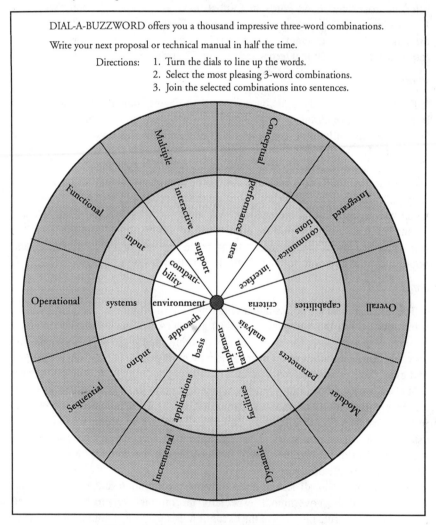

Figure 4. Gerald Cohen's Dial-A-Buzzword.

Acronyms — Of course, some argue that jargon is appropriate for a specific audience; indeed, one's use of jargon can indicate just how knowledgeable about the field one is. Acronyms and initialisms are probably the most obvious form of jargon because they are so recognizable and so incomprehensible to outsiders. And sometimes outsiders can't distinguish acronyms from initialisms: for example, SOW is an initialism, not an acronym, for a *statement of work*; it is not, therefore called "a SOW" but "an S-O-W." Similarly, a *table of contents* is a T-O-C, not a TOC. I know of no standard rule for this; one just has to learn the jargon. On the other hand, MIRV, multiple independently targetable reentry vehicle, is an acronym (the *t* is omitted because it would spoil the acronym, I guess), and some even write and speak of "MIRVs" and of "MIRVed warheads" [13, p. 386]. Pluralized acronyms are understandable, but acronyms should not, I think, be used as adjectives and verbs. At any rate, acronyms are much like code-insiders' lingo. But most technical documents are not intended for an elite club or clan. Technical documents convey information to audiences with rather diverse skills and backgrounds, audiences who usually need to use the information in one way or another—to repair a machine or make a decision or understand an experiment.

Ironically, those who most frequently use acronyms and other jargon are those who least frequently are aware of it—they are so immersed in their subject that they forget others are not. Consequently, technical writers are usually responsible for translating and obviating jargon, a task that is not always easy. ADA, for example, can stand for the American Dental Association, the American Diabetes Association, the American Disabilities Act, or Americans for Democratic Action. And ADA probably has other local or in-house meanings as well. A case in point: when I worked at New Mexico State University's Physical Science Laboratory (PSL), PMS stood for publication management system, an in-house quality control system for contracts and related documents. Of course, to most Americans, PMS is a commonly known initialism for premenstrual syndrome. When there was a PMS meeting or a document had to "go through PMS," we women at PSL used to chuckle, and probably many of the men did too. The point is that acronyms and initialisms often have specialized in-house or in-division or otherwise exclusive meanings, and context does not always indicate which meaning is correct.

Acronyms and initialisms also may change meaning. I once worked on a SADARM proposal. "What is SADARM?" I asked. Someone answered, "Search and destroy armor." Someone else offered, "Search and destroy armament." No one was sure. After finding it defined both ways in numerous documents, to get the correct answer, I called the customer and learned that SADARM stands for sense and destroy armament. However, prior to the new sensing instrumentation, SAD did mean search and destroy. (A rather appropriate moniker for such a mission, I suppose.)

One Word, One Meaning

Acronyms and initialisms are not alone in having more than one meaning. English is a rich and expansive language. One word can mean many different things depending on its context and use. *Clear,* for example, can be a noun, a verb, an adverb, or an adjective. As a noun, *clear* can mean remove ("clear the screen before entering the command"); as an adverb, *clear* can mean out of the way ("stand clear of the door"); and as an adjective, *clear* can mean transparent ("the glass must be clear and untinted"). These are only a few meanings and uses of *clear.* The Random House *Webster's College Dictionary* [14] lists sixty-five definitions of *clear,* including its use in several idioms, such as "in the clear."

Two very common terms in technical documents are *test* and *project.* Sometimes it is difficult not to use *test* as both a noun ("each product must undergo a series of tests") and a verb ("we must test the product first"). *Test,* however, means much the same thing in either context, so it probably does not confuse most readers, and *testing* can often substitute for the noun *test* ("serial testing is a contractual requirement"). *Project,* on the other hand, can disrupt readability, especially when used as a noun and verb in the same sentence or paragraph. The following is such an example:

This project has five tasks:

1. Test the equipment.
2. Repair all nonfunctioning parts.
3. Develop and implement a maintenance program.
4. Document all procedures.
5. Project future test sites and dates.

Of course, context helps us recognize the use and understand the meaning of a word; but the audience of a technical document does not have time to reorient according to context and to shift back and forth from meaning to meaning. Furthermore, the audience of many technical documents includes international—nonnative—speakers of English. Idiomatic expressions and multiple meanings and uses of a word are not only unsuitable for such an audience, their use is inconsiderate [15]. In a given document, then, each word should ideally have only one meaning.

Synonyms

Just as words can have more than one meaning, several words can have similar meanings—similar, but not the same. *Rocket, missile, projectile*—synonyms? Roughly speaking, yes. Accurately speaking, no. Accuracy is critical in a technical document; consequently, synonyms for technical terms are rarely acceptable.

Usage

Determining the right words is a major step in standardizing the terminology of a document, but using words correctly is also important. Matters such as gender-biased language, narrative perspective, voice, and articles all affect the standardization of terminology.

Gender-Biased Language

Gender-biased language is no longer acceptable in technical documents. All evidence shows that *he* is not a neutral-gender pronoun and *man* is not a neutral-gender noun, whether in *chairman* or *mankind* or *manpower*; therefore, writers should use these words only when referring specifically to males. A number of good books [16-19] are available to help writers recognize and correct gender-biased language. And, I am pleased to note, nearly all recently published technical writing textbooks include a section on sexist or gender-biased language.

Narrative Perspective

Most technical documents are written from a third-person or first-person narrative perspective, or a combined first/third perspective. An example of third-peson perspective is, "XYZ Company will be responsible for managing the project. They will oversee all aspects of production." An example of the combined perspective is, "XYZ Company will be responsible for managing the project. We will oversee all aspects of production." Either way is correct, with the latter being more personal. Establishing the narrative perspective early will save time and ensure consistency.

Voice

Some writers, editors, and authors prefer active voice, while others prefer passive voice. Few documents adhere to either one exclusively. Nonetheless, the document manager should indicate the preferred voice; and adherence to it, as much as possible, should lend consistency to and enhance the grace and flow of the document's language. For example, replacing the passive "the motherboards will be fabricated by the Electronics Section," with the active "the Electronics Section will fabricate the motherboards" streamlines the verb forms, clarifies the meaning, and quickens the pace of the sentence. However, the passive voice is necessary when the writer does not know who the actor/agent is/was or when including the actor/agent distracts or alters emphasis. For example, the difference between "the space shuttle launch was postponed because of foul weather," a passive construction, and "foul weather postponed the space shuttle launch," an active construction, is one of emphasis. The former, passive sentence emphasizes the space shuttle launch; the latter, active sentence emphasizes the foul weather. The choice belongs to the writer, who should know which emphasis is important in the context of the document.

Articles

The use of articles is fairly well standardized by the rules of grammar. But sometimes usage is questionable and clarification at the outset lessens mistakes and inconsistencies and saves time. For example, when referring to the Physical Science Laboratory by its complete name, *the* precedes the name. But when referring to the Laboratory by its acronym, PSL, no article precedes the name—not "the PSL," but "the Physical Science Laboratory." On the other hand, sometimes *the* precedes both the name and the acronym, as in "the Environmental Protection Agency" and "the EPA."

Mechanics

Naturally no discussion of terminology can exclude some mention of mechanics. Capitals, abbreviations and units of measure, plurals, spellings, and hyphens usually require standardizing as their use is so often inconsistent.

Capitals

Capitals are overused in most documents. Professionals frequently want to capitalize their own specialties—Electrical Engineering, Computer Science, Geology, and so on. But, capitals disrupt reading, calling attention to words that don't need attention. Proper names require capitals, as do words that begin sentences, and initialisms and acronyms. On the whole, however, fewer capitals mean smoother reading. Besides, some capitals are simply incorrect, as in the specialties mentioned above and as in the names of some computer languages. Fortran, for example, is not a true acronym, but an abbreviated and combined form of *formula translator*. Ada is not an acronym at all, but the name given to a computer-programming language in memory of Augusta Ada Byron, an English mathematician. BASIC is an acronym, standing for *beginners all-purpose symbolic instruction code*. COBOL, too, is an acronym, standing for *common business oriented language*. Nonetheless, nowadays, Basic and Cobol are often not fully capitalized, and perhaps one day will not even have initial capitalization, just as radar (radio detecting and ranging) is no longer capitalized, and seldom even thought of as an acronym. Again, the document manager should set the standard, and writers and editors should strive for consistency.

Abbreviations and Units of Measure

Whenever there is more than one way to abbreviate a term or more than one standard abbreviation for a unit of measure, the document manager should set the standard for the document. For example, if writers are going to use abbreviations for states, they should know which form: most use the post office abbreviations because they are familiar worldwide and have no periods, saving keystrokes and time—NM, CO, TX, and so forth. But some writers still use the old abbreviations,

N.M., Colo., Tex. Again, the point is to know the preferred abbreviation at the outset and be consistent.

Units of measure, interestingly enough, vary among disciplines. Engineers, for example, usually use cm^3 for centimeter cubed, while many scientists often use cc [20, pp. 392-95]. If authors from different disciplines are contributing to a document, the units of measure may appear both ways. The writers and editors need to know which is correct for the particular document at hand.

Plurals and Singulars

When standardizing nouns, writers often overlook such factors as plural endings. Many Latinate nouns have two correct (acceptable) plural endings. Memoranda or memorandums? Appendices or appendixes? Cacti or cactuses? No doubt all writers have preferences. What is important is knowing which form to use in a particular document. *Data* raises another issue. Is it a plural or a singular (collective) noun? "Data are" or "data is"? "This data" or "these data"? The document manager must decide.

Spelling

English spellings (and pronunciations), as we all well know, can be peculiar and inconsistent. First of all, there are British spellings and American spellings (e.g., colour, color; grey, gray; realise, realize). Then, as mentioned above, there are Latin spellings and English spellings (e.g., memoranda, memorandums). And, of course, there are homophones, words that sound alike but have different meanings and spellings (e.g., do, due, dew); homonyms, words that sound alike and have the same spelling but different meanings (e.g., cleave, meaning to sever, and cleave, meaning to adhere closely); and homographs, words that have the same spelling and may have the same pronunciation but do not have the same meaning (e.g., lead, meaning to show the way, and lead, meaning metal; read and read, the present tense and the past tense, respectively, the former pronounced reed, the latter pronounced red). Every good writer/editor should know the correct spelling of most words but may not know the preferred spelling if there is a choice between correct spellings, as with the Latinate and Anglicized plurals or with a foreign customer. For example, if the customer is British and terms in the RFP have British spelling, does the proposing American contractor use British or American spelling? The project manager and the document manager need to decide and inform team writers and editors.

Hyphenation

Hyphens are probably the most controversial marks of punctuation. As H. W. Fowler says of modern English usage of hyphens, "its infinite variety defies description. No two dictionaries and no two sets of style rules would be found to give consistently the same advice" [21, p. 255]. In technical documents, hyphens are particularly troubling with strings of words in titles and names and events.

Take for example high power microwave (HPM). In this example should *high power* be hyphenated? According to most books on usage, yes. But according to common practice, no. And what about high power microwave tests, or The High Power Microwave Laboratory, which becomes the *High Power Microwave Laboratory Report*? The rule, of course, is that coordinate adjectives should be hyphenated, thus high-power microwave tests. But if there is no hyphen in the name of the laboratory, should the writer insert one? Rather than answer this question, let me just say, the document manager needs to answer it, and other such questions, to avoid inconsistencies in the document. Again, a specification sheet is useful for establishing document standards, informing all team members of the standards, and updating the standards as necessary.

STANDARDIZATION

Standardizing document design—establishing the format and typography—and standardizing terminology—determining the right words, obviating jargon, standardizing usage and mechanics—are the tasks of the document manager. Completing these tasks early in document production will not only improve the management of that document but also create harmony among team members and assure document quality and effectiveness.

REFERENCES

1. T. M. Bernstein, recalled in *New York Times* on his death, 27 June 1979.
2. M. E. Barker, *Book Design and Production for the Small Publisher,* Londonborn Publications, San Francisco, 1990.
3. R. C. Eckhardt, R. Weibel, and T. Nace, *Desktop Publishing Secrets*, Peachpit Press, Berkeley, California, 1992.
4. M. Hill and W. Cochron, *Into Print: A Practical Guide to Writing, Illustrating, and Publishing,* William Kaufman, Inc., Los Altos, California, 1977.
5. R. C. Parker, *Newsletters from the Desktop: Designing Effective Publications with Your Computer,* Ventana Press, Chapel Hill, North Carolina, 1990.
6. *Standards,* American Society for Testing and Materials, Philadelphia, 1993.
7. T. C. Collocott and A. B. Dobson (eds.), *Chambers Science and Technology Dictionary,* Barnes and Noble, New York, 1974.
8. H. J. Gray (ed.), *Dictionary of Physics,* Longmans, Green, London, 1958.
9. K. G. Jackson (ed.), *Dictionary of Electrical Engineering,* Butterworths, London, 1973.
10. D. D. Polon, *Dictionary of Physics and Mathematics Abbreviations, Signs, and Symbols,* Odyssey Press, New York, 1965.
11. J. C. Sager, *A Practical Course in Terminology Processing,* John Benjamins Publishing Company, Philadelphia, 1990.
12. W. Safire, Vogue Words Are Trific, Right? in *Language Awareness* (4th Edition), P. Eschholz, A. Rosa, and V. Clark (eds.), St. Martin's Press, New York, pp. 164-168, 1986.

13. S. Hilgartner, R. C. Bell, and R. O'Connor, The Language of Nuclear War Strategists, in *Language Awareness* (4th Edition), P. Eschholz, A. Rosa, and V. Clark (eds.), St. Martin's Press, New York, pp. 381-388, 1986.

14. *Webster's College Dictionary,* Random House, New York, 1991.

15. L. H. Deming, Writing: Standard, Nonidiomatic English, *Proceedings of the ASTM Symposium on Standardizing Terminology for Better Communication: Practice, Applied Theory, and Results,* American Society for Testing and Material, Cleveland, pp. 106-112, 1993.

16. L. P. Arliss, *Gender Communication,* Prentice Hall, Englewood Cliffs, New Jersey, 1991.

17. C. Miller and K. Swift, *The Handbook of Nonsexist Writing,* Lippincott & Crowell Publishers, New York, 1980.

18. F. W. Frank and P. A. Treichler, *Language, Gender, and Professional Writing: Theoretical Approaches and Guidelines for Nonsexist Usage,* Modern Language Association of America, New York, 1989.

19. A. P. Nilsen, H. Bosmajian, H. L. Gershuny, and J. P. Stanley, *Sexism and Language,* National Council of Teachers of English, Urbana, Illinois, 1977.

20. *The Chicago Manual of Style,* The University of Chicago Press, Chicago, 1982.

21. H. W. Fowler, *A Dictionary of Modern English Usage* (2nd Edition), Oxford University Press, New York, 1965.

CHAPTER 12

Estimating Costs for Documentation Projects

DAVID L. SMITH

Probably anyone who has worked in the technical writing business for more than one month has been asked, "How much will it cost to prepare a_____?" (Fill in the blank with users manual, software specification, installation manual, maintenance manual, modification change order, memorandum, letter, ...) Of course, the immediate response that comes to mind—"Gee, I dunno"—does not inspire much confidence. But then the question does not provide nearly enough information for one to respond intelligently. A quick, glib answer—"Oh, about $437,256.98"—would not be trusted either. Documents are such idiosyncratic, complicated, variable things that a reasonable response to the question requires a lot of information and some time to process it. This chapter presents a method for providing a reasonable estimate for the cost of a document.

This method demonstrates how to estimate the cost of a single document. It is based on identifying the smallest units possible within a document and estimating the time required for each. The method agrees with J. Lasecke's assertion that for the customer to be comfortable with an estimate, the estimate must be based on concrete items [1]. Similarly, the estimate of an entire documentation project must be based on small units, one document at a time. Then the sum of the estimated costs for the individual documents will be the total estimated cost for the entire project.

This method is based on information gathered from several colleagues in the technical writing field as well as from a workshop presented by Norman W. Hempling at the 1985 International Technical Communication Conference. Building on Hempling's premise, I have refined and expanded it to include forms, spreadsheets, and tables with average labor times required for various tasks. The total package has proved valuable and generally accurate. As with any tool, increased experience in its use improves accuracy in the result.

The method is flexible and allows the user to apply his or her experience in considering how the participants (writers, engineers, editors) and the complexity of a project will affect the cost. However, it does not account for problems of multiple revisions caused by inadequate planning in the technical project or in the documentation project.

DETERMINING THE SCOPE OF THE PROJECT

To estimate the cost of the documentation effort, you must understand the scope of the task at hand. Four factors affect the cost of a document:

1. The complexity of the subject matter
2. The size of the document
3. The amount of work required in each labor category
4. The level of quality required

The best immediate response to the customer's "How much will it cost?" question is to ask the customer several questions. First, you want to find out what the document's specifications are. If the document is being produced for an agency of the Department of Defense in the United States government, the contract probably has a Contract Data Requirements List (CDRL) that specifies what document should be produced. The CDRL refers to a DID (Data Item Description), which defines the format and content of the document. As soporific as government specifications can be to read, they do provide the rules for the game. If there are no guidelines or specifications like these, you and the customer will have to define the document specifications before you can estimate how much preparation of the document will cost.

The document specifications should determine the content, establish the format, and define the level of quality required for the document. From the specifications, you can prepare a preliminary outline for the document. The outline is the basis for estimating the size of the document. It will indicate the complexity of the subject matter and the type of content, which will help determine the amount of work required in each labor category.

The form shown in Figure 1 is a tool for calculating the cost of the document. The following discussion refers to this form and its use. To begin, fill in the blanks on the form for the title and author. You will notice that the form can easily be prepared as a spreadsheet for electronically calculating the document estimate total.

Document Name:

Principal Author:

Complexity level: Simple __ Medium __ Complex __

Outline Sections						Time Required (hr/page)			
No	Heading	Fact		Pages		Write	Edit	Proof	Draw
		1	2	txt	fig	__	__	__	__
Base Labor Hours									
Quality Factor: Routine __ Professional __ Slick __									
Qualified Labor Hours									
Labor Rates						__	__	__	__
Cost by Labor Category									
	Total Pages			Total Document Cost					

Figure 1. Blank cost estimation form.

ESTIMATING COMPLEXITY

When you know the type of content, you can broadly categorize the complexity of the document as simple, medium, or complex. For most documents, complexity is the main cost factor. It also affects what resources must be assigned to the task. The following are examples of the three levels of complexity:

1. Simple subject matter: function and maintenance descriptions or operation instructions for mechanical devices.
2. Medium subject matter: troubleshooting descriptions or operation instructions for electromechanical devices.
3. Complex subject matter: theory of operation descriptions or operation instructions for electronic devices.

After studying the document specifications, you will have a good idea of how complex the subject matter is. After some experience with documents of the various types, you will be able to further refine your evaluation of the complexity level within these three broad categories. Table 1 lists labor hours required per page for four labor categories across the three levels of complexity. You will have to rely on experience and intuition to select an exact hours-per-page rate for each labor category. Also the working dynamics of each organization will affect these figures. You will want to adjust the figures in Table 1 according to your experience in your organization.

The ranges of required labor hours indicated in Table 1 have proved reliable for routine, standard-quality documents. Table 1 indicates a range of hours required

Table 1. Document Labor Estimates

Work Category	Labor Hours		
	Simple	Subject Matter Complexity Medium	Complex
Writing[a]	4-6 hr/page	5-8 hr/page	6-10 hr/page
Editing	0.2 hr/page	0.25 hr/page	0.33 hr/page
Proofreading	0.26 hr/page	0.26 hr/page	0.26 hr/page
Illustrating[b]	2 hr/page	4 hr/page	6 hr/page

[a] The writing work category includes time required for researching. This also assumes that the writing is done on a word processing system; hence, no work category for word processing is included.

[b] The illustrating category assumes that graphics are drawn with computer-aided tools.

per page for writing. Along with determining the general complexity of the section, you must decide where in the indicated range the required hours-per-page should be set. On the form, mark an X for the complexity level beside the term (Simple, Medium, Complex), and fill in the hours-per-page values under the labor categories with the figures you derive from Table 1.

ESTIMATING SIZE AND NATURE OF CONTENT

Using the outline prepared from the documentation specifications and discussing the requirements with the appropriate technical developer, you can determine the nature of the content and estimate the required number of text pages and of illustrations for each section in the outline. Enter the information on the form shown in Figure 1. Figure 2 is an example of a completed form.

On the form, fill in the numbers and heading titles for each section of the document outline. Then estimate how many pages of text and graphics each section will require. The Factor columns 1 and 2 are used to shorten the form when the outline contains multiple sections of an identical type. For example, in software documents, due to the repetitive nature of computer programs, many equivalent sections may be required for iterations of similar parts of the program, as shown in Figure 3.

If the specification calls for a section 4.X to describe the required input for each function in a computer program and the software designer estimates that there will be seven functions in the program, enter 7 in the Factor 1 column for that section and the following subsections. If you estimate that each function will require two pages of text and one page of graphics, enter 2 in the text column and 1 in the "fig" column on the same line. If there will be subsections—4.X.Y, 4.X.Z, etc.—to the required input description, such as three different possible formats, enter 7 in the Factor 1 column and 3 in the Factor 2 column along with the appropriate numbers for text and graphic pages.

DETERMINING THE AMOUNT OF WORK REQUIRED

Writing, editing, proofreading, and illustrating may all be required. For each outline section entered on the cost estimation form, multiply the number of text pages by the hours-per-page rate for writing and by the two factors, and enter the product in the Write column. Similarly, multiply the number of graphics pages by the hours-per-page rate for illustrating and by the two factors, and enter the product in the "Draw" column. Because all pages need to be edited and proofread, for the "Edit" and "Proof" columns, add the text and graphics pages and multiply the sum by the two factors. Figure 4 demonstrates the results. To find the total labor hours required for each labor category, add the time required for all the sections and put the sum at the bottom of each column on the "Base Labor Hours" line.

Document Name: Software Design Document

Principal Author: Senior Programmer

Complexity level: Simple __ Medium __ Complex X

	Outline Sections					Time Required (hr/page)			
No	Heading	Fact		Pages		Write	Edit	Proof	Draw
		1	2	txt	fig	10	.33	.26	6
	Cover, Title and TOC			.25		2.5	0.08	0.07	0
1.0	Scope					0	0	0	0
1.1	Identification			.13		1.3	0.04	0.03	0
1.2	System Overview			.25		2.5	0.08	0.07	0
2.0	Referenced Documents			1		10.0	0.33	0.26	0
3.0	Preliminary Design					0	0	0	0
3.1	CSCI Overview			.5	1	5.0	0.50	0.39	6.0
3.1.1	CSCI Architecture			1	1	10.0	0.66	0.52	6.0
3.1.2	System Status and Modes			1	2	10.0	0.99	0.78	12.0
3.1.3	Mem & Process Allocation			.5	1	5.0	0.50	0.39	6.0
3.2	CSCI Design Description			.5		5.0	0.17	0.13	0
3.2.X	CSCI Name and Id	2		1		20.0	0.66	.52	0
3.2.X.Y	Sub CSC Name and Id	2	2	1		40.0	1.32	1.04	0
4.0	Detailed Design			.5		5.0	0.17	0.13	0
4.X	Function Input Description	7		1		70.0	2.31	1.82	0
4.X.Y	Function Input Format Req	7	3	.25		52.5	1.73	1.37	0
4.X.Y.1	Function Input Format Specs	7	3	1		210.0	6.93	5.46	0
4.X.Y.2	Function Input Format Design	7	3	3	1	630.0	27.72	21.84	126.0
5.0	CSCI Data			.5	2	5.0	0.83	0.65	12.0
6.0	CSCI Data Files					0	0	0	0
6.1	CSC/CSU Cross Reference			.5		5.0	0.17	0.13	0
6.X	Data File Name and Id	2		.5	.5	10.0	0.66	0.52	6.0
7.0	Requirements Traceability			1		10.0	0.33	0.26	0
Base Labor Hours						1109.0	46.20	36.40	174.0
Quality Factor: Routine _X Professional __ Slick __					1				
Qualified Labor Hours						1109.0	46.20	36.40	174.0
Labor Rates						52.48	27.92	27.92	27.24
Cost by Labor Category						58190	1290	1016	4740
	Total Pages	23.9			Total Document Cost			$65,236.00	

Figure 2. Completed cost estimation form.

Outline Sections						Time Required (hr/page)			
No	Heading	Fact		Pages		Write	Edit	Proof	Draw
		1	2	txt	fig	10	.33	.26	6
4.X	Function Input Description	7		2	1				
4.X.Y	Function Input Format Req	7	3	.25	.5				

Figure 3. Illustration of factor columns.

Outline Sections						Time Required (hr/page)			
No	Heading	Fact		Pages		Write	Edit	Proof	Draw
		1	2	txt	fig	10	.33	.26	6
4.X	Function Input Description	7		2	1	140.0	6.93	5.46	6.0
4.X.Y	Function Input Format Req	7	3	.25	.5	52.5	5.20	4.10	63.0

Figure 4. Results of factor calculation.

DETERMINING REQUIRED LEVELS OF DOCUMENT QUALITY

As used here, quality refers to the degree of exactness in the text and amount of polish in the format of the document. Table 2 indicates criteria for four quality levels in technical documents: minimum, routine, professional, and slick.

1. Minimum quality requirements are appropriate only for internal documents that do not need to impress anyone, rather like casual conversation.
2. Routine quality is appropriate for internal documents that are part of the working processes of an organization, such as standards, policies, and procedures.
3. Professional quality is appropriate for documents intended for external distribution. These documents reflect the quality standards of the organization. Their formats are enhanced to convey the technical information and reflect professionalism.
4. Slick quality is appropriate for documents that have a sales function beyond merely communicating information. These documents must be appealing in order to convey information to a less-than-avid audience. Their organization and format will be carefully designed to achieve a specific purpose with a specific audience.

Table 2. Criteria for Document Quality Level*

ASPECT OF DOCUMENT	LEVEL OF QUALITY			
	Minimum	Routine	Professional	Slick
Content				
Technical Requirements	Accurate, complete, and appropriate			
Customer Specifications	Complies with CDRLs, DIDs, and other requirements			
Form				
Organization	Coherent	Accessible	Focused	Designed
Format	Generic for equipment		Enhanced	Designed
Special Effects	None	Added for information	Added for enhancement	Added for appeal
Language and Style				
Level of Edit	Screening	Mechanical style	Language	Substantive
Readability	Little concern	Moderate effort	Special effort	Strong emphasis
Appearance				
Legibility	Legible size and contrast		Enhanced size and contrast	
Impression	Little concern	Consideration	Moderate effort	Strong emphasis

*These quality criteria were developed by Dr. Susan Dressel and are used here with permission.

Naturally, a slick commercial user manual to be shipped with a package of computer software will cost more per page to produce than a routine report (or even a professional users manual to be delivered with a prototype or one-of-a-kind computer system). The required quality level affects cost across all four labor categories shown in Table 1. A useful rule of thumb is to add 30 percent to the estimated base cost if the document must be professional level and 150 percent if the document must be slick.

After determining the quality level, mark the form with an X beside the appropriate level and enter a factor in the box on the line. Enter 1 for Routine, 1.3 for Professional, or 2.5 for Slick. Then multiply the base-labor-hour totals by the quality factor, and enter the results on the "Qualified Labor Hours" line.

CALCULATING COST

Once complexity, size, and the quality factor are established, you can calculate the cost to develop the document. In the boxes on the labor rates line of the form, enter the hourly rates charged to your customer for the labor of whoever will be doing the work. Multiply the qualified labor hours by the corresponding labor rates, and enter the result on the "Cost by Labor Category" line. The total document cost is the sum of the Costs by Labor Category. Add the estimated costs for each of the individual documents in a project, and you have the total project cost.

Of course, unless the requester is experienced enough to know that document preparation requires more than hiring a typist, the cost will greatly exceed the requester's expectations. However, with this method, you have a concrete basis for the estimate that should prevent the requester from spreading rumors of your madness.

One of the benefits of this method is that it breaks the estimate down into small pieces, based on the document specification, so you can easily show the customer how you determined the costs. And if the cost estimate must be reduced because of a budget constraint, you have a basis for negotiating changes to the document's specification requirements.

Using the cost estimate form to compute documentation costs permits you to respond to the question "How much will it cost for _____?" with specific, realistic figures.

REFERENCE

1. J. Lasecke, Cost Estimating with Confidence, *STC Intercom, 37*:8, pp. 3-4, 1992.

SELECTED READING

Caernarven-Smith, P., A Cost and Price Model for Technical Publishing, *Technical Communication, 37*:3, pp. 268-274, 1990.

Frederickson, L., and R. G. Fuller, Calculating an Estimate for a Technical Writing Project, *Proceedings of the 35th ITCC,* Society for Technical Communication, Washington, DC, pp. MPD37-MPD40, 1988.

Heiss, J. M., Estimating Required Effort: Putting Weight Behind Your Predictions, *Proceedings of the 35th ITCC,* Society for Technical Communication, Washington, DC, pp. MPD44-MPD46, 1988.

Herrstrom, D. S., An Approach to Estimating the Cost of Product Documentation, with Some Hypotheses, *Proceedings of the 34th ITCC,* Society for Technical Communication, Washington, DC, pp. MPD24-MPD27, 1987.

Prekeges, J. G., Accurate Estimating and Scheduling, *Proceedings of the 35th ITCC,* Society for Technical Communication, Washington, DC, pp. MPD47-MPD49, 1988.

Sachs, I. M., Estimating Publication Costs, *Proceedings of the 34th ITCC*, Society for Technical Communication, Washington, DC, pp. MPD20-MPD23, 1987.

Schultz, G. E., A Method of Estimating Publication Costs, *Technical Communication, 34*:4, pp. 219-224, 1987.

CHAPTER 13

Team Conferences: Full Collaboration in the Report Writing Process

ROBERT M. BROWN

Research on writing in nonacademic settings has demonstrated that numerous factors influence the development of a report, including a considerable amount of social interaction. Lee Odell's suggestion in 1985 that "the process of composing may entail a great deal of social interaction" [1, p. 250] has been substantiated in study after study of document development in the workplace. Recent studies have particularly noted two important social dynamics affecting the composing process in nonacademic settings: collaborative writing and document review.

Writing in the workplace has become increasingly collaborative and complex. Surveys of writers in the workplace have shown not only that writers in various disciplines spend a substantial portion of their work week writing, but also that they often write as part of a team [2]. Much of what has been reported as collaborative writing, however, may not be group composing as much as interaction with others—especially supervisors—about a draft [3]. And most of the interaction between writers and their supervisors evidently occurs after a draft has been produced [4]. Collaboration, therefore, can be thought of as extending beyond the core of writers who generated the report and as occurring after the initial composing [5].

Postdrafting collaboration is a fact of life in many firms because reports and other documents generally undergo an elaborate approval process in the work world. Before a report can be issued, most organizations send the draft up through a series of increasingly senior managers for comment and approval. The document often shuttles back and forth between the writer and a hierarchy of reviewers. Reviewers typically see at least two iterations of a draft—first to critique it, a second time to ensure that the writer has made the requested improvements [6]. In some firms, external sponsors as well as internal reviewers may see multiple drafts and suggest textual changes [5].

James Paradis, David Dobrin, and Richard Miller coined the phrase "document cycling" to describe the process of passing a document between writers and supervisors to restructure and clarify their message [7, p. 285]. Although this process is not what is generally meant by collaborative writing, they suggest that this cycling is a form of collaborative document production. It is, more specifically, what Ede and Lunsford call hierarchical collaboration, as opposed to dialogic collaboration [8].

The number of reviews a document receives varies from firm to firm. In a 1991 survey of reviewers in various firms, reviewers at a think tank had the fewest reviews—two—and those at a government auditing agency had the most—an average of ten—with the overall average being between three and four [9]. This number coincides with earlier reports that the cycle is generally repeated three times, though it can be repeated as many as six times [7]. One report at a government agency was reviewed by nine different reviewers and received thirty-one reviews [6], and proposals at a manufacturing firm reportedly undergo up to fifty review and editing cycles [10]. The number of reviewers and the number of cycles often strike one as being excessive.

In this chapter, I explore two questions relating to collaborative report writing and reviewing: What problems, if any, accompany collaborative writing in firms that have hierarchical reviews? How can firms overcome those problems and better integrate the writing and reviewing processes?

THE PROBLEM: MANAGEMENT BY REVIEW

The argument for document cycling has been that reviewers not only improve the immediate product being scrutinized, but also communicate important corporate values to less experienced personnel [11]. Granted, it is important to indoctrinate junior staff into the corporate culture, and certainly there must be a quality mechanism to ensure that a report meets institutional standards. The real issue, however, is whether *cycling* documents is the most efficient and effective means of accomplishing those goals. I suggest that it is not.

Relying primarily on document cycling to ensure that a report meets corporate standards is what I call management by review. That is, instead of building quality into a report by guiding the team's analysis and arrangement of data, management reserves its input until after the team has created a draft. According to this model, the draft is a way of redefining a project and of deciding *what should have been written*. In essence, drafts are used for planning, which, of course, is backwards.

Almost all researchers who have studied the review process have found document cycling to be seriously flawed. Paradis, Dobrin, and Miller are critical of the counterproductive tension created by document cycling [7]. Roger Grice describes what he sees as multiple problems with traditional document reviews [12], as does David Farkas, who provides an extensive list of negative consequences ensuing from the "excessive reworking" of drafts in document cycling [10, p. 18]. Barbara Couture and Jone Rymer comment that managers as well as writers describe their interaction patterns as ineffective [4]. And James Weber provides perhaps the most condemning evidence when he states: "Writers interviewed rarely mentioned having achieved project goals as gauges of accomplishment. Instead they cited a document's clearance of organizational hurdles" [5, p. 58].

The problems resulting from document cycling or management by review are numerous and consequential:

- *Morale suffers.* Junior staff members interviewed said they "thought cycling painful, immensely time-consuming, and even mystifying" [7, p. 294]. When their work is repeatedly changed, writers may grow resentful and even "disengage themselves from their writing, as in 'What does it matter what I write, they'll only change it anyway'" [10, p. 18].
- *Tensions arise between staff and management.* When management allows writers to struggle in isolation for weeks or months creating what is their best effort, and then informs them that the resulting draft is inadequate, staff-management relations are strained [7, 13]. One writer described his view of reviewers to me this way: "A reviewer is someone who comes in after the battle and shoots all the wounded."
- *The team wastes time drafting.* Not having a full understanding of the needs of the organization and lacking management guidance, the team often does not produce a draft that meets reviewers' approval. Only after submitting it for review do they discover they have not met management's expectations [13].
- *The review process is inordinately lengthy.* The review process is lengthy for three basic reasons. First, when writers are not atuned to management's concerns, reviewers spend considerable time improving drafts that have, in their view, major problems. Second, the more levels of review, the longer the reviewing time. Susan Kleimann documents one report that took four months to go through the reviewing system [6]. Third, each reviewer usually sees the draft more than once.
- *Decisions are made in the managers' absence.* By the time the draft reaches the reviewers, major decisions about content issues and rhetorical issues have long ago been made. It is often too late for the team to collect new data or address new issues.
- *Reviewers are isolated from each other.* Reviewers have no way of knowing what other reviewers have changed about the draft [12]. They may even contradict what previous reviewers have suggested.

Since document cycling is rife with problems, can a firm replace that system with a more efficient one that achieves the same goals? Can it transform what most authors perceive as a trial by fire into a partnership in which exchange of ideas culminates in meaning? Would interaction between managers and writers before drafting help? If so, how can an organization bring managers into the process earlier and make them key participants in report development, instead of end-of-the-line faultfinders?

A POSSIBLE SOLUTION: THE WRITING CONFERENCE

Transactions between writers and managers about a text can occur before, while, or after the text is written. Ideally, perhaps, they should occur at all points. Suggestions for fostering better interaction throughout the report process include a variety of mechanisms, all of which would help to cut down on the review time and document cycling.

At project initiation, for example, firms can utilize kick-off meetings, clarification memos [13], and group brainstorming sessions [14]. Meetings, memos, and brainstorming sessions, if they involve both writers and managers, can help to ensure consensus about purpose, audience, and message.

During the data-gathering stages, teams can use "lead sheets," which are preliminary results distributed to managers to keep them informed; progress reports; oral briefings to management [15]; report-in-progress discussions [16]; and prenegotiation of controversial issues [17].

All of these mechanisms encourage collaborative planning and early involvement by management. As a result, much of the postdrafting conflict and document cycling can be eliminated. According to Paradis, Dobrin, and Miller, "The most common source of conflict was the failure of supervisor and staff to discuss matters of organization, purpose, and audience before the document was written" [7, p. 300]. Couture and Rymer also blame extensive reworking of documents on management's failure to become involved prior to report writing: "managers see little connection between lack of interaction beforehand and the extent of revisions required after drafting" [4, p. 101].

One of the most effective vehicles for ensuring consensus and document quality is the writing conference. What follows is a description of a conference in which the team and its management first reach consensus on the report's message and structure and then actually draft and review the full report during the conference. This mechanism is intended as a partial solution to the problem of miscommunication between managers and writers and the resulting forfeiture of time and money.

A writing conference is a meeting of all the members of the research team and the reviewers who are delegated to critique and approve the report. The conference, which occurs after the team has gathered all the data but before they have begun drafting the report, consists of nine basic steps:

1. Decide on the message.
2. Outline the chapters.
3. Meet, discuss, and revise the outline.
4. Draft an executive summary.
5. Meet, discuss, and revise the executive summary.
6. Draft the full report.
7. Meet, discuss, and revise each chapter.
8. Turn the draft over to the principal investigator (PI).
9. Review and polish the draft.

Using a Predrafting Conference

Holding a predrafting conference to agree on substance and structure is not a new idea, though it goes by different names in different firms. It is variously called a "pre-writing management" meeting [18], a "strategy meeting" [19], a "presubmission conference" [7], a "presentation plan" [20], and an "inspection meeting" [12]. Each of these meetings has as its goal the formation of early consensus and the avoidance of conflict and wasted effort.

I was introduced to the idea of a writing conference at the U.S. General Accounting Office (GAO), though GAO uses only the first three steps, which it refers to as a message conference. A message conference is a half-day meeting during which writers and reviewers talk through the issues and attempt to integrate context and fact. Their primary task at this predrafting session is to decide on the report's message. Often it is assumed that the message is fixed this late in the analysis, and sometimes it is. But just as often it is not, as evinced by massive changes during document cycling.

The Purpose of the Predrafting Conference

Besides determining the overall message, the group discusses other matters, large and small. For example, they ask questions about audience, methodology, the integrity of the data gathered, and the political implications of the findings. They discuss how much detail is needed, whether causal relationships can be firmly established, how many chapters the report will have, how strong the language will be, how conservative the recommendations will be, and what should go into an appendix. They challenge each other, prompt each other, critique each other, and negotiate "collectively toward new paradigms of perception, thought, feeling, and expression" [21, p. 646]. They generate ideas, offer alternative views of issues, raise objections, test logic, discuss structural options, and develop rhetorical strategies. And through this process of interaction, they establish knowledge and reach consensus.

In addition to making decisions and verbal agreements, the group generates various prereport documents to help later in the drafting stage. For instance, an expanded outline (with overview paragraphs for each chapter and topic sentences for all support paragraphs) helps reviewers evaluate the content and organization of a document before drafting begins [11]. If the group developed a tentative outline at an earlier meeting, they reexamine and revise that outline to reflect changes in project scope, data, and findings [13]. When the predrafting conference concludes, team members should sign off on the outline and be ready to externalize the group's newly created knowledge in a logical form. These are important tasks that by themselves help to avoid much of the blood on the floor during the reviewing stage.

Participants in the Predrafting Conference

The key to a successful writing conference is getting the right people to attend. The list of attendees should include all the team members, the PI, the first-line manager (e.g., project manager, program director), the second-line manager (e.g., assistant regional director or associate director), and the third-line manager (the highest person in the reviewing chain). Another important participant should be the technical editor [13, 22, 23]. The ideal policy should be that anyone who does not attend the conference forfeits his or her right to comment later on the draft, though the political likelihood of excluding a high-level reviewer is small.

How the Predrafting Conference Works

What happens in a predrafting conference is that a community of thinkers/writers begins the process of creating themselves in a document. People who have derived individual messages collaborate to derive a communal message and create a logical, communal self. They try to agree on what they will tell the larger community and how they will arrange the data to corroborate their story. They try to agree on an explanation of their communal, logical self and a form for that explanation. Writing, then, becomes a means of externalizing the interpretive community's beliefs and their justification for those beliefs.

At the predrafting conference, managers and writers collaboratively arrange and rearrange their perception of the immediate reality, and that agreed-upon reality becomes their report—the representation to the world of themselves. Rather than being a mere presentation of facts, the draft is a social artifact, much in the way that Thomas Kuhn has explained scientific knowledge as agreed-upon interpretations [24].

If writers and managers do not hold a predrafting meeting, the team creates its own—limited—knowledge. In that case, part of the community that is attempting to define itself is missing, and therefore the representation of themselves that they create will be incomplete. The result will be that the larger interpretive community, which includes the reviewers, will override that representation. Holding a predrafting conference is intended to encourage group interpretation of facts in order to create a full consensus of the knowledge created.

What the Predrafting Conference Cannot Do

Although a predrafting meeting improves the probability of producing a higher quality report with fewer major revisions, holding such a meeting does not guarantee a smooth ride through the organization's hierarchy. Evidence of this fact appears in Kleimann's case study; the draft cited earlier that received thirty-one reviews was at GAO, where message conferences are mandatory.

Specifically, the predrafting conference does not solve two major problems about drafting and reviewing. The first problem is that managers who attend conferences can—and often do—change their minds about a report's conclusions and presentation. Weeks after the predrafting meeting, they have been known to reverse their decisions about message and structure once they see those decisions implemented into language.

The second unsolved problem is the drafting burden. In many firms, the actual composing of a first draft is not collaborative at all; rather, the task typically falls to one person, the PI. Although a predrafting conference certainly helps to ease the PI's task by providing him or her with a socially constructed thesis and structure, the routine difficulty of drafting is still daunting. Although the PI is knowledgeable about the whole project, he or she is not the most knowledgeable person about individual parts of the project. The true expert is the team member who compiled the data for that part of the work plan. And that is the person who is most capable of constructing a plausible story from the data, perceiving the inherent structure within the data, and most efficiently drafting the chapter or section concerning that material.

Expanding the Collaborative Effort to a Full Report Writing Conference

Looking for ways to expand on and improve the conferencing concept, and after having participated in perhaps twenty or more useful but imperfect predrafting conferences, I approached a PI about trying a more intensive type of conference in which participants continue the collaborative effort. She agreed. At this expanded conference, which was a full writing conference, the participants not only agreed on the message and outlined it, but then went on to draft the entire report and reviewed it immediately. We compressed what is sometimes a four- to six-month process into six very intense days.

Instead of everyone disbanding after the predrafting conference (steps 1-3), team writers go on to step 4, drafting an executive summary. Managers, on the other hand, are temporarily dismissed from the conference to attend to other tasks. Their role in the writing conference becomes that of the traditional reviewer: to wait for a draft, comment on it, and provide recommendations for improvement. They reenter the process only when the team has a product ready for review. To help managers plan their schedules, the conference moderator sets time limits on the team's drafting and revising activities.

Drafting the Executive Summary

The team is given four hours to draft an executive summary. The writers may choose whatever team-writing arrangement they are comfortable with to develop the summary. For example, they can develop a communal outline and then have each person draft a section. Another option is to have the team's best writer or the PI draft each section and turn it over to the entire team to critique and revise. A third option is to gather around one computer and take turns at the keyboard while onlookers provide suggestions. The system that works most quickly for the particular team is the one they should use since time is critical.

Although most writers prefer to draft an executive summary after they have written a report, there is a good reason for requiring an executive summary first: Because the executive summary is the report in miniature, most problems will surface in the smaller document and can be resolved before attempting to write the longer version. Writers can see in the summary how well their ideas translated into prose and perhaps reevaluate some of their rhetorical decisions. Much later, after they have drafted the full report, the writers will need to revisit this summary to ensure that it still represents the emphases and findings of the completed report.

If half of Day One of the writing conference is devoted to message and outlining, the second half of that day is devoted to drafting the summary. (I recommend that Day One be a Tuesday if possible.) The four hours allotted to drafting the summary generally are not enough time, but the team can stay as late as they need to. By the start of Day Two, however, they must have a rough draft of the executive summary for all conferees to review.

The reviewers show up early on Day Two and the traditional review process begins. Because summaries are usually no more than five or six pages, reviewing this document should take only one to three hours, depending on how well the plan worked and how well the writers translated the message into prose. (Participants should be encouraged not to worry about the style of this document; it will be revised and polished later.) Everyone should be allowed to provide suggestions, and it is essential that any disagreements be resolved before moving on to the next step. Once agreement is reached and the team has clear directions for proceeding, the reviewers are set free again.

Drafting the Full Report

For the next several days—the rest of Day Two, all of Day Three, and all of Day Four—the team maniacally drafts the full report. Because of time pressures, each person must draft one section. Obviously, everyone must have his or her own computer and a quiet place to compose. How they divvy up the parts of the report is inconsequential, but typically one person drafts the objectives, background, and methodology, and, if there are enough members on the team, the others divide up the results, discussion, conclusions, and recommendations. If the team is small, writers must be responsible for larger assignments or the team must be given more than two-and-a-half days to generate a full draft. (By starting Day One on Tuesday, the team would have the weekend as well for drafting.)

Reviewing the Report

At the beginning of Day Five (Monday morning), multiple copies of the rough draft are made and distributed to reviewers' offices. Reviewers have Day Five to read through the assembled report, write notes in the margins, reconsider the structure and logic, and prepare for Day Six.

Day Six, the culmination of all the previous planning and conferring, is a roundtable discussion of the report, concentrating on higher-level concerns at first, eventually focusing on lower-level concerns. Discussions of style should be limited to recurring faults, not isolated sentences, and copyediting is better left until later. Questions that might be raised include: Is the level of detail appropriate? Do we need more information to substantiate conclusion four? Are the conclusions and recommendations explicit? Does the material we thought should go into an appendix work as an appendix, or does it go better in chapter two?

The goal is to complete the reviewing by the end of Day Six, though of the nine writing conferences I have attended, only four have concluded their business by the end of that day.

Preparing the Revised Draft

When the reviewing of the draft is completed, the next step is to turn the draft over to the PI, who has full responsibility for synthesizing and incorporating the group's suggestions into the second draft, which he or she is then responsible for polishing. Other team members may well be assigned to other projects at the end of Day Six.

The final step, which may take place as much as a week later, is to allow all reviewers to read and approve or disapprove of the revised draft. Since there should be few or no major changes to this draft, one option is to route it through the traditional document cycling process, whereby each manager reviews it and passes it along to the next level. A better option, I think, is to conduct a concurrent review—that is, send the draft to all reviewers simultaneously. This way the PI can compile all their suggestions at once and resolve any discrepancies in the suggestions. The best option for handling the review process, however, is to call all the reviewers back together one final time and have a brief approval meeting and sign off on the product. Assembling the full group has the added benefit of mutual congratulations and joint approval of the team's performance.

Potential Problems of Writing Conferences

The writing conference is not without potential problems. Following are some objections that writers, managers, and executives have voiced to me, over several years, concerning the writing conference.

Impossible Task

The foremost objection to this concept, and the one I have heard from a number of managers, is "It can't be done." Drafting a sixty-page report in just a few days, they said, is impossible. My response is that what has been done can be done. Of the nine writing conferences I have attended, seven achieved their goal—a quick rough draft of a report that everyone approved.

Lack of Attendance

The most significant difficulty is not deciding on the message or drafting the report, but getting the right people to attend. Although we must respect the multiple demands on upper management's time, upper management must recognize the advantages of remaining actively involved in the development of the message and the report. If those who review reports do not get involved early in the process, they will end up spending much more than two days trying to recreate the report in their own image.

Staff Reassigned

A third objection I hear is that quite often all staff except the PI are pulled off a project as soon as they complete their data gathering. Keeping the full staff on the project another six days would throw off the scheduling for a series of projects. The counterargument is that keeping the team on the project an extra six days will use up no more total staff days than if the PI were to write the report by himself or herself. Net time may actually be saved. In addition, this kind of conference can be planned into the annual scheduling of projects.

Excessive Financial Costs

Another objection is that meetings are expensive, and indeed they are. The collective salaries of everyone from junior team member through PI on up to Division Director can amount to a considerable cost. I once quickly computed the cost—just in salaries of the participants in one conference with eleven participants—at being $263 an hour, or $2104 a day. Then if participants must be flown in from regional offices, there are airfare, hotel costs, and per diem expenses to cover.

Emotional Cost

The full writing conference is a grueling, draining experience. Tempers occasionally flare, days are long, egos are bruised. The pressure of generating a ten- or fifteen-page chapter in two and a half days is intense. But then, the emotional cost of undergoing four months of document cycling is also high.

These objections are based on valid concerns. I think, however, each can be overcome by a progressive and knowledgeable manager. Even if a manager and PI are willing to try it, the first few attempts may not run as smoothly as hoped because the participants will be working their way through a new and strange system. But if writing conferences were standard practice, as document cycling is now, I believe writers and managers would work out any flaws in the initial attempts and adapt conferencing to their particular environment.

Benefits of Writing Conferences

The advantages of bringing all the participants together are enormous. The predrafting session and the periodic regroupings—after outlining, after drafting the summary, and after drafting the chapters—allow for incremental building of a message and incremental consensus. As a result, authors know what is expected of them because management has ample opportunity to present its perspective. Following are some specific advantages for writers, reviewers, and the firm.

Better Communication between Staff and Management

By providing "a tighter communication loop" [16, p. 13], writing conferences encourage communication and cooperation between writers and supervisors. A face-to-face conference allows all parties to state their assumptions and openly debate critical issues. The people closest to the investigation, the authors, can explain their views to managers who are sitting across the table. For their part, managers can listen to writers' ideas and respond in person. Team members educate managers about the data; managers educate team members about broader issues, including corporate culture.

Acculturation of Staff

Recent case studies of workplace writing have documented that personnel in different positions within an organization have different types of knowledge and view problems from different perspectives. In general, the persons who have more knowledge about corporate culture and political constraints are managers, not the technical staff who write reports [6, 7, 11, 25]. In fact, team members often lack "sufficient knowledge about social and political constraints to make intelligent composing decisions aimed at appealing to all members of a multiple audience" [11, p. 218]. Gaining this knowledge is one of the goals of a writing conference.

When writers sit in a room and negotiate a message with middle and upper management, the writers acquire a heightened awareness of the political issues surrounding their project and of the cultural values of the organization. Managers implicitly and explicitly share their perspectives with those below them in the hierarchy, communicating corporate culture and the effects of that culture on choices of data, strategy, and word choice [26]. In this sense, a writing conference becomes a means by which less experienced personnel join a more experienced community and its values, language, and perceptions [21]. Some evidence suggests that authors who listen carefully to more experienced managers about the social and political constraints of a situation perform their writing tasks more successfully [11].

Buy-In by Management

Interacting with managers to discuss content, structure, and strategy helps authors gain "initial audience adherence" [27, p. 58]. When managers have had an opportunity to preview ideas, they often develop a sense of shared authorship with the writers and feel a stronger allegiance to the report's conclusions.

Immediate Feedback

A major advantage of the writing conference is that reviewers can inform authors whether they have captured the agreed-upon knowledge. Unlike in traditional reviewing, they even have an opportunity to intervene in the composing process [16]. The authors' tasks are therefore eased considerably because the reviewers are present to help them make rhetorical decisions—offering options for structuring chapters, providing insights about political constraints, and demonstrating better ways of finessing sensitive issues.

Better Sense of Audience

When reviewers respond immediately to writers' ideas and drafts, writers develop a more realistic sense of audience. Talking with reviewers at length enhances writers' audience awareness, helps them "determine how readers' orientations and impressions differ from their own," and allows them to "use this knowledge to plan intelligent, socially sensitive audience-adaptation strategies" [27, p. 62].

Contradictions Resolved

Because the managers collectively review the draft in the meeting, they hear their colleagues' comments and suggestions. If differences in review comments exist, the reviewers themselves can resolve them, face to face. The resulting advantage to the team is that they "receive one agreed-upon solution rather than having to decide among a number of alternatives" [12, p. 236].

Time Savings

My assumption is that time invested in communal message agreement will pay off in fewer rewrites, and therefore there will be a net savings in time. There is anecdotal evidence [12, 16, 18, 27] but no empirical data to document this assertion; however, I believe that studies will eventually substantiate that predrafting meetings and full writing conferences are cost-effective.

Of the nine writing conferences I have attended, the large majority of the drafts sailed through the review process without major reworkings. Reduced reviewing time and fewer rewrites obviously translate into financial savings for an organization.

In addition, an excellent report benefits the firm not only by achieving the intended results, but also by enhancing the firm's ethos and credibility. As an added benefit, the firm emerges from the process with technical people who are better writers and who are more aware of corporate needs.

MAKING WRITING CONFERENCES WORK

The most convincing argument for using writing conferences is that the current way of managing report development is inefficient and costly. In a period when American business is emphasizing quality assurance, the report development process remains fixed on quality control, characterized by endless document cycling. Conferencing, on the other hand, is based on values most American firms strongly endorse: collaboration, expediency, and quality.

Logic suggests that a system will be superior to document cycling if it

- Allows both writers and reviewers to express their views and negotiate a consensus
- Lets authors know in advance what is expected of them
- Allows managers a chance to influence the direction and focus of a draft
- Provides face-to-face, immediate feedback
- Prevents crisis management at the end of a project.

Writing conferences, I think, are such a system. I believe that if writers and managers reach group agreement on audience, data, message, structure, and tone before the team starts drafting, the team will produce a better initial draft. I further believe that if management intervenes in the composing process and collectively reviews the report while in progress, fewer massive rewrites will be necessary.

To make conferences succeed, management must be willing to make three types of commitment. First, upper management must commit resources in personnel and budget. Second, middle management must be willing to commit themselves to working with teams to make collaborative decisions in advance of and during composing. And third, training divisions must make a commitment to incorporate collaboration and conferencing into their in–house programs.

Academe as well as industry needs to teach different models of managing report development. It is not enough simply to inform students that document review and cycling are realities within organizations. Instructors must also teach ways of making the review process more efficient. Management courses as well as writing courses must demonstrate that there are ways of ensuring quality in a document through effective project management. In short, managers must be taught that the best reviewer is a planner.

Finally, for new ideas to find acceptance, researchers in technical writing need to conduct empirical studies testing their effectiveness. Regarding conferences, we need to compare cases using traditional reviewing with those using conferences to determine if conferencing is indeed more efficient. And there are questions we need to address: Do teams that use conferences have fewer major rewrites? Is there a net savings in time when teams use writing conferences? Do writing conferences produce higher quality reports?

I am optimistic that research will demonstrate that when managers interact early with authors, integrate their various perspectives, and develop socially constructed documents, the firm saves time and issues higher quality reports.

REFERENCES

1. L. Odell, Beyond the Text: Relations between Writing and Social Context, in *Writing in Nonacademic Settings*, L. Odell and D. Goswami (eds.), Guilford Press, New York, pp. 249-280, 1985.
2. P. Anderson, What Survey Research Tells Us about Writing at Work, in *Writing in Nonacademic Settings*, L. Odell and D. Goswami (eds.), Guilford Press, New York, pp. 3-83, 1985.
3. B. Couture and J. Rymer, Interactive Writing on the Job: Definitions and Implications of "Collaboration," in *Writing in the Business Professions*, M. Kogen (ed.), National Council of Teachers of English/Association for Business Communication, Urbana, Illinois, pp. 73-93, 1989.
4. B. Couture and J. Rymer, Discourse Interaction between Writer and Supervisor: A Primary Collaboration in Workplace Writing, in *Collaborative Writing in Industry: Investigations in Theory and Practice*, M. M. Lay and W. M. Karis (eds.), Baywood Publishing Company, Amityville, New York, pp. 87-108, 1991.
5. J. Weber, The Construction of Multi-Authored Texts in One Laboratory Setting, in *Collaborative Writing in Industry: Investigations in Theory and Practice*, M. M. Lay and W. M. Karis (eds.), Baywood Publishing Company, Amityville, New York, pp. 49-63, 1991.
6. S. Kleimann, The Complexity of Workplace Review, *Technical Communication, 38*:4, pp. 520-526, 1991.
7. J. Paradis, D. Dobrin, and R. Miller, Writing at Exxon ITD: Notes on the Writing Environment of an R&D Organization, in *Writing in Nonacademic Settings*, L. Odell and D. Goswami (eds.), Guilford Press, New York, pp. 281-307, 1985.
8. L. Ede and A. Lunsford, *Singular Texts/Plural Authors: Perspectives on Collaborative Writing*, Southern Illinois University Press, Carbondale, Illinois, 1990.
9. R. Brown, *What Report Reviewers Say about Reviewing: A Survey*, paper presented at the 56th Annual Convention of the Association for Business Communication, Honolulu, Hawaii, November 30, 1991.
10. D. Farkas, Collaborative Writing, Software Development, and the Universe of Collaborative Activity, in *Collaborative Writing in Industry: Investigations in Theory and Practice*, M. M. Lay and W. M. Karis (eds.), Baywood Publishing Company, Amityville, New York, pp. 13-30, 1991.
11. R. Spilka, Studying Writer-Reader Interactions in the Workplace, *Technical Writing Teacher, 15*:3, 208-221, 1988.
12. R. Grice, Verifying Technical Information: Issues in Information-Development Collaboration, in *Collaborative Writing in Industry: Investigations in Theory and Practice*,

M. M. Lay and W. M. Karis (eds.), Baywood Publishing Company, Amityville, New York, pp. 224-241, 1991.

13. J. T. Hackos, Project Management—An Expanded Role for the Technical Communicator, *Proceedings of the 28th ITCC,* Society for Technical Communication, Washington, DC, pp. W34-W37, 1981.

14. J. Selzer, The Composing Processes of an Engineer, *College Composition and Communication, 34*:2, pp. 178-187, 1983.

15. D. A. Winsor, Engineering Writing/Writing Engineering, *College Composition and Communication, 41*:1, pp. 58-70, 1990.

16. A. Moorehead, The Conference Approach to Engineers' Report Writing, *IEEE Transactions on Professional Communication, 28*:3, pp. 13-16, 1985.

17. G. Henkel, Problems of Communication in Project Planning and Development, *Journal of Technical Writing and Communication, 11:*1, pp. 9-12, 1981.

18. T. Manyak, The Management of Business Writing, *Journal of Technical Writing and Communication 16*:4, pp. 355-361, 1986.

19. G. Broadhead and R. Freed, *Variables of Composition: Process and Product in a Business Setting,* Southern Illinois University Press, Carbondale, 1986.

20. R. Hartshorn, Building Rapport with Reviewers, *Proceedings of the 35th ITCC,* Society for Technical Communication, Washington, DC, pp. WE122-WE124, 1988.

21. K. Bruffee, Collaborative Learning and the "Conversation of Mankind," *College English, 46*:7, pp. 635-652, 1984.

22. J. Knapp, A New Role for the Technical Communicator: Member of a Design Team, *Proceedings of the 31st ITCC,* Society for Technical Communication, Washington, DC, pp. WE30-WE33, 1984.

23. R. Brown, Late in the Century, But Early in the Draft, in *The Writer in the Workplace: New Roles for the '90s,* Society for Technical Communication, Sacramento Chapter, Sacramento, California, pp. 4-9, 1991.

24. T. Kuhn, *The Structure of Scientific Revolutions* (2nd Edition), University of Chicago Press, Chicago, 1970.

25. L. Odell, D. Goswami, A. Herrington, and D. Quick, Studying Writing in Nonacademic Settings, in *New Essays in Technical and Scientific Communication: Research, Theory, and Practice,* P. V. Anderson, R. J. Brockmann, and C. R. Miller (eds.), Baywood Publishing Company, Amityville, New York, pp. 17-40, 1983.

26. L. Driskill, Understanding the Writing Context in Organizations, in *Writing in the Business Professions,* M. Kogen (ed.), National Council of Teachers of English/Association for Business Communication, Urbana, Illinois, pp. 125-145, 1989.

27. R. Spilka, Orality and Literacy in the Workplace: Process- and Text-Based Strategies for Multiple-Audience Adaptation, *Journal of Business and Technical Communication, 4*:1, pp. 44-67, 1990.

PART IV

Legal and Ethical Issues

Law and ethics are important considerations for publications staff. Publications managers need especially to be aware of the legal aspects of publications development as well as the implications of professional codes of ethics and the role of the publications unit in creating organizational *ethos*.

Carolyn D. Rude, in "Managing Publications According to Legal and Ethical Standards," provides an overview of some of these legal and ethical matters, including intellectual property, product liability, and contracts. In a section on professional codes and ethics, Rude, associate professor and director of technical communication at Texas Tech University, discusses the relationship between employer and employee with regard to intellectual property or ideas, conflicts of interest, and favoritism. A closing note on environmental ethics considers the publications manager's responsibility to eliminate waste when producing documents.

Stuart Brown, assistant professor of English at New Mexico State University, takes a theoretical look at organizational *ethos* in "Rhetoric, Ethical Codes, and the Revival of *Ethos* in Publications Management." Brown discusses organizational codes of ethics in the light of contemporary scholarly work on ethics and professional communication, and points to some of the implications for publications managers.

CHAPTER 14

Managing Publications According to Legal and Ethical Standards

CAROLYN D. RUDE

Law and ethics originate in questions of right and wrong, good and bad, fair and unfair. Problems in law and ethics arise because the right, good, and fair often conflict with personal advantage—profit, advancement, convenience, or expediency. Resolving these conflicts is complex because profit is an incentive to development of improvements in thought, systems of organization, and products. Although "right," "good," and "fair" are not absolutes, the concepts all assume some balancing of the individual will with the welfare of other individuals and groups.

The law has established protections and limits on some practices, such as the protection of an author through copyright, based on judgments and traditions about what is right, good, and fair. People who violate laws may be prosecuted in court. Ethical standards are broader and less formally encoded. Ethical standards may be written (as in the Code for Communicators of the Society for Technical Communication), or they may reflect common values of a culture or society and not necessarily be encoded formally. Violators of ethical codes may be censured by a professional group or by their employers. The best motive for ethical conduct, however, is not fear of sanction but the commitment one makes as a professional person to the well-being of the profession and its members as well as to people who are affected by the actions of the profession.

This chapter provides an overview of legal and ethical issues that relate to the development of publications. The legal issues are intellectual property, product liability, and contracts. The chapter excludes issues of personnel and employment, such as discrimination and harrassment. The chapter also omits issues of libel, censorship, obscenity, and First Amendment protections that may concern journalists, novelists, poets, playwrights, and screenwriters more than managers of technical publications. The chapter considers federal law, but state law may be more restrictive. The overview of ethics is also limited to professional (rather than personal) issues, especially professional standards, obligations to an employer, and environmental ethics.

LEGAL ISSUES

The production of documents involves three types of legal issues: intellectual property, product liability, and contracts.

Intellectual Property

Intellectual property includes products of research and creative work, such as publications, software, inventions, and manufacturing processes. Intellectual property law provides writers, inventors, researchers, and artists with the incentive to accept the risks and costs of development by giving them the right to profit from their work. Like property in land or equipment, intellectual property may be owned, sold, and donated. It is protected by laws regarding copyright, trademarks and patents, and trade secrets.

Copyright Law and Procedures

The United States Copyright Act of 1976 protects "original works of authorship fixed in any tangible medium of expression," including books, videos, slide shows, graphics, recordings, musical works, computer programs, and other types of expression. The creator of any such expression has the exclusive right to control reproductions or performances of the work. Publications managers need to know this law for two reasons: to protect the company's publications from unfair use by others, and to ensure fair use of the materials created by others that the company uses in publishing.

In the United States, the Copyright Act of 1976 and its 1988 amendments protect expressions published or created after 1977. The Copyright Act of 1909, which established somewhat different terms of protection, protects materials published before 1978. The 1976 act provides automatic copyright as soon as the work is fixed in a form of expression, even at the manuscript stage. Copyright protection lasts for fifty years after the author's death. In the case of work made for hire (see the section following) or anonymous work, the copyright term is seventy-five years from publication or 100 years from creation, whichever is shorter.

Publications managers may obtain useful information from the Publications Section LM-455, Copyright Office, Library of Congress, Washington, DC 20559. Particularly useful are Circular 1, "Copyright Basics"; Circular 2, "Publications on Copyright"; and Circular 3, "Copyright Notice." The circulars are free; other publications, some of which have a charge, are listed in Circular 2. In addition to the government publications, the copyright handbooks by William Strong [1] and Stephen Fishman [2] are useful sources for laypersons.

Copyright notice — Any work published before March 1, 1989, must bear a copyright notice. The notice includes three elements: the symbol © , the word "Copyright," or the abbreviation "Copr."; the year of first publication; and the name of the copyright owner. The notice is optional but recommended for work published after March 1, 1989. Typically the notice appears in a book or manual on the verso of the title page. Use of the copyright notice does not require registration with the Copyright Office.

Copyright registration — Registration with the Copyright Office offers legal advantages (evidence and awards) in case of an infringement. Registration requires that the following three items be sent in the same envelope to the Register of Copyrights: completed application form, filing fee ($10 in 1992), and two copies of a published work. The application form depends on the type of work. Form TX is for published and unpublished nondramatic literary works; Form SE is for serials. Other forms are used for performing arts, visual arts, and sound recordings. Computer programs are considered literary works.

International copyright protection — The United States has agreements with other countries to extend reciprocal copyright protection through the Berne Convention and the Universal Copyright Convention. Most countries belong to one or both of these international conventions. Work protected by copyright in the United States shares protection in other countries that have signed the treaties. Likewise, copyrighted work produced in other countries is subject to the same fair-use guidelines that govern use of work copyrighted in the United States. If a publication will be distributed in countries other than the United States, the publications manager should find out the terms of protection in those countries before first publication. In Circular 38a, the Copyright Office provides a list of countries that maintain copyright relations with the United States.

Work made for hire — An employer owns the copyright on any material an employee creates as part of employment. Thus, computer manuals are copyrighted by the computer company, not by the writers who work for the company. If a company contracts with a freelance writer or artist to produce material for a publication, the contract may specify that the work is made for hire. If the employer provides significant supervision and the work is a contribution to a larger project, the contracted work would probably be considered made for hire. In some contract situations, the writer may be considered an independent contractor and not an employee.

Permission to publish — Work protected by copyright can be reproduced only by permission of the copyright owner, except under conditions of fair use. A publications manager should obtain signed permissions before reproducing all or parts of the copyrighted material, including text, visuals, recordings, or any other expression. The permission statement should specify the terms of use, including the exact material to be reproduced and the title and distribution plans of the work in which the copyrighted material will be reproduced. Some copyright owners charge a fee for use. The permissions agreement should be kept.

Fair use — Some uses of copyrighted material without permission are legitimate. An example is photocopying an article from a periodical for personal research. Photocopying an entire book, however, exceeds the boundaries of fair use because that deprives the author of profit from sale of the book. Likewise, distributing photocopies of a periodical through an office deprives the publisher of subscriptions. Quoting parts of a work in a review or as evidence to support an argument is fair use so long as the quotation is short and the source is documented. Some works specify a word limit for quotation. Illustrations and text are separate objects in the eyes of the law [3, p. 61]. Reproducing an entire line drawing from a publication with copyright protection would exceed the boundaries of fair use. Even though the drawing may be a small part of a document, it is complete in itself. If there is any doubt about what is fair, formal permission should be obtained.

Public domain — Some published work does not meet the requirements for copyright protection and is therefore in the public domain. Work whose copyright has expired and work by the U.S. government is in the public domain. This material may be used without permission.

Trademarks and Patents

Trademarks and patents, like copyrights, identify and protect intellectual property. A patent protects an invention, which may be an object, process, composition of matter, or design. A trademark is any word, phrase, logo, or graphic symbol that identifies a product or process. A business that uses a trademark in interstate commerce may claim an exclusive right to use the mark and register it with the U.S. Patent and Trademark Office (PTO). The validity of the claim must be established. Once a mark is formally registered and certified, the symbol ® may be placed next to the mark whenever it is used [4, p. 100]. This symbol means that the trademark is registered with the PTO and alerts others to restricted use of the mark. The symbol ™ denotes a mark registered on a state basis only or one that has not been officially placed on the Principal Register in the PTO [4, p. 106]. Words that are registered trademarks are identified in dictionaries. Trademarks, such as Xerox, are capitalized in print. Publications managers must respect the restrictions on uses of trademarks just as they respect copyrights.

Trade Secrets

A trade secret is information that is not generally known and that can provide its owner with a competitive advantage [41, p. 1]. Trade secrets may include formulas, manufacturing processes, product designs, private computer programs, and lists of customers [5, p. 360]. The law protects owners of trade secrets if the owners take necessary steps to preserve the secrecy. Publications managers and employees should know and respect the legal protections of a company's trade secrets and their responsibilities to preserve secrecy. The protection of trade secrets is an exception to the First Amendment protection of freedom of speech.

An employee owes a "duty of trust" to current and former employers. It is illegal to share with a new employer the privileged information gained while working for a former employer. Some employers require employees to sign a confidentiality or nondisclosure agreement, which prohibits the release of information to others. Competitors may try to use employees as sources of information in industrial espionage. It is illegal for a firm to hire someone away from a competitor to gain information [6, p. 177].

If valuable information is not kept secret, anyone who innocently learns the information may use it. Judith Bronson [6] identifies five responsibilities of technical professionals in protecting trade secrets: protecting documents (including computer files) from easy access; keeping confidential information secret from competitors, reporters, and family members; reporting problems; avoiding conflicts of interest; and remembering obligations to former employers.

Computer Software

Computer programs may be protected by copyright, patent, and trade-secret law. Programs in development receive trade-secret protection. As a process or system, a computer program can be patented. As an expression, a program receives copyright protection. A work, however, cannot be both patented and copyrighted [1, p. 20].

Publications managers mainly need to know that using pirated versions of commercial software violates intellectual property law. Software piracy (unauthorized copying and use of programs) denies the creators of the programs their legal right to recover development costs and to profit from their creations. Ultimately such piracy discourages innovation and improvements. Software is also protected by contract law. Agreements printed on the package prohibit duplication and distribution. A user accepts the terms of the contract by opening the package. Software agreements typically specify that a purchaser may make a single copy to a disk or one hard drive. A separate package should be purchased for each user or machine.

Some software can be replicated legally. *Freeware* is software made for free distribution. It is legal to copy and distribute such programs but not to sell them. Some virus detection programs are freeware. *Shareware,* often distributed over networks, may be copied and used with minimal restrictions. Creators of such programs may request and are entitled to modest fees from users. *Clip art* programs provide graphics for reproduction, and the purchaser is entitled to copy and reproduce those graphics.

Product Liability

A consumer has a legally enforceable right to assume that a product will serve in normal use without causing injury [7, p. 6]. Product liability refers to the responsibility of a manufacturer or vendor of goods to compensate for injury caused by a product [8, p. 322]. Hazardous products not only include obvious ones such as heavy equipment, solvents, some medicines, and products that threaten users with electric shock, but also everyday objects including some wearing apparel, toys, and furniture. A defect may occur in design, materials, production, packaging, or labeling and instructions.

Some products that consumers want and need are inherently dangerous, even when well designed. Manufacturers may provide hazardous products that the public needs and wants if the risk can be made reasonable with directions and warnings [8, p. 322]. The law requires instructions for safe use and adequate warnings. Technical writers and editors who prepare instructions and warnings have some responsibility for ensuring safe use of the product. In addition, if an injury occurs and a lawsuit is filed, the words and illustrations will serve as evidence.

The Duty to Warn

A manufacturer or supplier must warn of any hazards of use when there is a reasonable probability of injury unless a warning is given [7, p. 38]. The duty to warn covers any foreseeable or reasonable anticipated use, including uses other than the intended use [7, p. 50]. If the hazard is a common danger known to users, the warning is not necessary. Thus, household knives do not carry a warning (users can be presumed to know that knives can cut). Manufacturers have a duty to warn even when the danger is to just a few persons from the total number of users [9, p. 1083). They also have a duty to warn against risk in incidental uses, such as storage or disposal [9, p. 1083), and against foreseeable misuse. Plastic bags from the dry cleaner are stamped with warnings against use as toys, even though their main use is not as toys. Because the manufacturer and vendor can anticipate that the bags might be offered to children, they must warn against the hazards of such use. The legal standard of strict tort liability holds manufacturers responsible for injury whether or not they know or foresee the danger. This responsibility imposes incentive to conduct safety research [10, pp. 214-215].

Manufacturers do not have the duty to warn against "remote possibility of injury in an isolated and unusual case" [9, p. 1085]. They are not liable if a user does not follow clear instructions [9, p. 1083], nor for normal wear and tear of the product [7, p. 48]. Manufacturers are charged to know the nature and quality of their products and thus cannot claim that they did not know a product's danger [9, p. 1086]. They also cannot avoid liability for defective products by writing disclaimers [5, p. 406].

Misrepresentation of a product, thus giving users a false sense of security about it, or concealment of dangers can be the basis for claims against a company [8, p. 319]. Also, words that give assurance may be negligent if they conceal danger. For example, labeling a dart package as "KIDDY TOY-PAK" is an indirect representation of safety [9, p. 1083]. In a case that led to bankruptcy of a pharmaceutical company, written product claims about safety and effectiveness of a birth control device were ruled by the courts to jeopardize public health because of their inaccuracy [11, p. 309]

Instructions and Safety Labels

Writers can inform users about hazards and proper use with instructions on product use and with warnings incorporated into the instructions or affixed to the product or both. Instructions tell how to use the product efficiently, effectively, and safely. Warnings alert users to the dangers involved and identify procedures for avoiding dangers. Instructions for use do not satisfy the duty to warn, and warnings do not discharge the duty to instruct [7, pp. 39-40]. Failure to give adequate and accurate instructions and warnings may constitute negligence [7, p. 46].

Preparing instructions and warnings requires analysis of the hazard itself, including hazards of misuse that is foreseeable and of incidental use, as well as the degree of harm that may result from misuse. Instructions and warnings must be understandable by the people who will come in contact with the product—installers, users, service persons, people who pass by, children. The expertise of these people with this product and their literacy determine choices of wording and visuals.

General principles of writing for comprehension also apply. For example, readers understand concrete outcomes ("birth defects") more readily than abstractions ("hazardous to your health"). "Use adequate ventilation" may require users to guess the meaning of "adequate," especially if they work in a building with no access to outside air. Parallel structure and consistent use of active voice help readers comprehend by minimizing steps in interpretation. Visuals can help all readers, but they are especially helpful when literacy and translation are problems.

Instructions for safe use and warnings must appear in a location where users will see them *before* performing the task. They should appear at the beginning of a procedure that requires precautions rather than as footnotes. They may need to be repeated as various procedures are repeated. If instructions for safe use require extra efforts, the instructions must be especially motivating. They should indicate the seriousness of the task.

On the other hand, concern about warnings may result in overwarning. Excessive warnings and exaggerated risks may diminish their effectiveness. Readers often ignore such warnings or fail to discriminate significant hazards from slight risks to property. If a user manual for a household electronic device begins with three pages of warnings randomly arranged, users are likely to skip all these pages.

The number and placement of warnings must be thoughtfully planned; ideally, the instructions and warnings are tested with representative users.

Safety labels may appear within printed instructions or on the product or both. Safety information within the instructions should correspond to warnings on the product. Labels on the product must be durable enough to last for the product's life. The American National Standards Institute (ANSI), the Occupational Safety and Health Administration (OSHA), and the International Standards Organization (ISO) have developed some standards of wording and layout for warnings. These standards identify different categories of hazards, symbols and pictographs that represent the hazards visually (especially important when translation or literacy are problems), layout, and wording of safety labels.

Westinghouse Electric Corporation (WEC) has summarized and compared standards of various organizations, including ANSI, Society of Automotive Engineers (SAE), and the ISO, in its *Product Safety Label Handbook* [12]. The handbook identifies seven elements of a safety label, including the hazard alert symbol (an exclamation point enclosed in a triangle), signal word, color, symbol of the hazard, verbal hazard identification, result of ignoring the warning, and how to avoid the hazard. The signal words DANGER, WARNING, and CAUTION indicate specific hazards of decreasing magnitude of risk. SAFETY INSTRUCTIONS indicates directions for safe operation, and NOTICE indicates information that needs emphasis but does not identify hazards. The words are respectively signaled by red, orange, yellow, green, and blue backgrounds. Herb Smith [11] notes that the signal words differ in the medical field.

There are useful sources on instructions and safety labels. The FMC *Product Safety Sign and Label System* [13] provides instructions for designing safety symbols. The special issue of *IEEE Transactions on Professional Communication* on legal and ethical issues edited by Stephen Doheny-Farina [14] includes useful essays. James Paradis [15] reviews lawsuits involving studguns and analyzes the operator's manuals rhetorically, illustrating the social context of laws and technology. He observes that conflicting institutional interests and rhetorical ineptitude result in failure to place priority on human consequences.

Personal Liability

Technical communicators may wonder about their personal liability in case a product causes injury. A product liability suit claiming faulty design, production, or packaging would not involve technical writers and editors. The designers, engineers, and manufacturers of the product have greater responsibility for product safety. Furthermore, most cases name a company rather than individuals because the company has greater resources.

Suits, however, usually claim inadequate instructions and warnings. Suits could conceivably charge an individual writer or editor with negligence, though the norm is to name the manufacturer. Everyone in the chain of distribution of a product owes a "duty of due care" to anyone who might be injured by a product [8, p. 319]. Technical communicators could be negligent, legally and ethically, if they knew that the product being documented could be hazardous, knew of the responsibility to provide clear instructions and adequate warnings but did not make an effort to do so, or did not investigate to determine hazards in the use of the product. Claiming ignorance of the law would not be a defense because a professional person is assumed to be informed about professional matters.

Technical communicators do not need to work in dread of legal action against them. They should, however, accept their responsibility for providing clear instructions and warnings for the use of any product that might injure a user. Publications managers can encourage writers and editors to meet these responsibilites by following the guidelines in Figure 1.

Freelance writers who document hazardous products should consider incorporation. This form of business helps protect personal assets in the case of an award for damages in a liability suit. In contracts with manufacturers, freelancers should ask for an indemnity clause that assigns liability for product defects to the manufacturer and that limits their own liability to violations of copyright.

Liability and language relate in areas other than product liability. Kristin Woolever [16] reviews liability aspects of investment information, goods and services marketing, and employee handbooks. Statements in all these areas may be contractual and interpreted legally as warranties.

Contracts

Contracts are agreements: one party offers a good or service, and the other party accepts the offer by agreeing to the terms of the offer. The offer and acceptance must be supported by a "consideration"—something of value. In a contract between a company and a freelance writer, the offer might be $10,000, and the acceptance is the writer's agreement to perform the work specified for that amount. The consideration is the item worth $10,000, perhaps the documentation of a software package consisting of 400 double-spaced typescript pages and disk version to be delivered within three months.

Once the parties have agreed to the terms, they have a legal obligation to fulfill their promises, and they have legal recourse if the other party breaches the contract (fails to fulfill the promises). As employees, publications managers work under contract with their employers, but they make contracts in the course of publications development as well: with vendors such as typesetters and printers, with graphic artists and freelance writers and editors, and with members of publications teams who are also employees.

Oral contracts as well as written ones are enforceable, but written ones are preferable especially if the contract involves a sale of more than $500 or the work cannot be performed within one year from the date when the contract is made [5, pp. 392, 400]. Both parties should sign written contracts. For a contract to be legally binding, both parties must have legal capacity; that is, they both must be

Guidelines: The Duty to Warn and Instruct

1. *Become informed about the law and standards for instructions and warnings.* Legal encyclopedias explain the law for laypersons. *The Guide to American Law* provides an understandable overview. The *Corpus Juris Secundum* provides details on specific cases, and volume 72 (supplement) provides information on safety requirements for specific products, such as bottles and containers, ladders, saws, and toys, that would be useful to manufacturers of that product. *Products Liability in a Nutshell* includes a chapter on warnings and instructions.

2. *Establish policies and guidelines for addressing safety in product documentation.* Make investigation of safety a routine part of documentation. Train employees–technical communicators, managers, product engineers and designers–in the requirements for safety and for adequate instruction and warnings.

3. *Add information about product liability and warnings to the company style guide.* ANSI, OSHA, and ISO guidelines and copies of relevant portions of the CJS defining legal responsibilities for specific products might be appropriate.

4. *Learn about the product that is being documented.* Existing documentation may provide information about company products, and the CJS includes information on categories of products. Consult the engineer or designer to determine any hazards of use.

5. *Include warnings and precautions in product instructions.* Determine whether a safety label is also needed. Categorize the hazard according to ANSI classifications, and include the seven elements of an effective warning.

6. *Test instructions and safety labels with representative users.*

7. *Keep a record of your efforts to become informed about the safety of the product and to provide sufficient information for safe use.*

Figure 1. The duty to warn and instruct: guidelines for publications managers.

able to understand what the contract is about. Contracts must not violate laws or concepts of good conduct, morals, and public policy, and they would be invalidated by fraud, misrepresentation, force, or undue influence [17, pp. 46, 50-53].

The terms of the consideration should be specific. Leonard DuBoff [18] reviews terms a freelance writer submitting an article to a magazine might expect and require; these are adaptable to contracts for technical publications. The terms specify advances, royalties or payment, format and content of the manuscript, due dates, author's alterations of galleys or proofs, ownership of the copyright, and author credit, copies, and purchases. In addition, the contract may include a "satisfactory manuscript" clause that allows a publisher to reject a manuscript of unsatisfactory quality. The test is whether a reasonable person would be satisfied, but the definitions of satisfactory, such as reasonably correct spelling and grammar, should be specified. A warranty and indemnity clause establishes the responsibility of the author and publisher in case of a lawsuit. If the work will require dangerous activities, the author may request Workers Compensation benefits. A covenant not to compete would prohibit the writer from working on a similar project for a competitor for a period of time. Linda Pinkerton [3] provides a sample publisher-author contract that publications managers could consult to determine contract terms and wording if the company has not previously developed a standard contract.

Contracts with printers will include printing specifications and the printer's promises regarding cost, time, and delivery. The specifications should cover all the document features about which there is a choice, including number of copies, number of pages, paper (weight, finish, color), ink (color, type), number and type of illustrations and whether they are camera-ready, cover, proof copies, folding, binding, delivery date, and method of payment. The specifications should also state policies regarding overruns, author's alterations (how charged), and subcontracting (whether the printer can subcontract to another vendor).

Public contracts (those made by public bodies such as government and school districts) must not show favoritism. Those contracts, in many cases, require competitive bidding. All prospective bidders must be given the same specifications [7, pp. 182, 186].

Contracts with members of a publications team reflect agreements about who will do what and when. Such contracts are probably not written in legal terms and signed, but project management plans and other written or oral assignments identify the offer and the consideration, and the employee's assent to the assignment is the acceptance. Employment contracts in general establish the broad expectations for job performance.

A contract may be altered if both parties agree. It terminates when both parties fulfill their promises. A breach of contract is failure by one of the parties to fulfill the stated promises. For example, the software program that the freelance writer is contracted to document may change substantially, causing delays in the documentation. The parties should try to renegotiate the contract. If that fails, the party that breached the contract may be sued for damages.

Written contracts are good management tools as well as legal documents because they require project planning and make expectations clear. By helping to prevent failures that result from misunderstanding, they protect working relationships.

ETHICAL ISSUES

Acting ethically often demands more than obeying the law. Some actions may be legal but also be unethical. Ethics in the world of work is sometimes equated with professional responsibility. Both concepts imply the ability to put the common good above personal gain. Ethical professionals respect the welfare of other members of the profession, employers, and the people the profession serves or affects.

Ethical conduct is important in all professions; its particular importance in technical communication relates to the power of technology and the power of language. Technology is powerful both for what it can do and because of a general reverence for it in society. Language is powerful because it shapes perception and action. Any group with power must use it responsibly.

Publications managers are responsible for their own ethical conduct and for creating environments that will not compromise the ethics of the people they supervise nor of the users of publications. Sometimes they must advocate on behalf of employees and readers or users to insist on accurate and complete information in publications. Sometimes they must enforce the employer's ethical guidelines.

The Law and Ethics

All the legal issues defined in this chapter have ethical counterparts. Conduct is governed by law when it is "actionable," that is, when violations can be settled in a court of law. Violations of intellectual property, product liability, and contract law are all actionable. Sometimes ethical behavior requires one to exceed the letter of the law. For example, the manufacturer of alcoholic beverages may post the mandatory warning about alcohol and pregnancy on all containers and thereby fulfill legal requirements but use tight letterspacing and all capital letters to discourage consumers from reading the warning. Such a practice supports sales more than the well-being of consumers and violates the principle of responsibility for human welfare. Some questionable conduct may be hard to enforce legally, such as sharing of trade secrets or excess photocopying. When legal enforcement is impractical or unavailable, professionals rely on ethical standards of right.

Professional Ethics

One defining characteristic of a profession is a code of ethics. The members of a profession agree on the conduct that is desirable and acceptable. These codes aim to maintain the stature of the profession and to ensure that members of the profession will serve the public according to high standards. The codes typically address performance of duties, relations with the public, and loyalty to the profession. The Society for Technical Communication anthology, *Technical Communication and Ethics* [19], includes the written codes of several professional associations in communication as well as a number of articles in which technical communicators explore the ethics of this profession.

Competent and Responsible Performance of Duties

The cornerstone of all codes of professional ethics, whether in medicine, law, business, or communication, is a commitment to perform the duties of the profession in a competent and responsible way. The central duty of the STC *Code for Communicators* is "responsibility to communicate technical information truthfully, clearly, and economically." Four of the seven specific responsibilities in that code cite means to the end of truthful, clear, and economical communication: using language and visuals with precision; preferring simple, direct expression of ideas; satisfying the audience's need for information; and accepting responsibiity for the audience's understanding. Textbooks and journal articles reflect the wide acceptance of these responsibities.

The predecessor to the STC Code, the *Canon of Ethics* of the Society of Technical Writers and Editors, was even more explicit about responsibility for content. In its section titled *Relations with the Public,* the Canon rejects "untrue, unfair, and exaggerated statements," affirms "due regard for the safety of life and health of those who may be affected by the work for which [the writer] is responsible," and insists that opinions be informed by "adequate knowledge" and "the facts." From an ethical standpoint, the Canon is stronger than the Code because its sphere of responsibility is wider. Communicators are responsible for the substance of the ideas and the way they are used by readers. By contrast, transmitters of ideas, as the Code describes technical communicators, are ethically neutral except for transmitting accurately. The Code reflects a positivist view of knowledge and the ideal of objective and transparent language. This view has collapsed under examination of linguists, philosophers, and rhetoricians.

Professional competence requires technical communicators to report accurately and clearly but also to verify information, research thoroughly, make informed decisions, refuse to disguise or distort negative information to serve some end of expediency, and edit thoughtfully to avoid intentional or inadvertent falsification.

Professional ethics also requires ongoing competence. The Code for Communicators specifies continual improvement of competence. Keeping knowledge and skills up to date reflects a commitment to the people served and affected by the profession.

Loyalty to the Profession

The STC Code requires respect for colleagues and conduct that will attract talented individuals to the profession. Some professional codes prohibit undue competition with other professionals, such as underbidding a competitor, especially when inside information (the bid of the competitor) is known in advance of the lower bid. Some self-interest is obvious in the items specifying loyalty to the profession and its members, but all professions guard their chance to exist and serve a public.

Limitations of Standards

Professional ethical standards are not necessarily benign. Written ethics codes may be public relations tools, used to discourage close scrutiny of professional practice, rather than ensurers of ethical standards [20, p. 345]. They are rarely enforced. Steven Katz [21] argues that an ethic of expediency underlies technical communication. This ethic sacrifices human welfare to technological efficacy. Still, the tradition in all the professions of declaring a commitment to competence, responsibility, and human welfare establishes an important basis for professional conduct.

Employee/Employer Ethics

As well as belonging to a profession and accepting its standards, technical communicators have specific responsibilities to their employers. Expectations for employees include all professions not just the employees who are technical communicators.

The Contractual Relationship of Employee and Employer

The contractual relationship of employee and employer establishes a basis for defining ethical conduct. Since contracts that violate good conduct, morals, and public policy are illegal, an employer cannot require employees to perform actions that violate these concepts. Neither can employees establish their own secret contract terms that violate the employer's offer of payment for work. Employees can breach the employment contract by theft of property and ideas, conflict of interest, and favoritism.

Theft. Theft by employees can be petty, as in taking office supplies for personal use, or more serious, as in embezzlement. Employees can take ideas as well as things by revealing trade secrets or by claiming the ideas of others as their own. Even when employees change jobs, they owe former employers the preservation of inside information that gives competitive advantage.

Conflict of interest. A conflict of interest pits one obligation against another. Writers who freelance for two competitors, or employees who consult for a competitor, invite conflict of interest because their work for one may jeopardize the interest of the other. Ethical professionals avoid these conflicts by determining expectations before accepting offers.

Favoritism. To achieve quality products and to use company resources efficiently, managers should award assignments and contracts to employees or vendors on the basis of qualifications rather than personal loyalties. Favoritism privileges personal favors over qualifications and compromises quality and efficiency.

Employee Loyalty and Whistleblowing

Employees owe loyalty to employers but not to the point of deceiving or misleading the public, especially if deception may jeopardize health and safety. Questionable or incomplete data or an apparent effort to disguise information that reflects negatively on a product or company should alert publications managers to a possible breach of ethics. If an employee is pressured to mislead the public, that employee must balance loyalty to the employer against professional ethics and the principle of due care. Employers themselves may feel the pressure of extreme competition and feel they have to cheat to compete. Open negotiation within the company should be the first choice of action. Information about the specific ethical infraction and its consequences to the public as well as to the employer's reputation may help publications managers persuade their own managers. This type of conflict is difficult because of the power an employer has over an employee. It requires thoughtful decision making and creative problem solving as well as courage.

If the problem cannot be solved within the company, employees have the option (and sometimes the obligation) of whistleblowing, or making public the breach of ethics. Whistleblowing is a pejorative term, suggesting a violation of loyalty, and whistleblowers risk sanction of coworkers as well as employers. Assessing the magnitude of the infraction and balancing the gains and costs of whistleblowing will help an employee determine the conduct that ethics demands.

Environmental Ethics

Environmental ethics has a shorter tradition than professional and employee ethics because the issues have emerged in recent decades. Standards of conduct, however, are based on the same principles of care for the welfare of people who are affected by the conduct. Publications use paper, ink, plastic, and electricity, all of which harm the environment. The manufacture of paper creates toxic pollutants and uses natural resources, especially trees and water. The manufacture of recycled paper is less toxic. Uncoated papers are more readily recycled than coated papers, and white paper is more readily recycled than colored. Inks made from soybean oil are less toxic than inks based on petroleum products. Plastic wrappers for periodicals will probably end up in landfills and may be superfluous. Electricity used for photocopies contributes to global warming. The use of these products is ethical, but misuse (including excessive use) is not because profit, convenience, and expediency overrule responsibility for the common good.

Publications groups can contribute to the welfare of the environment, and therefore to those who share the environment, by reducing unnecessary use of consumables, choosing inks and papers and other supplies that minimize enviromental destruction, and recycling. No law prohibits waste in publications development, but ethics does.

Law and ethics touch all the activities of a publications group. A manager should know enough of legal and ethical guidelines to articulate them and to use them in decision making. Doing so will help protect the people who are affected by the company's products. It will also help to create a work environment that rewards employees for the highest standards of performance.

REFERENCES

1. W. S. Strong, *The Copyright Book: A Practical Guide* (3rd Edition), MIT Press, Cambridge, Massachusetts, 1990.
2. S. Fishman, *The Copyright Handbook: How to Protect and Use Written Works,* Nolo Press, Berkeley, 1991.
3. L. F. Pinkerton, *The Writer's Law Primer,* Lyons and Burford, New York, 1990.
4. S. R. Elias, *Nolo's Intellectual Property Law Dictionary,* Nolo Press, Berkeley, 1985.
5. M. M. Belli and A. P. Wilkinson, *Everybody's Guide to the Law,* Harper and Row, New York, 1987.
6. J. G. Bronson, Unfriendly Eyes, *IEEE Transactions on Professional Communication,* *30*:3, pp. 173-178, 1987.
7. Products Liability, in *Corpus Juris Secundum, 72* (Supplement), West Publishing Company, St. Paul, pp. 4-106, 1975.
8. Product Liability, in *The Guide to American Law: Everyone's Legal Encyclopedia, 8,* West Publishing Company, St. Paul, pp. 318-324, 1984.
9. Negligence, in *Corpus Juris Secundum, 65,* West Publishing Company, St. Paul, pp. 423-1234, 1966.
10. J. J. Phillips, Warnings, Instructions, and Misrepresentations, in *Products Liability in a Nutshell* (3rd Edition), West Publishing Company, St. Paul, pp. 204-230, 1988.
11. H. Smith, Technical Communications and the Law: Product Liability and Safety Labels, *Journal of Technical Writing and Communication, 20*:3, pp. 307-319, 1990.
12. Westinghouse Electric Corporation, *Danger, Warning, Caution: Product Safety Label Handbook,* Westinghouse Printing Division, Trafford, Pennsylvania, 1985.
13. FMC Corporation, *Product Safety Sign and Label System,* Santa Clara, 1990.
14. S. Doheny-Farina (ed.), Legal and Ethical Aspects of Technical Communication: A Special Issue, *IEEE Transactions on Professional Communication, 30*:3, pp. 119-211, 1987.
15. J. Paradis, Text and Action: The Operator's Manual in Context and in Court, in *Textual Dynamic of Professions,* C. Bazerman and J. Paradis (eds.), University of Wisconsin Press, Madison, pp. 256-278, 1991.
16. K. R. Woolever, Corporate Language and the Law: Avoiding Liability in Corporate Communications, *IEEE Transactions on Professional Communication, 33*:2, pp. 94-98, 1990.
17. M. J. Ross, *Handbook of Everyday Law* (3rd Edition), Harper and Row, New York, 1975.
18. L. D. DuBoff, *The Law (in Plain English) for Writers,* Madrona Publishers, Seattle, 1987.
19. R. J. Brockmann and F. Rook (eds.), *Technical Communication and Ethics,* Society for Technical Communication, Arlington, Virginia, 1989.

20. M. Markel, A Basic Unit on Ethics for Technical Communicators, *Journal of Technical Writing and Communication, 21*:4, pp. 327-350, 1991.
21. S. B. Katz, The Ethic of Expediency: Classical Rhetoric, Technology, and the Holocaust, *College English, 54*:3, pp. 255-275, 1992.

CHAPTER 15

Rhetoric, Ethical Codes, and the Revival of *Ethos* in Publications Management

STUART C. BROWN

Ethics is increasingly important to publications managers and technical communicators. Teaching ethics is now regarded as an important part of business and technical writing curricula. Yet ethical training, for the most part, has been left to the academy. The inclination in professional and organizational contexts has been to deal with ethics by formulating codes, stipulating that being a member of the profession means abiding by its standards of conduct. Nearly all professional organizations and three out of four of the largest U.S. corporations have some formal code of conduct [1, p. 91].

This chapter provides a primer on ethical codes, discusses recent scholarly work on ethics, and points to the implications these topics have for publications managers. It raises questions about the importance of meshing one's personal values with an organization's goals and about managerial and organizational responsibilities.

My purpose is to qualify ready responses to the above concerns, to complicate rather than endorse notions of using codes of conduct in publications management as a means of achieving ethical behavior. I suggest that such codes as the Society for Technical Communication (STC) *Code for Communicators* may enhance views of "rhetoric as technology" and inadvertently cause a root ethical dilemma by denying *ethos* or authorial character. I point to a revived conception of *ethos* as a way to attain more ethical communication practices.

As Edward Corbett suggests, "in the area of contingent human affairs, the area in which rhetoric commonly operates, we have to rely heavily on what the speaker or writer tells us is probably true, and cons [handwritten note: Quandries. // Dilema] ble to trust the speaker or writer" [2, p. 258].

A PRIMER ON ET

The core of the 1978 Society for Tech [obscured] Code for Communicators" stipulates, "My commitment to professional excellence and ethical behavior means that I will

- Use language and visuals with precision.
- Prefer simple, direct expression of ideas.
- Satisfy the audience's need for information, not my own need for self-expression.
- Hold myself responsible for how well my audience understands my message.
- Respect the work of colleagues, knowing that a communication problem may have more than one solution.
- Strive continually to improve my professional competence.
- Promote a climate that encourages the exercise of professional judgement and that attracts talented individuals to careers in technical communication."

This action-oriented, bulleted list specifies how a professional communicator is to behave.

Richard Johannesen points to several benefits of having a formal code of ethics. A code has the potential to educate new members of the profession; to "narrow problematic areas with which a person has to struggle"; to provide a basis to reflect on personal and institutional goals, means, and obligations; and to reduce the threat of outside regulatory action [3, p. 173].

But, as Johannesen notes, perhaps a more critical feature is that effective codes can be generative: "they can serve as a starting point to stimulate professional and public scrutiny of major ethical quandries," or to create public debate over specific practices, or to initiate discussion *prior to* adoption or approval" of policy. Having a formal code in place also provides a communicator with justification for refusing to participate or perpetuate a communication practice [3, pp. 173-174].

The difficulty is in creating a code that will satisfy the above functions and avoid creating problems in itself. For example, the vague and abstract language of the STC code makes adherence a problem. What does it mean to "[p]refer simple, direct expression of ideas"? We can recognize the need to attract others to the profession as indicated in the last item, but what kind of climate "encourages the exercise of professional judgement"? Internal consistency is also a difficulty here—the code is set in the first person, yet self-expression is seconded to that of audience need. If the communicator takes on the responsibility for audience understanding, yet is denied "self-expression," what takes place?

Unfortunately, professional ethical codes are typically rules of behavior, action-oriented dictation "to do this" or "don't do that." Instead, Karen Lebacqz argues, codes need to be reconceived as portraits of the moral character expected of professionals in a discipline [4]. A code should act not only to determine how a person is to be, but to help that person become. In short, an ethical code must allow an individual's *ethos* as well as the larger, more encompassing character of the community if it is to be ethical itself.

Technical writers, notes John Bryan, "have traditionally relied on the ethical orientation of the organizational families that adopt us" [5, p. 73]. Questioning the use of such codes, he argues that codes of conduct and consciousness raising are not in themselves effective, concluding that the classroom is the only place where students "will receive guidance and preparation for the ethical choices they must make" [5, p. 87]. Ethical training, it seems, is being added to all the other responsibilities educators face.

Knowing ethical behavior as specified by a code and knowing how to act ethically are obviously different. Codes determined in the abstract, by others, and imposed either explicitly or implicitly seem to have little chance of providing guidance, much less consciousness raising, in the everyday work world. How aware are we of the formal ethical codes in our professional lives? How often do we consult them as aids to our decision making?

Situational constraints intrude. A writer developing fact sheets for a nuclear power plant may not have the opportunity to question too closely safety standards and waste disposal procedures. A proposal developer for a defense contractor may not have the latitude (or expertise) to contest cost estimates. Even more mundane document tasks, however, are ethically complicated simply because organizations are complex.

As J. Michael Sproule notes, "an organization is always in flux, changing through the process of enactment as people constantly modify the institutional landscape through their actions. Rules are therefore not the dominant reality in an organization" [6, pp. 260-261]. If nothing else, codes are rendered ineffectual because they necessarily lag behind institutional and situational change.

A CONFLICT OF RHETORICS

Some of the recent scholarly work on ethics has significant implications for professional communicators and publications managers. One of the more obvious concerns has to do with how rhetoric is defined and the responsibility this definition assigns to the professional communicator. The research points to the complex relationship between writer and audience and to the ways this relationship complicates the communications produced by an organization.

Codes that exist now, such as STC's, are written from an institutional perspective—the code represents the profession to its members and to the world at large. But in a profession as newly dynamic as technical communication, a code may date rather quickly, portraying objectives that do not necessarily take into account changing conceptions of professional communication practices. Foremost are questions about the underlying ethicality of some basic communication premises in the workplace, especially the idea that what is rhetorically effective is right [7].

S. Michael Halloran sees two competing roles for rhetoric in professional writing: rhetoric as a set of tools or skills and rhetoric as virtue [8].

Rhetoric as a Set of Tools or Skills

The first role, more common in institutional settings and advocated by organizational communication theorists such as Sproule, views rhetoric as "reducible to sets of discrete motions learned in sequence" [8, p. 223]. This view mirrors the ethically neutral stance of tools suggested by the National Rifle Association's bumpersticker: "Guns Don't Kill People, People Kill People."

The role of professional communicators bound by a conception of rhetoric as a set of tools or skills separates personal ethics from adherence to institutional needs. Skills as discrete entities are easily subverted to immediate ends. It is difficult to stay aware of larger, more intangible concerns in the crush of deadlines and budgetary concerns. When a nail needs driven, one reaches for a hammer.

Rhetoric as Virtue

The tendency to reduce rhetoric to technique or skills, however, conflicts with more encompassing views of rhetoric. Richard Weaver argues that rhetoric "at its truest seeks to perfect men by showing them better versions of themselves, links in that chain extending up toward the ideal" [9, p. 82]. Or, as Halloran suggests, the implicit ethical dimension of rhetoric is in developing human capacities and the intellectual virtue of eloquence, the idea of "a good man speaking well." In classical terms, "method or technique was always subordinate to the native human capacity for persuasive speech, and the development of rhetorical skills was simply a means to perfecting that capacity and achieving eloquence" [8, pp. 226-227].

Technique versus Virtue

According to Halloran, a collection of techniques, because it is an extension of the person, separable and inessential, risks becoming autonomous so that it "begins to define its own ends." In contrast, a virtue is an "essential attribute," whose detachment from a person changes that person fundamentally [8, p. 227]. Rhetoric perceived as technology too easily accommodates a code of ethics as a separate and inessential additive, usable when expedient, discarded or replaced when not. Rhetoric as virtue is integral, deniable only by creating self-conflict. A truly ethical rhetoric makes codes superfluous.

The issue demonstrates the split between rhetoric seen as persuasion and rhetoric seen as identification [10], or rhetoric conceived as *techne* versus rhetoric conceived as *phronesis* [11, 12]. Carolyn Miller, summarizing Aristotle's position, notes that "the reasoning appropriate to production takes the form of *techne,* and the reasoning appropriate to performance, or conduct, takes the form of *phronesis*" [11, p. 22]. *Techne* is primarily concerned with what is useful; *phronesis* is concerned with what is good. A rhetoric conceived as *techne* is a rhetoric of tools, a technology directed at ends. The outcome is invariably that the tools take on their own purposes distinct from the people who use them. The aims or ends of the technology supplant individual ethical considerations for the supposed good of the organization. Technology, according to Miller, creates two related phenomena: "the goal of efficiency and the absorption of the individual person into the corporate group" [13, p. 232].

Applying this perspective to ethical communication practices reveals the tension created by subordinating individual consciousness to portray a group *ethos.* *Ethos* as such appears as a collective representation rather than the presentation of the inherent character of the writer. An individual's character and his or her accompanying sense of ethics are overshadowed by an organization's stipulated codes of conduct. Given the problematic nature of many ethical codes, individual capacity for ethical action is truncated to mirroring organizational *ethos.* The homogeneity of the group ethic obscures individual response.

THE HEGEMONY OF AUDIENCE

In most professional communication, success is often determined by providing a message that will be interpreted approximately the same by as many of the intended audience as possible, usually as innocuously as possible. A newsletter is designed to convey information *about* rather than *by.* The cost, however, in striving for as large a success ratio as possible is the loss of consideration for individual conscience, both reader's and writer's.

Audience is usually taught as the most critical feature in technical writing and document production. Current textbooks significantly weight attention to audience over attention to most other concerns, especially to ethics or to personal "voice" [14-17]. The reader or audience determines how a message is presented.

However, producing a text determined by its readership reduces the personal involvement of the author. Technical capability or craft counts for more than ethical integrity. Technique, rather than authorship, becomes the interaction; a document assumes an independence from both the identity and the participation of individuals for the sake of a specific community or intended audience. Unable to recognize an individual "voice" and its attendant contributions and responsibilities, the reader must animate an inanimate textual surface, in essence inventing the writer behind the document. The fewer textual clues available, the more invention required, or, what is more likely, the easier to ignore authorship entirely.

The ethical problem is the impersonal nature of the interaction. A writer, says the STC Code, is responsible for communicating "technical information truthfully, clearly, and economically." Language and visuals are to be used "precisely," preferably in the conveyance of "simple, direct expression of ideas." Content becomes a matter of technique, form over substance. "The aim" of such discourse, says Peter Hartley, "is to *minimize elaboration*" [18, p. 164]. Doing so minimizes the need for discussion, for exchange between writer and reader. Text is received as given. Readers too easily lose sight of the people operating behind the textual surface. Disembodied, so to speak, the text assumes its own authority. The writer necessarily must distance self from the content or substance of the message in such a role. If our individuality as writers shows, our documents fail. Corporate *ethos* is necessarily preeminent if *ethos* shows at all. In such cases, institutional appearance, although often cloaked in attention to audience's needs, predetermines the presentation of information.

Genre conventions further add to appearance constraints. An annual report, for example, looks and sounds like an annual report—its objective is to keep investors happy and trusting in the corporation, not have them question policy. In documents where action, rather than the message itself, is the desired outcome, authorial presence is even more intrusive. In an environmental impact study, the writer's apparentness may suggest bias, a bias contestable by opposition to the findings presented or being acted upon.

ETHICS AS COMPLICATION

Regard for ethical communication complicates organizational goals. Henry Johnstone proposes that most communication involves a social contract, one between an advocate and an audience. For ethical communication to occur, three criteria must be in place. First, the advocate or writer must assume that audiences are beyond control, thus granting a legitimacy to its decision-making capabilities. Second, both the writer and the audience must be open-minded. Third, both parties involved in the exchange must have a genuine interest in the outcome or the solution to the problem [19].

Direct mail appeals from environmental groups are an example of unethical communication practices. Requests to fill in "action surveys" or to write to government leaders along with enclosed decals, wildlife stamps, and other "freebies" cloak an agenda designed to generate funding for an organization. Highly sophisticated, these appeals establish an urgent need and provide a solution to resolve that need. Choice of response is limited to ignoring the message or cooperating by contributing. Provisions for questioning either the need or its solution are severely restricted. The writer falsely elevates shared interest with the reader in resolving the problem—whether the writer is genuinely interested in solving the problem or not, the immediate purpose is to satisfy the organization's needs, rather than the reader's. The writer has an accountability to the employer first.

The complication, especially for professional communicators, is in reconciling institutional needs (or sometimes, demands) with personal conduct. Most publications, aimed at providing a particular viewpoint to an audience, solicit agreements rather than dispute. Resolving dispute takes time, calls into question authority, and hinders goal satisfaction. Granting autonomy to the audience in reaching a decision is counter to the goals of the writer or advocate. Open-mindedness is desirable only in regard to getting the message read and accepted. The writer directs his or her rhetorical talents to converting the audience to a particular position or to accepting a certain representation. Interest in the solution is restricted to the audience agreeing to the solution proposed or the information presented. Any other outcome means failure. Consideration for the larger public good, if it exists at all, becomes a matter of appearance. Effectiveness subsumes personal integrity.

"A MATTER OF CONDUCT"

As Miller suggests, technical writing necessarily must become "a matter of conduct rather than of production, a matter of arguing in a prudent way toward the good of the community rather than of constructing texts" [11, p. 23]. Pragmatically, Cezar Ornatowski counters that audience analysis mechanisms are inadequate for "discerning and discussing the more subtle, and essentially political choices, pressures, and agendas" encountered in workplace environments [20, p. 99]. He notes that writers are expected to serve their employers "effectively" and "efficiently." Their documents are designed for specific purposes and those that do not meet the specifications are unsatisfactory, regardless of the values of the writer [20, p. 100].

One sees how (and why) the STC, for example, adopted in its Code the metaphor of a bridge: "As a technical communicator, I am the bridge between those who create ideas and those who use them." Scott Sanders furthers the comparison by suggesting that text acts as "a mediating bridge, a rhetorical construct, spanning the communication gap between writer and reader" [21, p. 64]. Corporate reports, newsletters, operations guides, technical specifications, promotional brochures, user manuals—the literatures found in a professional setting that publications managers produce—exist as institutional tools, rhetorical strategies designed to convey the character of entities larger than the individual. Ethical codes, rhetorical tools themselves, assist in this. The metaphor of "bridge" turns the writer into a conveyance, one implicitly neutral. Although Sanders argues that an effective document mediates between the writer's "logic and desires" and the writer's presumption of the "logic and desires" of the audience, the goal is reached when the readers of the document "are persuaded that they share a community of logical and effectual understanding with the writer" [21, p. 62]. The key event is the document taking on its own life distinct from the writer's. Techniques assume independent roles as rhetorical strategies serve to validate "the decisions readers will make about the data's use" [21, p. 64].

Given this audience-based approach to technical communication, rhetoric is reduced to a set of techniques to achieve reader acceptance or provide for a particular action. Documents take on their own purposes, ones suborned to perpetuating institutional goals rather than an individual's goals. The document and its strategies replace the writer as source of interaction. And since the document is limited in this capacity, ethical responsibility is surrendered entirely to the reader.

Hartley's distinction between academic writing and writing for industry further illustrates the animation of a document at the expense of authorial existence. He conceives academic writing, especially the essay, as a *reflective mode* not suited for industry. An essay traditionally demonstrates a personal point of view, or makes an argument. Instead, he proposes, technical and professional communication require a *presentational mode* that emphasizes the pragmatic and impersonal. Following the conventions of good technical writing, Hartley proposes that writing for industry be action oriented with easily assimilated "bursts of information. . . Its archetype is *advertising*" [18, p. 164]. Furthermore, he suggests, "*industrial communication aims to avoid argument . . .* The industrial writer wants the reader to *understand* the communication, *accept* it, and *react* favorably to it" [18, p. 165]. Favorable reader or audience regard determines a document's success. STC's requirements that technical communicators "[u]se language and visuals with precision" and "[p]refer simple, direct expression of ideas" follow Hartley's precepts.

But ethical considerations are left unrecognized. Ornatowski points out that technical communication is useful because it can provide a "mantle" of objectivity to agendas and interpretations that are often "in some measure political." The utility of rhetoric as *techne* becomes paramount. Organizational ends direct rhetorical means. The task of the technical writer or publications manager is to accomplish an institutional objective by denying individual attributes. "The fact that we do not commonly think that way about it is its greatest rhetorical asset," notes Ornatowski [20, p. 101]

Research, however, is beginning to suggest that efficiency is perhaps only the more apparent feature, that the production of a document is not just based on audience assessment and message content. Organizational setting or "culture" is receiving increasing attention as a determiner of textual content. Lee Odell, for example, has discovered three additional considerations that writers take into account: shared attitudes or values, prior actions or circumstances, and typical ways or procedures within the organization [22, p. 252]. Writers in such institutional settings, it appears, implicitly assume the privatized sphere of an organizational *ethos* rather than that derived from personal ethics or the public good.

THE PLACE FOR *ETHOS* IN
PROFESSIONAL COMMUNICATION

As suggested by the STC's dictum to "[s]atisfy the audience's need for information, not my own need for self-expression," the technical writer denies his or her existence in the text. One rarely sees the individuals who work behind the corporate logo or under the letterhead. The continued debate over use of first person is not surprising. Isolating the reader from a sense of writer as individual rather than the implied neutrality of a spokesperson enables a greater sense of the rational and the detached. Or as Paul Campbell suggests in his discussion of *personae* and scientific discourse, "only by disentangling whatever it is one wishes to study from the traces of personal values, emotions, biases, etc., is it possible to see clearly and to agree about anything at all" [23, p. 398]. Objectivity is recognized as paramount in decision making. Given the facts, one is able to make reasoned judgments.

The problem, aside from how to determine what is objective and whether objectivity is possible, is the ethical concerns raised by such views. Theresa Enos argues that striving for objectivity "creates dangerous ethical issues: personality devaluation, the suppression of the author, no discernible voice. The result is a nonresponsible attitude, intended or not, an abdication of human responsibility for what humans have created" [24, p. 99]. Her solution is to revive *ethos* as a determining feature in professional communication.

Enos and others are exploring the role of *ethos* in professional communication [10, 13, 24-29]. Turning to the work of rhetorical scholars such as Corbett, Jim Corder, and George Yoos [2, 30-32], professional communication theorists are now questioning, as Philip Rubens suggests, the ethical effect of character devaluation stemming from emphasis on a supposed objectivity [33]. Assuming an objective stance precludes, by definition, ethical considerations. Values, morals, virtues, and other ethical concerns are regarded as subjective criteria that hinder rational decisions and observations. Restricting the appearance of self or character in documents lends to a greater sense of objectivity.

Questioning the validity of objectivity, Enos draws on the work of Kenneth Burke. She suggests that awareness of *ethos* enables

> the writer to create audience and, inversely, for the reader to re-create this audience. Consubstantiation—that is, presence—is necessary for the writer to become part of this creation and for the reader, in turn, to *become* the audience; thus through identification, persuasion is effected [10, p. 99].

Ethos is generative in her scheme, providing for reciprocity by elevating identification over persuasion as the primary means of communication. People meet people through a text rather than succumb to rhetorical strategies. Reader and writer more openly collaborate when each has a better sense of who the other is. Integrity is more easily established between reader and writer. Such recognition lends itself to a more equitable sense of responsibility for the interpretation of the text and for any resulting actions. With authorial presence more openly apparent, deception is also more accountable.

My explorations here are not designed to deny the practical and applied notions of audience attention in technical and professional communication, nor to discount entirely the value of ethical codes. Achieving purposes is a critical feature for which rhetoric provides tools. We also must consider M. Jimmie Killingsworth and P. L. Walter's idea of invocation and evocation: "As the author's involvement [with the text] increases, the audience becomes more detached . . . . As the *I* withdraws, the *you* fills it; but if the *I* is fully present, the *you* remains distant" [34, p. 35]. They argue an author-dominated text is an *invocative* text while a reader-oriented text is an *evocative* one, noting the now distrusted New Critic's view of text as an embodied person [34, p. 27]. But if we too fully disavow the notion of text as an embodied person in attempts to justify impersonal text, we run the risk of text becoming authorless. By corrupting ideas of *ethos* in professional communication, if not outrightly denying its existence, we call into question the place for ethics in our documents. We leave ourselves with ethical rules rather than responsibilities.

The near elimination of the *invocative* has created its problems. In our roles as publications managers and professional communicators we must recognize that we are knowledge makers as well as knowledge brokers. The danger of not doing so, Miller argues, is closed-system thinking that "substitutes 'effective procedures' for invention and self-contained knowledge of the system (isolated expertise) for dialectical discovery of agreements" [13, p. 235]. And in times of crisis or uncertainty, Johannesen reminds us, "ethical communication stems less from deliberation than from our 'character'" [35, p. 73]. Reviving a sense of authorship in our documents will not only enliven them, but could assist in enhancing ethical well-being for both readers and writers.

REFERENCES

1. R. J. Brockmann and F. Rook (eds.), *Technical Communication and Ethics,* Society for Technical Communication, Arlington, Virginia, 1989.
2. E. P. J. Corbett, The Ethical Dimensions of Rhetoric, in *Selected Essays of Edward P. J. Corbett,* R. J. Connors (ed.), Southern Methodist University Press, Dallas, pp. 255-266, 1989.
3. R. L. Johannesen, *Ethics in Human Communication* (3rd Edition), Waveland, Prospect Heights, Illinois, 1990.
4. K. Lebacqz, *Professional Ethics: Power and Paradox,* Abingdon Press, Nashville, 1985.
5. J. Bryan, Down the Slippery Slope: Ethics and the Technical Writer as Marketer, *Technical Communication Quarterly, 1*:1, pp. 73-88, 1992.
6. J. M. Sproule, Organizational Rhetoric and the Public Sphere, *Communication Studies, 40*:4, pp. 258-265, 1989.

7. A. E. Walzer, The Ethics of False *Implicature* in Technical and Professional Writing Courses, *Journal of Technical Writing and Communication, 19*:2, pp. 149-160, 1989.
8. S. M. Halloran, Eloquence in a Technological Society, *Central States Speech Journal, 29*:4, pp. 221-227, 1978.
9. R. M. Weaver, The *Phaedrus* and the Nature of Rhetoric, in *Language Is Sermonic: Richard M. Weaver on the Nature of Rhetoric,* R. L. Johannesen, R. Strickland, and R. T. Eubanks (eds.), Louisiana State University Press, Baton Rouge, pp. 57-83, 1970.
10. T. Enos, "An Eternal Golden Braid": Rhetor as Audience, Audience as Rhetor, in *Sense of Audience in Written Communication,* G. Kirsch and D. H. Roen (eds.), Sage, Newbury Park, California, pp. 99-114, 1990.
11. C. Miller, What's Practical about Technical Writing? in *Technical Writing: Theory and Practice,* B. E. Fearing and W. K. Sparrow (eds.), Modern Language Association, New York, pp. 14-26, 1989.
12. E. Garver, Teaching Writing and Teaching Virtue, *Journal of Business Communication, 22*:1, pp. 51-73, 1985.
13. C. Miller, Technology as a Form of Consciousness: A Study of Contemporary *Ethos, Central States Speech Journal, 29*:4, pp. 228-236, 1978.
14. P. V. Anderson, *Technical Writing: A Reader-Centered Approach* (2nd Edition), Harcourt Brace Jovanovich, San Diego, 1991.
15. A. Eisenberg, *Effective Technical Communication* (2nd Edition), McGraw-Hill, New York, 1992.
16. L. A. Olsen and T. N. Huckin, *Technical Writing and Professional Communication* (2nd Edition), McGraw-Hill, New York, 1991.
17. M. H. Markel, *Technical Writing: Situations and Strategies* (3rd Edition), St. Martin's Press, New York, 1992.
18. P. Hartley, Writing for Industry: The Presentational Mode Versus the Reflective Mode, *Technical Writing Teacher, 18*:1, pp. 162-169, 1991.
19. H. W. Johnstone, Jr., Some Reflections on Argumentation, in *Philosophy, Rhetoric, and Argumentation,* M. Natanson and H. W. Johnstone, Jr. (eds.), Pennsylvania State University Press, University Park, pp. 1-10, 1965.
20. C. M. Ornatowski, Between Efficiency and Politics: Rhetoric and Ethics in Technical Writing, *Technical Communication Quarterly, 1*:1, pp. 91-103, 1992.
21. S. P. Sanders, How Can Technical Writing Be Persuasive? in *Solving Problems in Technical Writing,* L. Beene and P. White (eds.), Oxford University Press, New York, pp. 55-78, 1988.
22. L. Odell, Beyond the Text: Relations Between Writing and Social Context, in *Writing in Nonacademic Settings,* L. Odell and D. Goswami (eds.), Guilford Press, New York, pp. 249-307, 1985.
23. P. N. Campbell, The *Personae* of Scientific Discourse, *Quarterly Journal of Speech, 61*:4, pp. 391-405, 1975.
24. T. Enos, Rhetoric and the Discourse of Technology, in *Worlds of Writing: Teaching and Learning in Discourse Communities of Work,* C. B. Matalene (ed.), Random House, New York, pp. 93-109, 1989.
25. L. Beason, Strategies for Establishing an Effective Persona: An Analysis of Appeals to *Ethos* in Business Speeches, *Journal of Business Communication, 28*:4, pp. 326-346, 1991.

26. C. Kallendorf and C. Kallendorf, The Figures of Speech, *Ethos,* and Aristotle: Notes Towards a Rhetoric of Business Communication, *Journal of Business Communication, 22:*1, pp. 35-50, 1985.

27. D. M. Guinn, *Ethos* in Technical Discourse, *Technical Writing Teacher, 11:*1, pp. 31-37, 1983.

28. E. W. Stoddard, The Role of *Ethos* in the Theory of Technical Writing, *Technical Writing Teacher, 11:*3, pp. 229-241, 1985.

29. A. E. Walzer, *Ethos,* Technical Writing, and the Liberal Arts, *Technical Writing Teacher, 8:*3, pp. 50-53, 1981.

30. J. W. Corder, Hunting for *Ethos* Where They Say It Can't Be Found, *Rhetoric Review, 7:*2, pp. 299-316, 1989.

31. J. W. Corder, Varieties of Ethical Argument, with Some Account of the Significance of *Ethos* in the Teaching of Composition, *Freshman English News, 6:*3, pp. 1-23, 1978.

32. G. Yoos, A Revision of the Concept of Ethical Appeal, *Philosophy and Rhetoric, 12:*1, pp. 41-58, 1979.

33. P. M. Rubens, Reinventing the Wheel? Ethics for Technical Communicators, *Journal of Technical Writing and Communication, 11:*4, pp. 698-711, 1981.

34. M. J. Killingsworth and P. L. Walter, A Grammar of Person for Technical Writing, *Technical Writing Teacher, 17:*1, pp. 26-40, 1990.

35. R. L. Johannesen, Virtue, Ethics, Character, and Political Communication, in *Ethical Dimensions of Political Communication,* R. E. Denton, Jr. (ed.), Praeger Publishers, New York, pp. 69-90, 1991.

PART V

Pedagogy

Although the title of this section reflects the editors' concern with teaching technical and professional communication, we believe these three essays contain information that will be useful to both academics and workplace professionals. All three examine issues of interest to publications staff and provide bibliographic information that should be helpful in solving some of the problems that challenge writers, editors, and publications managers.

Carole Yee's "Can We Be Partners? Industry/Corporate Advisory Boards for Academic Technical Communication Programs" encourages enlisting a corporate board. Yee, who chairs the Department of Humanities and teaches in the technical communication program at New Mexico Institute of Mining and Technology, advocates the use of corporate boards to support academic programs in technical and professional communication and notes their benefit to both academic and industry participants.

The final chapters of the book, Paul V. Anderson's "Teaching Technical Communication Majors about Organizational Management" and O. Jane Allen's "A Design for a Graduate Seminar in Publications Management," describe courses taught at Miami University (Ohio) and New Mexico State University, respectively.

Anderson provides a rationale for teaching organizational management courses tailored to the specific needs of writers and editors. In describing his course, which is part of Miami University's master's program in technical and scientific communication, he points to a wealth of literature that should be useful to instructors designing courses as well as to publications managers seeking resources for solving management problems in the workplace.

The seminar Allen describes is designed for students in New Mexico State University's master's program in technical and professional communication and doctoral program in rhetoric and professional communication. One of the objectives of this course is to bring students into contact with professionals in the field by giving them a context in which to explore some of the realities of the workplace. Allen also provides useful bibliographic material.

CHAPTER 16

Can We Be Partners? Industry/Corporate Advisory Boards for Academic Technical Communication Programs

CAROLE YEE

In response to a need in government and industry, technical communication programs have burgeoned in universities all over the United States in the past two decades. Without that demand by employers, academic technical communication programs certainly would not have flourished as they have. Yet despite the healthy market—so far—for their graduates, academics by and large have designed these new academic programs themselves.

Frequently, government and industry organizations who employ the graduates of these programs have been invited to consult with the academic programs after the fact. Of course, government and industry have at times trained their own technical communicators with in-house education programs. Employers, however, often do not want merely a few skills added to their workers' qualifications; many prefer college-educated employees knowledgeable about communicating scientific and technical information.

Academic and industry professionals hold a mutual interest in managing the education of future technical communication professionals, and representatives from both camps wish to share their interests and concerns. The questions are how and in what way(s). One answer is an advisory board. But can academic and industry professionals be useful to one another on an advisory board? And can this be a true partnership, one of shared information and advice? Can they share information across the table with true understanding and effect?

A number of universities are finding industry advisory boards useful in guiding their technical communication programs. At New Mexico Tech our experience with an advisory board has proved profitable to our undergraduate program and to our students. With interaction from our industry representatives, we provide students with the skills and understanding they need to make important contributions to industry. In this chapter, I discuss some of the issues surrounding the use of advisory boards and point to some of the ways advisory boards can benefit both their corporate representatives and academic institutions. The chapter concludes with suggestions for forming and managing advisory boards.

ON FORMING THE PARTNERSHIP

Many academics who designed technical communications programs at their universities had their own vision for program goals, curricula, and requirements. They may have consulted with government and industry people, either as independent professional consultants or in some other capacity, but then most created their own programs. Ultimately, academics have been responsible for designing, organizing, implementing, and teaching in the new technical communication programs themselves.

Many feel that this is as it should be, that these programs should be first and foremost academic, and who better than academics to design them. Charlotte Thralls, for example, cautions that academics need to be discerning about industry-university collaboration. "[R]ather than prepare our students to fit into their workplace communities, we should show them how to scrutinize, and perhaps resist, normative practices within these communities." Indeed, Thralls says, "the most important debate in our profession today" may be "the appropriate relationship between academe and professional practice" [1, p. 247]. Academics, then, do not all agree that technical communication programs should seek and accept the advice of industry about courses, class assignments, or even industry expectations for graduates.

On the other hand, while some industry professionals may be eager to advise academic programs, others may feel unsure that they know how to advise and direct university programs. Wanting to serve but uncertain how to do so effectively, many industry board members may wonder exactly how to contribute, how to make a difference. In other words, both university and industry representatives may seriously question just how they can help one another manage the education and training of future technical communicators.

From both the academic and the industry sides comes the feeling that it is a mistake for academic technical communication programs to be feeders to specific industries or corporations, and, in turn, for specific industries and corporations to depend too heavily upon specific neighboring universities to provide their employees. Because their focus is a single industry, the feeder programs, their critics claim, are limited in depth and scope. Despite the practical nature of technical communication programs and the high demand for their graduates, many professionals believe technical communication programs should be independent from the future employers of their graduates.

Granted, too close or too provincial a connection between a university technical communication program and an industry is not a good thing. Still, some sort of cooperative relationship with government and industry can have many benefits for a technical communication program as well as for the government organization or industry involved. An advisory board designed *to suit the specific needs* of a particular program can be a definite asset to that program, its students, and the industries that are on the board. The trick is for the academic and the government and industry representatives to seek a collaborative, egalitarian relationship. With a focused and specific set of goals for the advisory board, a productive collaborative relationship can be achieved.

Any technical communication program, then, deciding to form an industry advisory board needs first to determine what specific benefits such an advisory board is expected to provide to that program. And in turn, the academic program needs to ask what benefits they can provide to the industries involved. A program considering the use of an advisory board should understand the different kinds of benefits to be derived from different kinds of advisory boards. In addition, the program professionals should be able to define for themselves and for board members the specific nature of their program and its needs. Mutual management of the advisory board then becomes not only possible but also productive for both.

Academic and industry cultures are vastly *different* from each other. As Chris Anson and L. Forsberg document, student technical writers who recently moved from academic communities into professional communities for internships struggled with corporate writing. The students discovered that the sort of writing they learned in their professional courses did not necessarily prepare them for the subtle and sometimes frustrating challenge of learning to write for a new audience of multiple readers within an unfamiliar culture. For new employees, learning to function successfully within the corporate culture, Anson and Forsberg suggest, may well be more about "social and intellectual adaptations" than about rules of grammar and usage [2, p. 201].

The irony is that we in the academic community cannot provide students with the experience that prepares them for this challenge of reading social context, except by describing the social nature of writing and, of course, by requiring students to complete an internship. The differences between the academic world and the corporate culture—the academic concerned primarily with the students' learning and the corporate representative concerned with the organization's production and profit—can thwart communication on an industry advisory board. However, with careful management and a clear definition of purpose, an industry advisory board can prove mutually beneficial, offering representatives from both the academic program and the government or industrial organization opportunities for employment, research, education, and resources, opportunities not available without that academic-industry collaboration.

USING AN ADVISORY BOARD:
SOME PURPOSES AND BENEFITS

Four possible, perhaps even overlapping, purposes might be considerations for any academic-industry advisory board: curriculum planning and review, internships and employment for students, equipment support, and research opportunities. In the end, any of these purposes can result in shared benefits for the academic and industry/corporate communities.

Curriculum Planning and Review:
Keeping Industry and the Academy Current

A collaboration with government and industry representatives can offer valuable insights into a program's curriculum, but several safeguards assure that the relationship will be collaborative, providing guidance for the program and benefits for the corporate organization.

First, the academic representatives need to formulate the program's philosophy and approach to its curriculum. That academics know more about the academic side of curriculum than the industry representatives goes without saying, and yet if the academic representatives are not clear about their program goals and philosophy, they may find industry representatives are more than willing to define the program's philosopy and direction for them. Defining the philosophy requires reading about other academic programs and consulting with their staffs. But defining the intellectual content of the program is the main business of the academic representatives who must determine whether a program is philosophically rhetorical, linguistic, cognitive, literary, or otherwise.

Second, curriculum review and planning requires that academics *explain* to their industry colleagues how they define their program. This is exactly where the representatives to the board from the nonacademic side can offer insight, advice, and guidance. But they can do this only if the academics can satisfactorily and confidently define and explain who and what they are.

Curriculum review should be a truly collaborative exchange. The industry board members bring the academics up to date on developments in the field from the industry side. And academics inform industry about developments in pedagogy and research. Together, they should be able to keep a technical communication program's curriculum current and each other informed about important new industry and academic trends and concerns.

For example, New Mexico Tech's Corporate Advisory Board, although formed some years after the program itself came into being, offers the New Mexico Tech technical communication program both annual review and update on its curriculum, keeping the academic program current with the industries closely associated with it. As the field of technical communication becomes more or less based in cognitive research, in the psychology of collaboration, or in the sociological concerns of multiculturalism, the industry-university discussions at the advisory board meetings change. This exchange about current concerns on both sides—academic and industrial/corporate—makes annual advisory board meetings lively and even exciting on both sides of the table.

Internships and Employment for Students

Surely placing students and graduates in internships and employment is the most popular reason for advisory boards with industry. Most industries eagerly tap the talent pool of recent graduates and internship candidates. Moreover, board members often exert extra effort to hire students from the programs they advise, knowing the program as well as they do. These industry representatives trust the education and training of the graduates as well as the recommendations of the faculty they know.

Indeed, many board members will request that their programs regularly send them the resumes of students looking for internships or employment so they can consider those students first for any openings in their departments. Additionally, students may visit the industry board members at their places of work for insight into the working world outside the academic walls. Students may wish to practice interviewing techniques and audience analysis with industry board members, or ask board members to critique their classroom work and portfolios. In other words, industry board members can actively help students prepare for the employment market and for employment itself.

New Mexico Tech's student STC chapter has developed an activity called Shadow Days that would work well with an advisory board as well. This activity allows a technical communication student to spend a workday following a professional technical communicator around. Although many students claim the best part of the day is lunch at a restaurant with the professional, many Shadow Days have led to New Mexico Tech students landing summer internships and, for some, full-time permanent employment.

Because most of our advisory board members live and work at least two and sometimes several states away from New Mexico, we have not suggested this idea to our board members. However, I am confident that it would be a highly workable program with in-state advisory board members. This is the sort of direct contact between technical communication students and professionals that an advisory board focused on internships and employment for students might foster.

Equipment Support: Experience for Academics and Exposure for Corporations

Managing a technical communication program usually requires expensive computer equipment for students and faculty to produce documents. This equipment is too costly for academic programs to purchase from their budgets, and programs frequently seek industry support for equipment through grants and donations. Indeed, many corporations have programs for making just such equipment grants to schools. Board members from those corporations certainly may review proposals for program equipment grants, guide those proposals through the corporate review process, and sponsor those proposals within the corporation.

New Mexico Tech's Corporate Advisory Board, for instance, has a representative from Hewlett-Packard Corporation, and Hewlett-Packard has generously provided the technical communication program with several major equipment grants, starting with a fourteen-terminal word processing and desktop publishing laboratory some years ago. A recent grant included a multimedia lab of Apollo workstations with multiple X-window terminals.

This sort of equipment support only a major computer corporation can provide; in return, the academic program teaches students on the corporation's equipment, which often becomes the familiar and favored equipment of those students and their teachers. Additionally, industry representatives can offer valuable suggestions for upgrading program equipment, guiding laboratory development, and deciding how best to use existing equipment. Technical communication programs with industry advisory boards may find themselves the lucky recipients of gifts of used equipment as well.

Research Opportunities for Faculty, Students, and Industry

Advisory board members may also provide valuable opportunities for faculty to conduct research at their industrial or corporate sites. Or the industry/corporation might invite faculty to collaborate on industry/corporate research projects. Studies of usability testing, ethnography, and writing processes are only a few examples of research topics that may very well engage university and industry people to work together on projects. Finally, faculty might consider seeking industry financial underwriting for their research projects.

Board meetings can keep members abreast of research interests of faculty and industry and help to build bridges for collaborative projects. Naturally, technical communication programs whose representatives are from large corporations nearby are at an advantage for research projects supported by these industries. In any event, research interests of both academic and industry sides of the board should be on the board's meeting agendas.

In 1992, for example, our Advisory Board and the New Mexico Tech technical communication program began discussing the possibility of hosting at New

Mexico Tech a conference on multiculturalism in technical communication. The conference would enable industry and university people to discuss the problems, concerns, and advantages of developing a multicultural curriculum; to examine student populations; and to evaluate approaches to the study of technical communication. This conference we expect to provide research opportunities for both university and corporate professionals.

FORMING AN ADVISORY BOARD:
SOME CONSIDERATIONS

Sherry Little and Deborah Bosley both describe processes for forming an industry board to help new technical communication programs get started [3-6]. As Little points out, people from industry usually do not have to be persuaded to serve on such a board:

> Most industrial people are delighted to be asked for their advice and are eager participants in such activities. In most, there is a strong commitment to their profession and serving on an advisory committee allows them an outlet for this commitment, a commitment that they take seriously [5, p. 34].

Little and Bosley both say that industrial advisory committees or boards can provide new programs with useful advice about industry expectations for graduates, internships and employment for students and graduates, support for research and equipment, even ideas for class assignments [3-6]. In other words, the advantages of such a board to the industries the board members represent apparently are obvious to them, and they are usually eager to serve. And Lynn Deming describes how New Mexico Tech's technical communication program sought its corporate advisory board's advice about how to promote the academic program to corporate and industrial employers. The board's counsel and advice proved valuable [7]. Most university programs find their board members serve responsibly and thoughtfully when they have been well chosen by the academic program they advise.

The college or university development office can be helpful to a program thinking about forming an industry advisory board because that office should know what industries and businesses support the school. The development office should be able to recommend good people as well as interested companies. The first step an academic program can take is, then, to talk to the people at the school's development office where that different culture of industry and business intersects with the school's.

A small board (fewer than ten people) that includes only one or two official representatives from the academic program will be able to accomplish much. If board members must travel long distances to attend meetings, annual meetings are probably adequate. If, however, board members are nearby, the board may prefer to meet two or three times a year. Partial-day meetings seem to be about the right length, even for annual meetings. The representatives serving on the board are busy people and the academic representatives, who usually set the agenda, need to generate a full agenda that does not waste time with unnecessary or trivial discussion.

Academic programs seeking to form a board will also want to consider whether industrial and corporate writers, managers, or alumni from the program should be invited to serve on the board. The choice probably will depend, again, on the specific purpose of the advisory board. Members should be invited for a limited term, one to three years, with the understanding that the membership of the board will change as the goals and needs of the program change. Corporate writers may be useful one year, whereas managers may be useful the next.

Finally, academic programs need to keep in mind that the industry/corporate representatives are serving on the board out of professional commitment, and the academic program must prepare carefully for the board meetings. Members should be sent directions, agendas, and preparation material in plenty of time before the meeting. Gestures of gratitude, from thank-you notes to small gifts, can help to make board members feel appreciated and valuable to the board. Academics and corporate/industry representatives alike will enjoy meeting in an atmosphere of mutual respect and comfort. This can be arranged by careful preparation, frequent review of the board's goals, and sincere gestures of appreciation.

In summary, an industry advisory board needs to consider what exactly that board can do for the specific program. Defining and explaining the program's academic mission ought to be the responsibility of the academic side of the board. Clarifying the board's purpose can help the academics to manage the selection of board members and industries, the meeting agendas, the equipment needs of the program, the contribution the industries represented on the board can make to faculty and student research, and the way the board can help students with internships and employment. To answer the questions raised at the beginning of this paper, yes, a well-managed advisory board can contribute to a successful academic program and can create a productive, successful partnership between academe and industry.

REFERENCES

1. C. Thralls, Rev. *Collaborative Writing in Industry: Investigations in Theory and Practice*, M. L. Lay and W. M. Karis (eds.), *Journal of Business and Technical Communication, 6*:2, pp. 247-250, 1992.
2. C. M. Anson and L. L. Forsberg, Moving Beyond the Academic Community: Transitional Stages in Professional Writing, *Written Communication, 7*:2, pp. 200-231, 1990.
3. D. S. Bosley, Articulating Goals for a University Corporate Advisory Board, *Proceedings 1991 CPTSC,* CPTSC, Cincinnati, pp. 59-65, 1991.

4. D. S. Bosley, Broadening the Base of a Technical Communication Program: An Industrial/Academic Alliance, *Technical Communication Quarterly, 1*:1, pp. 41-56, 1992.
5. S. B. Little, Industry and Education Working Together: The Use of Advisory Committees, *Proceedings 1985 CPTSC*, CPTSC, Miami, Ohio, pp. 32-40, 1985.
6. S. B. Little, Reaching Out: A Rationale for University and Industrial Collaboration in Planning and Evaluating Technical Communication Programs, *Proceedings 1987 CPTSC,* CPTSC, Orlando, pp. 21-35, 1987.
7. L. Deming, New Mexico Tech's Technical Communication Program: Introducing a Corporate Board, *Proceedings 1991 CPTSC,* CPTSC, Cincinnati, pp. 55-58, 1991.

CHAPTER 17

Teaching Technical Communication Majors about Organizational Management

PAUL V. ANDERSON

Among technical communicators, the word "management" designates two related but distinguishable areas of responsibility. The first is *project* management. Many technical communicators are project managers. They establish goals, create project schedules, coordinate their efforts with those of other people, assure that deadlines are met, and perform other managerial tasks required to complete their projects.

Second, there is *organizational* management. Organizational managers typically assign projects; establish priorities among competing projects; set policy; acquire needed resources; monitor budgets; and hire, train, motivate, and evaluate staff members. Many organizational managers have the word "manager" in their job titles (department manager, publications manager). Owners of technical communication companies are also organizational managers. Some managers supervise one or two individuals; however, high-level managers in large companies may oversee a technical communication staff of hundreds.

IMPORTANCE OF INSTRUCTION IN ORGANIZATIONAL MANAGEMENT

Most college programs in technical communication teach project management. Some even offer special courses on the topic. In contrast, organizational management is rarely taught. Instruction in it is not mentioned once in two collections of bibliographic essays about technical communication and its teaching [1, 2]. Yet, there are good reasons for us to teach organizational management to communication majors.

Most importantly, organizational management is an integral part of our profession. When some students (and some educators) think of technical communicators, they mistakenly include only the writer, editor, or graphics artist. According to this view, a writer, editor, or artist who advances to management leaves the profession of technical communication for some other realm. That's not the case.

Technical communication management is a specialty *within* our field. Twenty percent of the members of the Society for Technical Communication identify themselves as managers [3]. Every year, approximately one out of every six papers delivered at the International Technical Communication Conference appears in the management stem. Furthermore, as one can learn from talking with any group of experienced communicators, a poor manager hinders writers and editors from doing their jobs, thereby reducing the quality of the communications produced. Conversely, a knowledgeable and skilled manager makes the job more enjoyable and the resulting products more effective.

In many instances technical communication majors find themselves with managerial responsibility soon after graduation. Because technical communication is a rapidly growing profession with considerable upward mobility, recent graduates are sometimes promoted to fill vacated management positions. Graduates hired as a company's first technical communicator are sometimes asked to build a technical communication department.

Even students who aren't headed quickly to managerial responsibilities can benefit from studying organizational management. When writers, editors, and other communication specialists understand managers' concerns and goals, they can more readily provide information their managers need. And they can advocate more effectively for their own goals and projects. In addition, some technical communication programs attract practicing professionals returning to school expressly to increase their opportunities for advancement or to sharpen their performance in management positions they already hold.

To educate our technical communication majors about management, we might require them to take a management class taught by business-school faculty. These classes are undoubtedly valuable to technical communication majors. They provide a helpful introduction to the general responsibilities of managers and usefully digest current advice from management specialists and researchers. However, technical communication majors have some special needs that business-school courses don't meet. In the rest of this chapter, I discuss these needs and suggest some ways technical communication programs can address them.

SPECIAL NEEDS OF TECHNICAL COMMUNICATION MAJORS

Technical communication majors need four things that business-school management courses don't provide:

- Assistance in shifting from a writer's or editor's perspective to a manager's perspective
- An action-oriented approach to management
- The opportunity to explore the particular management issues and practices that arise in technical communication
- Discussion of a humane set of managerial values appropriate to our field

Help in Shifting to a Management Perspective

Unlike most business students, technical communication majors devote a large part of their study to learning the role of the entry-level person—the writer or editor. When they think of advancing, many imagine themselves becoming "senior writers" or "senior editors." Many identify so strongly with the writer's or editor's role that they need assistance in switching to a managerial perspective. Some even resist the shift.

Students have these difficulties for several reasons. First, management classes cover topics most technical communication students didn't envision as part of their careers when they chose their major, such topics as designing departmental mission statements, motivating and evaluating other people, and creating project and departmental budgets—to name but a few examples. To see these topics as relevant to their careers, students must revise their definition of their chosen profession.

Second, as they study these topics, students sometimes conclude that a manager's goals are foreign, even hostile, to those of writers and editors. For example, technical communication students generally enroll in management classes after spending at least a year learning how to polish their documents to a very high level of quality. In the management course, however, they must imagine themselves in the role of a person who, despite a commitment to quality, takes responsibility for seeing that projects are completed on time and within budget. They must envision themselves telling a writer or editor, "Even though I'm sure you could make this project much better if you spent more time on it, the project is now as good as we can afford to make it." No student wants to hear this from a manager, and many students don't want to think of themselves saying it to a writer or editor.

Students also experience difficulty in shifting to a managerial perspective because this perspective requires them to look at familiar topics from novel and sometimes disturbing standpoints. For example, students are accustomed to devising ways they can impressively present their qualifications to prospective employers. In a management class, they must consider how they would set up a screening process designed to penetrate behind these carefully crafted self-presentations to determine which candidate is best suited for a particular opening. Seen from the manager's perspective, the job search and other familiar topics take on new, strange, and (perhaps) forbidding appearances.

Students' reluctance to adopt a management perspective creates a pedagogical challenge: if students hesitate to think of themselves as future managers, they aren't fully prepared to learn what they need to know about managing. This problem doesn't arise in the typical management course offered by business schools because most business majors already see themselves headed for management. In technical communication programs, we must find our own ways of helping students make this shift.

An Action-Oriented Approach to Management

Technical communication majors need to learn an action-oriented approach to management. Business-school management courses take a topical approach. They typically skip from a chapter about organization to one on motivation to one on evaluation, without discussing the underlying sequence of activities managers perform when addressing any management problem. In this way, business-school management courses resemble product-based writing textbooks. Our students need a process approach, one that guides them through a sequence of steps they can follow when facing the practical, on-the-job management problems and decisions that arise in our profession.

Exploration of Management Issues and Practices in Technical Communication

Technical communication majors also need to learn how general management concepts and principles apply in our field. For example, in a business-school course, students study the relative merits of a bureaucratic organizational structure (in which people are arranged around functional specialties) and a matrix structure (where people from many specialties are organized around projects). Business-school courses discuss these alternatives from the vantage point of top executives of large corporations.

However, the alternatives are also important to technical communication managers, even if they manage only a small percentage of a company's overall workforce. A technical communication manager in a large company might have to decide whether to centralize her department or disperse the communicators throughout the various divisions they serve. In making the decision, the manager would need to consider factors peculiar to technical communication. A dispersed organization (which follows a bureaucratic model) enables writers and editors to specialize—a real benefit if the divisions work in quite distinct areas. However, a dispersed organization reduces the manager's ability to shift people among assignments (as can be done readily with matrix structures) if one division suddenly needs additional assistance because of upcoming proposal deadlines or the imminent release of a new product. Technical communication majors need to learn how such general management issues apply in our field.

Discussion of Managerial Values Appropriate to Technical Communication

Finally, when studying management, our students should learn how to address the distinctive ethical issues that arise for managers in technical communication. Business-school courses tend to discuss a wide variety of ethical concerns, ranging from product safety to corporate spying. All are important to technical communicators, and we take up many of them in our writing and editing courses.

The ethical question that arises specifically in a technical communication management course is this: How should managers treat the people in their departments and companies? Although this question may be addressed in business-school management courses, these courses aren't going to deal with specific applications to the management of professional communicators. Our majors should learn to manage in the same way they learn to write—namely, in a manner that promotes the satisfaction, increases the self-esteem, enhances the dignity, and supports the individual needs of the people affected by their actions. This doesn't mean that instruction in technical communication management should ignore such workplace values as profits and productivity. Instead, it requires us to teach our students to manage in ways that achieve business objectives while still being consistent with a humane set of values.

METHODS OF TAILORING MANAGEMENT INSTRUCTION TO TECHNICAL COMMUNICATION MAJORS

Here, then, is the challenge facing technical communication programs. On one hand, our students should learn about the topics covered in traditional, business-school management courses. On the other hand, these courses are not going to meet our students' needs in four critical areas: shifting from an entry-level to a managerial perspective, understanding the management issues and practices that particularly concern technical communication managers, learning an action-oriented approach to management, and developing a humane set of managerial values. Somehow, we must devise curricula that cover traditional management topics but also meet our students' special needs.

We can do that in several ways. We can create our own in-program management course that mixes standard business-school topics with material prepared specifically for our majors. Alternatively, we can require students to take a business-school course that we supplement with in-program management instruction, which we might weave into several courses or present in a single offering. The master's degree program at Miami University (Ohio) uses a variation of the latter strategy. During their first semester, students enroll in an organizational communication course where they study traditional management topics primarily from the standpoint of writers and editors who, to do their jobs effectively, need to know how organizations and managers function. In their second year, students take a half-semester (eight-week) course in which they switch to the managerial role.

In this half-semester management course, I use several strategies to address the special needs of technical communication majors. Although the overall course may not be readily adaptable by other programs, I believe the strategies I use can be incorporated easily elsewhere.

Helping Students Shift to a Management Perspective

In order to move from a writer's or editor's perspective to a manager's perspective, students need to learn what a manager does, how a manager's job is like (and unlike) the jobs of writer and editor, and why the manager's job is important to writers and editors.

Exploring Managerial Characteristics

One way to introduce these topics is to ask students to generate lists of the characteristics of good and bad managers, drawing on their own experiences working for managers. As I record the lists on the blackboard, the students illustrate their points with anecdotes. I highlight the way each story shows how a manager's actions helped or hindered the people reporting to him or her and point out that technical writers and editors need the same kind of help and can suffer from the same sorts of impediments from their managers.

Often students will offer contradictory entries for the lists. For instance, one might say that good managers plan other people's work so that employees can work without making errors or wasting time, while another student might say that good managers allow employees to approach their tasks creatively and tolerate errors because errors are essential to experimentation. Without trying to resolve these conflicts, I point them out, promising that future work in the course will provide ways of thinking them through. Similarly, I do not try to make sure the lists are complete; the lists inevitably grow as students learn more about the manager's job. I focus instead on getting students to see management as a set of skills and behaviors that make a difference to the success of the manager's organization and to the happiness and productivity of its employees.

Playing a Managerial Role as Technical Communicators

As another transitional activity, I ask students to play a managerial role in a simple case. In the case, students imagine they have been invited to edit a special issue of *Technical Communication* on the topic of education. Their assignment is to tell the journal's editor how they would manage the preparation of the issue—everything from how they would decide what topics to include, to how they would identify prospective authors, decide whether to solicit articles or issue an open call for submissions, instruct authors about what to write, obtain manuscript reviews, and evaluate the success of the issue once it is published. For each decision they make, the students must consider alternatives and offer a rationale for their choice. The case helps students appreciate the manager's role because it focuses their attention on what a manager contributes to the creation of a familiar result, a set of well-written and informative articles just like something they might have worked on in a writing or editing class. (I will gladly send copies of the cases mentioned in this chapter to people who request them.)

Reading the Literature

Readings can also help students shift to a managerial perspective. I like to use Patricia Caernarven-Smith's article from *Technical Communication* titled *What's Not to Like about Management?* [4] and the first three chapters of Margaret Hennig and Anne Jardim's *The Managerial Woman* [5]. Both publications discuss in an interesting and detailed way the differences between the entry-level job and the managerial one. Hennig and Jardim's chapters also support my effort to emphasize the importance of following equitable management practices that treat all employees fairly and respectfully. To ensure that students begin the course with a broad, systematic overview of the manager's role, I also have them read the introductory chapter from a traditional management textbook, such as the one by D. Hellriegel and J. W. Slocum [6]. (Incidentally, Arthur Martin [7] and John Fallon [8] provide background information about technical communication management that instructors may find helpful, though the chapters are not suited for student reading.)

Visiting Technical Communication Units

Field trips are another way to help students make the transition to a management perspective. I have found it very useful to visit managers of technical communication departments or the owners of technical communication companies as early as possible in my course—usually during the second class meeting. Such a visit, where students can hear a manager in their own field talk about such matters as hiring, organizing, motivating, billing, and scheduling can be far more effective than readings and classroom activities at engaging students' interest in managerial work.

Taking an Action-Oriented Approach to Management

In addition to helping students make the transition from the writer's and editor's perspective to the manager's, instruction in technical communication management should provide an action-oriented approach to management responsibilities. I provide this by using a problem-solving model employed throughout our program as a comprehensive description of the technical communicator's job, whether writing, editing, or managing [9]. Since I know of no comparable model suitable for management courses in our field, I'll describe my use of it in some detail.

The model conceptualizes technical communication as an effort to move from a present state (i.e., the current situation) to a goal state. In a writing course, we teach students how to move between these points by creating a document or other communication. For example, a computer company might be preparing a new product but need instructions for it. That would be the present state. We teach students how to write a manual that would help create a goal state in which people who have purchased the product are able to use it effectively. In the management course, students explore problems that are solved not through writing or editing, but through managerial action. These management problems fall into two groups.

The first group of problems involves a current state in which people are dissatisfied. Customers have been complaining about the instruction manuals a company is producing, or scientists in a research division have stopped bringing their manuscripts to the technical communication department for editing. The manager's problem is to take the managerial actions necessary to arrive at a goal state in which the source of the problem has been removed and those who had been dissatisfied are happy. We call these problems "problems of dissatisfaction."

We call the second group of problems "problems of aspiration": an individual or organization aspires to create something that does not exist, such as a new technical communication company or a new technical communication department in a corporation that does not yet have one. The manager's problem is to take the managerial actions necessary to move from a present state marked by desire to a goal state in which the desired entity exists and operates successfully.

As mentioned above, the problem-solving model I use employs the same general terms to describe the manager's problem-solving activities as it does to describe the writer's or editor's. These activities are defining the problem, designing a solution, implementing it, and evaluating the outcome. Of course, managers and writers perform these general activities differently. For example, writers define a writing problem by doing such things as describing the purpose of their communication, analyzing its audience, and identifying the resources and constraints that will affect the type of solution they can create. In contrast, a manager would define a problem of aspiration by identifying all the things that must be created for the goal state to be achieved. To start a new department, for instance, a manager would need (among other things) to create a mission statement, develop a budget, draft job descriptions, hire personnel, establish policies, obtain and arrange a work space, develop procedures for handling work, and so on (see Figure 1).

When teaching students how to define managerial problems, I pay special attention to techniques for defining problems of dissatisfaction—the ones that arise because something isn't working correctly. Such problems generally have numerous possible causes. The manager's first challenge is to identify the cause or causes that contribute most to the problem. That involves two steps: identifying the possible causes and then determining which are the real culprits. When managers act intuitively, without performing these steps, they can end up taking

AIM

To solve problems in the management and communication of specialized information, where that information is to be used for practical purposes.

ACTIVITIES

General Actions	Tasks for Managers
Define the Problem	Define the present state and goal state Identify things that need to be changed or created (e.g., budgets, job description, policies, mission statement) Communicate with decision makers about their aims and concerns Communicate with stakeholders (people affected by decision) Identify constraints and relevant ethical issues **Outcome:** Understanding of where we are, where we want to be, and what we need to consider to get from here to there
Design a Solution	Gather ideas about alternative solutions Compare alternatives and choose one Elaborate the solution by describing each of its elements in detail (e.g., features of completed solution; implementation of plan, including training, budget, schedule; quality control measures) **Outcome:** Draft of plan
Test the Solution	Gather ideas about possible problems and improvements to the plan Share plan with decision makers and stakeholders Possibly run pilot version Analyze results Recommend improvements **Outcome:** Final plan and support for it
Implement the Solution	Enact the implementation plan Monitor its success throughout implementation **Outcome:** Working solution plus data for evaluation
Evaluate the Solution	Design evaluation method Use the method Analyze results Formulate recommendations Make changes **Outcome:** Improved solution and insight about how to better solve similar problems in the future

CONTEXT

The context for problem solving is the particular situation in which a communicator works. Major features of context are kind of employer (research center, electronics firm, etc.), subject matter, medium, audience, culture (Western, Eastern), etc.

Figure 1. A problem-solving model for publications managers.

action that fails to touch the problem's source. For example, if a documentation department has been producing weak instructions for the past year, the problem's source might be that the newly hired writers aren't skilled communicators, or that they aren't given enough time on their projects, or that they aren't given the cooperation they need from the technical specialists. If the problem's real cause is that the communicators aren't getting sufficient cooperation from the technical specialists who are supposed to supply information and review drafts for accuracy, the shortcomings in the instructions won't disappear because the manager sends the writers to writing seminars or sees that they receive more reasonable deadlines. To help students learn how to avoid "correcting" the wrong cause, I teach them how to use back-step analysis to explore the universe of possible causes. Back-step analysis involves creating a diagram that resembles a tree diagram but involves exploring roots rather than branches. Then, using the Pareto Principle, the students learn to assess the likelihood that any particular cause is the most significant factor in the problem at hand. These procedures are described in S. M. Erickson's very useful book *Management Tools for Everyone* [10].

Of course, defining a problem and its causes is only the first step in managerial problem solving. As the students and I take up the various other topics in the course—motivation, organizational structure, etc.—we situate them in relation to all our model's activities, which (to repeat) include not only defining problems but also designing possible solutions, testing those solutions, implementing them, and evaluating the results.

Presenting Management Issues and Practices in Technical Communication

The problem-solving framework just described not only provides an action-oriented approach to management but also helps students focus on the specific management issues that arise in technical communication. Another way of achieving that focus is to have the students talk with practicing managers. For that reason, I arrange field trips or guest speakers for about half of the class sessions. Also, whenever possible, I have the students read articles written by technical communication managers. When I want them to read about topics for which adequate essays don't exist in the technical communication literature, I turn to popular management books and traditional management textbooks; I then guide the discussions of these readings toward their implications for technical communication managers. The following paragraphs briefly identify some readings and associated activities I've found useful.

Managerial Responsibilities

At the beginning of the course, I supplement readings about the nature of managerial responsibilities (mentioned above) with selected chapters from a popular management book, such as Thomas Peters and Robert Waterman's *In*

Search of Excellence [11] or James Kouzes and Barry Posner's *The Leadership Challenge* [12]. More than anything, these books convey advice about leadership style, and they do so with a zest that students find appealing. In discussing these readings, we talk about the impact that various managerial styles and strategies would have on the practical operation of technical communication departments and companies.

Management Functions

After the introductory portion of the course, I assign readings about traditional management functions: planning, organizing, and controlling. When reading about planning we pay special attention to the broadest of organizational plans: mission statements and the very general goals, objectives, and policies that outline the way the organization will pursue its mission. For an introduction to broad-scale planning, we turn to a management textbook, such as the one by Joseph Massie and John Douglas [13], and to Kenneth Cook's essay on strategic planning in technical communication [14]. Our discussion centers on such topics as the way the mission statement of a technical communication department relates to the mission statement of the overall organization and the ways mission statements can extend or limit the ability of a department to gain the resources and cooperation it needs from the rest of the organization. We also talk about the mission statements people creating their own technical communication companies might devise.

When we study the organizing function of managers, we look at the ways technical communication managers organize people and processes to achieve organizational objectives. We read M. Jimmie Killingsworth and Betsy Jones's discussion of whether it is better to gather the communicators in a centralized department or disperse them throughout the divisions they serve [15]. We also read Thomas Duffy, Theodore Post, and Gregory Smith's description of the processes used by several organizations to develop manuals [16], and John Barr and Stephanie Rosenbaum's suggestions for assessing organizational productivity [17]. We then consider the manager's efforts to find qualified people to work in the organization. On this topic we read a paper by L. C. McKinley that describes the hiring process used by NCR Corporation to hire technical communicators [18].

In our readings on managerial control, we look at financial, schedule, and quality control. With respect to financial control, we begin with Caernarven-Smith's discussion of departmental budgets and their significance [19]. Then we read Stello Jordan and H. Lee Shimberg's [20] old but conceptually useful description of one method for estimating and controlling the costs of individual projects. We contrast that method with two variations on an alternative way of estimating project costs described by George Schultz [21] and David Herrstrom [22]. Our work on financial control culminates with the students working on a case in which they must tell how they would proceed if they worked for a technical communication company and were assigned to create a budget for technical sales and instructional materials requested by a client for a product it has developed and will manufacture in Japan but sell in the United States also.

When studying schedule control, we are able to skip over many of the things that managers need to know about managing projects completed by one person or a few people. Students have already learned those things in their writing and editing classes. In the management course, we focus instead on creating schedules for large projects that require contributions of many people working in parallel, for instance when several writers work simultaneously on different chapters of the same document and graphics are handled by a separate group of specialists. For this purpose, we turn again to Erickson's *Management Tools for Everyone* [23] to learn the concepts and procedures associated with the Critical Path Method (CPM) of scheduling. Students then create a schedule using a computerized scheduling program (MacProject). Our work on scheduling ends with a discussion of staff loading, the process by which a manager calculates for individual workers the specific days they must work on each of the various projects underway in a department to be sure that all the projects are completed on time.

In our look at quality control, we begin by briefly reprising what students have already learned in other courses about reviewing, testing, and other activities involved with assuring the quality of single projects. I remind students of how important it is for managers to include sufficient time for these quality-control activities in the schedules they create. Then we turn to another issue of quality control: evaluating staff to assure that they are performing to the top of their abilities. Our readings include articles by Charles McCaleb [24] and Kent Cummings [25] about evaluation methods they use.

Management Situations

In the final part of the course, we look at two special management situations. The first is the management of technical and scientific journals, which usually involves the same considerations as department or company management plus some additional responsibilities. The most significant additional considerations are that the manager must create and maintain a system for producing a new issue of the publication at regular intervals and that the manager must deal not only with employees but also authors who submit articles and expert reviewers who determine whether or not the articles will be published. Our readings include chapters by M. O'Connor [26] and an internship report by M. Zerbe [27], a graduate of our program who performed his internship at the *Journal of the National Cancer Institute*. Also, each year we invite the editor of a scientific or medical journal to meet with us.

The second special area is policy. Here we think about such things as how to manage the flow of information in a company. We talk about the possible tension between the desire to circulate technical information as widely as possible within the organization and the corresponding need to keep proprietary information from circulating to competitors. One valuable reading in this area is a chapter on formal and informal communication channels in Thomas Allen's *Managing the Flow of Technologyy* [28]. Another good source is Terrance Skelton's "Designing Communication Systems for Decentralized Organizations: A New Role for Technical Communicators" [29].

Besides the readings already mentioned, we also look throughout the term at articles and chapters that provide general advice for handling the myriad problems managers face [30-35]. Good sources for additional articles are the other chapters in this book, the *Institute of Electrical and Electronics Engineers Proceedings on Professional Communication,* the *Proceedings of the International Technical Communication Conference*, and *Technical Communication* (including Caernarven-Smith's column on management).

Encouraging Humane Managerial Values

Much of the class discussion of ethical values centers around our consideration of management styles. That's because each management style is built upon a distinctive set of assumptions about the relationships managers ought to have with employees and the obligations managers ought to feel toward other people. Although I familiarize students with autocratic managerial styles, I don't advocate them, and when I arrange field trips and guest speakers, I select companies and individuals who can serve as examples of humane management.

I also emphasize the importance to managers of seeing things from the perspective of the persons they manage. For instance, students sometimes focus on the imagined efficiency of requiring every writer in a department to follow a rigid and elaborate style guide, especially if the style guide reflects the good communication practices the students have learned in their writing and editing courses. However, such restrictions look much less appealing to students when they consider how little their own talents would be used if *they* were required to write under such restrictions and how little they would enjoy their work—a consideration that by itself is sufficient cause to question the desirability of such practices. In this way, I emphasize that one key to ethical management is sensitivity to the needs and desires of the individuals with whom one is working. I also point out that managers are especially influential members of an organization, so they have a greater than average opportunity (and responsibility) to influence company policy and procedures so that all people—employees, customers, vendors, community members—are treated in an ethical and respectful way.

Graded Projects

My course includes three graded projects, each attuned to the course's special objectives. The first project occurs early in the class and supports the effort to help students re-see their profession and their experiences from a management perspective. Students have three options. Those who have already worked as technical communicators can describe and assess the management practices in their employer's organization. Those without technical communication experience can describe management practices they have encountered in a summer job, former career or other employment, and then discuss the extent to which those practices would be successful in our field. Finally, students without any managerial experience can pick one of the chapters in the popular management book we read at the beginning of the term, summarize its main points, and then talk about how the chapter's advice might be applied when managing technical communicators.

The second of the course's three graded projects asks students to conduct library research on any management topic of importance or interest to them, summarize their findings, and explain the application of their findings to our field. Topics students have selected include controlling burnout, managing ethically, managing the introduction of new technology, using humor in management, and applying Japanese management techniques to technical communication in the U.S.

The third graded project is a final exam that provides students an opportunity to use the problem-solving model to integrate what they have learned about the variety of topics studied in the course. This take-home exam presents students with a case (usually about five pages) of one of the two types described above: a problem of dissatisfaction or one of aspiration. For example, one case asked students to tell how they would design a six-person technical communication department for a multidivisional manufacturing company. The company and its communication needs and current practices were described in detail to provide students with practice at applying general principles to a specific situation. Another case asked students to serve as a management consultant to a research company whose success rate with proposals for outside funding had dropped rapidly in the past two years.

In these cases, there is no "correct" answer. I evaluate the students' work in terms of the soundness of the problem-solving processes they describe, the reasons they offer for what they decide to do, and the skill with which they draw upon the material taught in the course.

As several essays in this volume indicate, the field of technical communication management is evolving rapidly. As technical communication managers take on new roles, as new media evolve, as new management tools are created, and as our theoretical and practical knowledge continues to grow, we will see many changes in what we might want technical communication majors to study about organizational management. One thing will remain constant, however: the importance of providing instruction on this topic for our future writers, editors, graphics designers—and managers.

REFERENCES

1. M. G. Moran and D. Journet, *Research in Technical Communication: A Bibliographic Sourcebook*, Greenwood, Westport, Connecticut, 1985.
2. C. H. Sides, *Technical and Business Communication: Bibliographic Essays for Teachers and Corporate Trainers*, National Council of Teachers of English and Society for Technical Communication, Urbana, Illinois, and Washington, DC, 1989.
3. *Profile 92*, Society for Technical Communication, Washington, DC, p. 5, 1992.
4. P. Caernarven-Smith, What's Not to Like about Management? *Technical Communication, 37*:2, pp. 180-181, 1990.
5. M. Hennig and A. Jardim, What This Book Is About, The Way It Is: Men and Women in Management Jobs, Patterns of Difference and Their Implications, and The Middle Management Career Path, in *The Managerial Woman,* Anchor/Doubleday, Garden City, New York, pp. 1-68, 1977.
6. D. Hellriegel and J. W. Slocum, Jr., The Importance of Management and Managers, in *Management* (3rd Edition), Addison-Wesley, Redding, Massachusetts, pp. 3-36, 1982.
7. A. C. Martin, The Roles and Responsibilities of Management and Supervision, in *Handbook of Technical Writing Practices*, Vol. 2, S. Jordan, J. M. Kleinman, and H. L. Shimberg (eds.), Society for Technical Communication, Washington, DC, pp. 969-1027, 1971.
8. J. Fallon, General Management Considerations, in *Handbook of Technical Writing Practices,* Vol. 2, S. Jordan, J. M. Kleinman, and H. Shimberg (eds.), Society for Technical Communication, Washington, DC, pp. 927-943, 1971.
9. P. V. Anderson, What Technical and Scientific Communicators Do: A Comprehensive Model for Developing Academic Programs, *IEEE Transactions on Professional Communication, 27:*4, pp. 161-167, 1984.
10. S. M. Erickson, Problem? I Don't See a Problem, in *Management Tools for Everyone: Twenty Analytical Techniques,* Petrocelli, New York, pp. 13-27, 1981.
11. T. J. Peters and R. H. Waterman, Jr., *In Search of Excellence: Lessons from America's Best-Run Companies,* Warner Books, New York, 1982.
12. J. M. Kouzes and B. Z. Posner, *The Leadership Challenge: How to Get Extraordinary Things Done in Organizations,* Jossey-Bass, San Francisco, 1987.
13. J. L. Massie and J. Douglas, Organizing: Designing the Formal Structure, in *Managing: A Contemporary Introduction* (5th Edition), Prentice-Hall, Englewood Cliffs, New Jersey, pp. 156-184, 1992.
14. K. J. Cook, Jr., How Strategic Planning Can Work in Your Organization, *Technical Communication, 37:*4, pp. 381-385, 1990.
15. M. J. Killingsworth and B. G. Jones, Division of Labor or Integrated Teams: A Crux in the Management of Technical Communication? *Technical Communication, 36*:3, pp. 210-221, 1989.
16. T. M. Duffy, T. Post, and G. Smith, An Analysis of the Process of Developing Military Technical Manuals, *Technical Communication, 34*:2, pp. 70-78, 1987.
17. J. P. Barr and S. Rosenbaum. Documentation and Training Productivity Benchmarks, *Technical Communication, 37*:4, pp. 399-408, 1990.
18. L. C. McKinley, You Can Hire Super Writers, unpublished manuscript.
19. P. Caernarven-Smith, What Your Budget Knows About You, *Technical Communication, 37*:1, pp. 74-77, 1990.

20. S. Jordan and H. L. Shimberg, Estimating and Cost Control, in *Handbook of Technical Writing Practices,* Vol. 2, S. Jordan, J. M. Kleinman and H. L. Shimberg (eds.), Society for Technical Communication, Washington, DC, pp. 1103-1157, 1971.

21. G. E. Schultz, a Method of Estimating Publication Costs, *Technical Communication, 34*:4, pp. 219-224, 1987.

22. D. S. Herrstrom, An Approach to Estimating the Cost of Product Documentation, with Some Hypotheses, *Proceedings of the 34th ITCC,* Society for Technical Communication, Washington, DC, pp. MPD24-MPD27, 1987.

23. S. M. Erickson, You Want It When? And It Can't Be Done by Then, in *Management Tools for Everyone: Twenty Analytical Techniques,* Petrocelli, New York, pp. 29-64, 1981.

24. C. S. McCaleb, Positive, Participatory Performance Appraisals, *Proceedings of the 31st ITCC,* Society for Technical Communication, Washington, DC, pp. MPD14-MPD16, 1984.

25. K. Cummings, Performance Ranking of Technical Editors/Writers, *Proceedings of the 31st ITCC,* Society for Technical Communication, Washington, DC, pp. MPD8-MPD11, 1984.

26. M. O'Connor, Editing Outlined, Guiding Authors, Keeping Papers Moving, and Working with Referees, in *Editing Scientific Books and Journals,* Pitman Medical Publishing, Tunbridge Wells, England, pp. 1-35, 1978.

27. M. Zerbe, *An Internship in Technical Communication with the Journal of the National Cancer Institute,* Miami University, Oxford, Ohio, pp. 1-21, 1990.

28. T. J. Allen, Structuring Organizational Communication Networks I: The Influence of Formal and Informal Organization, in *Managing the Flow of Technology: Technology Transfer and the Dissemination of Technological Information with the R & D Organization,* MIT Press, Cambridge, Massachusetts, pp. 182-233, 1977.

29. T. M. Skelton, Designing Communication Systems for Decentralized Organizations: A New Role for Technical Communicators, *IEEE Transactions on Professional Communication, 33*:2, pp. 83-88, 1990.

30. J. T. Hackos, Documentation Management: Why Should We Manage? *Proceedings of the 36th ITCC,* Society for Technical Communication, Washington, DC, pp. MG12-MG14, 1989.

31. P. Caernarven-Smith, Architect or Builder? *Technical Communication 37*:3, pp. 310-312, 1990.

32. J. T. Hackos, Managing Creative People, *Technical Communication 37*:4, pp. 375-380, 1990.

33. J. J. K. Polson, A Model for Management: Defending Yourself Against Murphy, *Proceedings of the 35th ITCC,* Society for Technical Communication, Washington, DC, pp. MPD100-MPD103, 1988.

34. J. C. Redish, A Dozen Helpful Hints for Managers, *Proceedings of the 36th ITCC,* Society for Technical Communication, Washington, DC, pp. MG20-MG23, 1989.

35. L. M. Zook, Making and Breaking Rules—A Manager's Viewpoint, *Technical Communication, 33*:3, pp. 144-148, 1986.

CHAPTER 18

A Design for a Graduate Seminar in Publications Management

O. JANE ALLEN

As Paul Anderson emphasizes in the preceding chapter, programs in technical and professional communication should prepare students for management responsibilities in the workplace. Many of our graduates find themselves with supervisory and other management responsibilities soon after they enter the workforce. Even those who do not can be better writers and editors if they understand their work from a management perspective.

Business colleges offer management courses, some of which are useful to technical and professional communication students. However, as Anderson notes, such courses often do not deal with issues specific to publications management. Moreover, students can devote only a limited number of credit hours to course work outside the technical/professional communication major. Consequently, academic programs must offer courses that, at the very least, develop students' awareness of the corporate environment and of the management issues they will face in the workplace.

New Mexico State University offers both a master of arts degree in English with an emphasis in technical and professional communication and a doctorate in rhetoric and professional communication. To help prepare students for management responsibilities in the workplace, we offer a three-semester-hour graduate seminar in publications management. The seminar, which meets for two and a half hours once a week, complements a six-semester-hour internship requirement. Both the seminar and the internship are designed to help students in their transition from the classroom to the workplace.

The course is described here to help others who wish to adapt parts of it to fit their needs and to generate an exchange among readers from the academic and the corporate spheres. The description includes bibliography that students as well as publications staff may find useful.

The seminar in publications management involves both theory and practice, providing students with resources that will support them on the job and help them develop a sense of the larger context of corporate culture through the opportunity to study the publications processes within an organization. Research and reading assignments concentrate on six major topics of interest to publications professionals: communication in organizations, management and supervision, project management, technology and professional communication, legal and ethical issues, and contract employment.

RESEARCH ASSIGNMENTS

Research assignments for the course include 1) a study of a publications unit within an organization, and 2) a review of the literature on a topic related to publications management. Students orally present results of both assignments to the class, gaining experience in oral presentation and receiving the benefit of one another's research.

Study of a Publications Unit

The publications unit research assignment requires students to study a publications unit within an organization, write a report of the study, and present the report orally to the class.

Purpose and Benefits to Students

The purpose of having students study a publications unit is to provide them with information about the various ways a publications group can function within an organization, the types of documents that may be developed, and the management strategies pursued and issues faced by publications managers. The study of an organization's publications unit fills a gap for students who have been in internships but who haven't had the time or the opportunity to study the workings of the publications unit within which they interned. Their stance as researchers permits them to ask questions they might not have felt free to ask as student interns.

Students must collaborate with at least one other student in the class, thus giving them the experience of working with others and cooperating to complete their research, write their reports, and present their reports to the class. They learn the benefits of sharing ideas to get a job done. They also learn about the problems associated with collaboration and the importance of representing themselves as a team both to the organization they are researching and to the class.

Preparation for the Study

I caution students that the main focus of their research must be on how a publications unit functions within an organization and that, unlike more formal studies they might do for a thesis or dissertation, they may have to subordinate the method of the study to the exigencies of the organization they are studying and the circumstances of a college semester. Some of our students, especially those in the Ph.D. program, already have taken courses on ethnographic study methods. For those who have not, I include readings, discussed below, to guide them. However, time and the availability of the appropriate people within the organization being studied may not lend themselves to optimum ethnographic study methods. The important point is that students gain information that they can share with the class about how a publications unit functions within an organization.

The course syllabus includes guidelines for the study and requires students to turn in a memorandum, by the fourth week of the semester, listing team members and the organization to be studied. The last three or four weeks of the semester are reserved for oral reports, allotting forty-five minutes to an hour for each report and the subsequent discussion.

Students are responsible for selecting an appropriate organization and securing written permission from the manager of the unit they study. Class discussions the first week or two of the semester help students settle on appropriate organizations. They arrange interviews with organization supervisors to explain their projects and obtain permission. They follow up the oral permission with a written agreement that describes the purpose and scope of their study and stipulations they may agree upon with the organization supervisor. A few students are already employed in full-time jobs or as interns in professional communication positions. Hence I require them to perform their study in an organization in which they are not employed. At the same time, these students provide important contacts for other students looking for an organization to study.

Both campus and corporate groups in the area have been especially cooperative in accommodating students. Among the on-campus publications units are the Agricultural Information Office, the Sports Information Office, the Physical Science Laboratory, Information Services, and the NMSU Foundation offices. Students have gone off campus to study several organizations, including a printing plant, the Education Services Division at the White Sands Missile Range, the Bureau of Land Management, and the publications unit at El Paso Natural Gas Company. Part of our success in getting the cooperation of these organizations derives from the fact that local organizations are hiring our graduates and appreciate the importance of corporate participation in their education. In addition, the class discusses the importance of professional conduct in performing every phase of their study in an organization.

Readings, which are discussed later, and class discussion assist students in their research. Early class discussion of literature and the work experience they bring to the class helps students arrive at a plan for their study and a list of questions they need to have answered. Semester exigencies naturally limit the thoroughness of some of the studies; nevertheless, students as well as the publications units they study benefit from the experience.

Written and Oral Reports

Students write a formal report of the study following instructions for formal reports in a reputable handbook. The assignment, however, could as well be to write a paper for publication in an essay collection or journal, using models available in the literature.

To guide students in their studies, contents of the reports are detailed in the syllabus. The reports must contain a general description of the organization, its mission, its products and services, its size, and its internal organization. Students must show how the publications unit functions within the larger organization and describe the scope of its responsibility for developing documentation within the organization. Information about the number of writers, editors, illustrators, and other staff within the publications unit, along with general information about their backgrounds, must also be included. Other required information includes the types of documents handled, support equipment and personnel available, and processes used to produce documents. In the analysis section of the report, students must include an assessment of the strengths and weaknesses of the written products and of the organization and management of the publications unit. Where appropriate, students also include recommendations for change.

In presenting findings to the class, students give a professional presentation, with all members of the team participating. The presentation involves the use of appropriate visual materials. Finally, students provide an outline of their findings as a handout so that classmates will have it for future reference.

Review of the Literature

The second research assignment is a review of the literature on a topic related to publications management. Students have the option of writing a review essay or preparing an annotated bibliography prefaced with an appropriate introduction. Each student completes this assignment individually, reports on it to the class, and provides the class with a bibliography that would be useful to a publications manager. Topics are scheduled for presentation to coincide with a series of assigned readings that fall under the six general topics around which the course is organized.

Students must turn in a memorandum by the second week of the course indicating their choice of topic from a list included with the syllabus. From these memos the presentations for the semester are scheduled. Each student works on a separate topic, one that is of interest to communication professionals, and presents the results of the research to the class. A brief list of topics follows, but the possibilities are obviously numerous.

Management Communication
   Nonverbal Communication
   Gender Issues and Professional Communication
Management and Supervision
   Conducting Employment Interviews
   Evaluating Productivity
   Evaluating Employee Performance
   Conducting a Meeting
   Developing Procedures
   Managing Conflict
Project Management
   Estimating Publication Costs
   Collaborative Writing and Editing
   Coordinating a Documentation Project
Technology and Professional Communication
   Artificial Intelligence and Professional Communication
   Hypermedia and Professional Communication
   Desktop Publishing and Professional Communication
Legal and Ethical Issues
   Copyright Law
   Management Communication and the Law
   Equal Employment Opportunity
   Ethics and the Professional Communicator
Contract Employment
   Setting Up a Freelance Business
   Preparing a Proposal for a Contract Project
   Hiring Contract Employees

These presentations, and the bibliographies that accompany them, provide the entire class with a broad base of information about management issues that publications professionals need to be aware of. At the same time, the presentations expand on assigned reading topics and contribute to the discussions of the readings.

READING ASSIGNMENTS

Reading assignments coincide with students' presentations of their literature reviews in the various subject areas. To supplement discussion of the reading and students' presentations, I also invite guest lecturers, often graduates of our program who are publications managers, to speak on related topics. The final weeks of the semester, as mentioned above, are reserved for students' presentations of their studies of publications units.

I look forward to using this collection of essays as an assigned text for the course. Other materials suitable for assigned reading, for faculty use in facilitating discussion, or to get students started on their literature reviews can be found in essay collections, professional society journals and proceedings, management journals, and organizational communication texts. Some of these materials that I have found useful are referenced in the discussion and bibliography that follows.

Communication in Organizations

One of the first readings I assign is Stephen Doheny-Farina and Lee Odell's "Ethnographic Research on Writing: Assumptions and Methodology" [1]. Although this article is not directly related to management communication, it is useful in helping students understand the nature of the research they will be doing in their study of a publications unit.

We also read and discuss several other articles about organizational context and corporate culture to help students organize their research projects and arrive at appropriate questions for their research. Among the useful pieces I have found are David A. Nadler and Michael L. Tushman's "A Model for Diagnosing Organizational Behavior" [2], Lawrence B. Levine's "Corporate Culture, Technical Documentation, and Organization Diagnosis" [3], J. C. Mathes' "Written Communication: The Industrial Context" [4], and Jean Ann Lutz's "Writers in Organizations and How They Learn the Image: Theory, Research, and Implications" [5].

Additional topics introduced in this unit include gender issues in professional communication, informal lines of communication, listening, nonverbal communication, and techniques for holding cost-effective meetings.

In dealing with gender issues in professional communication, Francine Wattman Frank and Paula A. Treichler's *Language, Gender, and Professional Writing* is a valuable resource [6]. Another source is the October 1991 issue of *Journal of Business and Technical Communication,* which is devoted to "Gender and Professional Communication" [7]. Readings from these sources provide opportunities to discuss management styles, language issues, and other sensitive matters related to gender.

Useful articles about managerial communication include John L. DiGaetani's "The Business of Listening" [8], Keith Davis' "The Care and Culture of the Corporate Grapevine" [9], John E. Baird, Jr., and Gretchen K. Wieting's "Nonverbal Communication Can Be a Motivational Tool" [10], all included in *Communication for Management and Business,* 4th Ed., by Norman B. Sigband and Arthur H. Bell. In addition, Milo O. Frank's *How to Run a Successful Meeting in Half the Time* [11] contains information on organizing and conducting meetings.

Management and Supervision

The broad area of management and supervision covers responsibilities students may face as supervisors of communication staff. Appropriate assignments for this unit include JoAnn T. Hackos' "Managing Creative People," which suggests management styles that are effective in working with publications staff [12], and David C. Leonard's "Understanding and Managing Conflict in a Technical Communication Department," which discusses the causes of conflict and suggests keys to conflict resolution [13].

Employee performance evaluation is an especially sensitive topic for students because they are concerned both about being evaluated and about their responsiblities as evaluators. Articles useful in helping students come to terms with the need for performance evaluations both as evaluators and as evaluatees include Patricia Buhler's "Evaluating an Employee's Performance" [14], which points out that employee evaluation involves dialogue between the supervisor and the employee; T. M. Dalla Santa's "The Whys and Hows of Effective Performance Appraisals" [15], which explains the use of performance evaluation and suggests effective techniques; and Jill Kanin-Lovers' "Making Performance Evaluation Work" [16], which discusses organizational goals for performance evaluation and includes suggestions for encouraging dialogue and providing appropriate documentation as a defense against law suits. Also informative is William C. Howell's chapter on performance evaluation in *Business and Management Communication: New Perspectives* [17]. Howell discusses how performance appraisal affects employee motivation and attitudes and how different appraisal systems and techniques work.

Project Management

Project management is an important topic for publications managers. Publications staff who are not called managers or who have no supervisory responsibilities may find themselves supervising projects, from brochures to entire libraries of documentation. Under this general topic area, students need to be concerned with such issues as the role of professional communicators in the documentation development cycle, collaborative work, cost estimating, measuring productivity, and documentation planning.

One source of information on collaborative writing that provides a model for students writing literature reviews is Mary Beth Debs's "Recent Research on Collaborative Writing in Industry" [18]. Deborah Bosley's "Designing Effective Technical Communication Teams" [19] contains useful suggestions for facilitating collaboration. Both articles are included in a special issue of *Technical Communication* on collaboration. Carol Barnum's "Working with People" [20] discusses how technical communicators perform collaborative work and some problems that can develop, and offers suggestions for successful collaborative work.

Mary M. Lay and William M. Karis' *Collaborative Writing in Industry: Theory and Practice* is a collection of twelve essays that describe recent practice in industry and provide insight into the theories that inform collaboration. The Winter 1993 *Technical Communication Quarterly,* edited by Rebecca E.

Burnett and Ann Hill Duin, is a special issue devoted to collaboration in technical communication. It contains a selected, annotated bibliography on collaboration compiled by Linda A. Jorn [23].

James G. Prekeges' "Planning and Tracking a Project" [24] offers guidelines for the various stages of project development, including planning, scheduling, budgeting, and quality control. Karen A. Schriver's "Quality in Document Design: Issues and Controversies" [25] provides an overview of the quality movement and the implications for document design. Shriver includes "An Annotated Bibliography on Quality Issues in Document Design and Technical Communication" in her article. George E. Schultz's "A Method of Estimating Publication Costs" [26] describes a unit cost system for estimating publications costs based on historical data and a computerized job-by-job accounting system. All these pieces provide practical suggestions that should be helpful in the workplace.

Technology and Professional Communication

The reading unit on technology and professional communication is included to ensure students' awareness that a publications manager is often responsible for acquiring and using production equipment for an organization's publications. Students likewise need to be aware of current technology that affects document design and production.

Several recent collections contain articles that discuss the implications of developing technologies for professional communication. Examples of useful articles include Roger Grice's "Online Information: What Do People Want? What Do People Need?" [27], Philip Rubens' "Online Information, Hypermedia, and the Idea of Literacy" [28], and Robert Krull's "Online Writing from an Organizational Perspective" [29], in *The Society of Text: Hypertext, Hypermedia, and the Social Construction of Information*; and Rubens' "Writing for an On-Line Age: The Influence of Electronic Text on Writing," from *Worlds of Writing [30]*.

Current management communication textbooks sometimes include chapters on technology as it relates to professional communication. One such chapter is H. Albert Napier and Linda Driskill's "The Technological Context for Business Communication" [31] in *Business and Managerial Communication*, edited by Driskill. This chapter discusses the effects of technology on communication processes and productivity and the use of electronic equipment including voice mail, electronic mail, videoconferencing, and FAX. In addition, Norman B. Sigband and Arthur H. Bell include a chapter on "The Electronic Communication Revolution" in their 5th edition of *Communication for Management and Business* [32].

Legal and Ethical Issues

In the unit on legal and ethical issues, students study some of the more complex ethical issues with which professional communicators are faced. They also read about some of the practical legal matters with which they need to be concerned.

The Society for Technical Communication Code for Communicators and its implications for publications staff is a good place to begin in discussing ethical issues. The chapters on ethics by Carolyn Rude and Stuart Brown in this collection both look at the implications of this code as well as other related topics. Gregory Clark's "Ethics in Technical Communication: A Rhetorical Perspective" [33] and Mark Wicclair and David Farkas' "Ethical Reasoning in Technical Communication: A Practical Framework" [34] are interesting pieces for technical communication students. The Wicclair and Farkas essay, originally published in *Technical Communication,* is reprinted in the Society for Technical Communication anthology *Technical Communication and Ethics* [35], along with several other useful pieces, including a selected bibliography.

On a more practical level, and to raise students' awareness of some of the legal issues associated with professional communication, I have assigned Charles Walter and Thomas F. Marsteller's "Liability for the Dissemination of Defective Information" [36] and Russell W. Driver's "A Communication Model for Determining the Appropriateness of On-Product Warnings" [37]. In addition, Larry Strate and Skip Swerdlow's "The Maze of the Law: How Technical Writers Can Research and Understand Legal Matters" [38] provides students with a resource for legal research. The September 1987 *IEEE Transactions on Professional Communication,* in which the articles by Walter and Marsteller, Driver, and Strate and Swerdlow appear, is a special issue devoted to "Legal and Ethical Aspects of Technical Communication."

Sigband and Bell include readings on legal issues of interest to professional communicators in *Communication for Business and Management.* Their chapter "Legal Considerations: Products, Promotion, and the Law" [39] alerts managers to the contractual implications of various forms of communication, and lists "Major Federal Legislation, Executive Orders, and Supreme Court Decisions Relating to Managerial Communication." Richard B. Sypher's "Communication and the Law" [40], reprinted in Sigband and Bell's text, cautions executives about the legal implications of documents such as personnel manuals that communicate company policy. James Paradis' "Text and Action: The Operator's Manual in Context and in Court" [41] examines some of the legal and ethical implications of the documentation that accompanies technical products.

Jacquelyn L. Monday's recent "Protecting Your Work—Professional Ethics and the Copyright Law" [42] summarizes and offers advice on a variety of matters related to copyright law, including rights and obligations in using material by others, copyright ownership, and protecting one's own work.

Contract Employment

Contract employment is important to students from two perspectives. Many of them already are freelance communicators and are concerned about managing their own businesses. They also need to be aware of the issues associated with using contract employes as resources in an organizational publications unit.

Donald D. Clayton's chapter on "Consultants' Communications in Business and Managerial Communication: New Perspectives" [43] defines the role of the consultant and offers suggestions for writing effective project proposals and reports. The November 1986 issue of *Technical Communication*, a special issue on "Freelancing in Technical Communication" (which carried an earlier version of Armbruster's chapter in this book), contains several useful articles [44], as does *Communication Training and Consulting in Business, Industry, and Government*, edited by William J. Buchholz [45]. Students will also be interested in books such as Herman Holtz's *How to Start and Run a Writing and Editing Business* [46] and Robert O. Metzger's *Developing a Consulting Practice* [47].

All these materials can be used either as assigned readings or for reference to inform class discussion and to encourage students to supplement the assigned readings with additional materials in their literature reviews and presentations. Publications staff in the workplace may also find them useful.

Clearly, academic programs in technical and professional communication must help students to integrate their classroom experience with the realities of the workplace. The course described here offers students a wide range of information about the role of publications units in organizations and affords them the opportunity to investigate first hand the complexity of corporate culture. It allows faculty and students to combine classroom study with knowledge about workplace duties and environments. Students leave the course with a resource file, problem-solving skills, and information about many of the issues they will face as writers, editors, and publications managers.

REFERENCES

1. S. Doheny-Farina and L. Odell, Ethnographic Research on Writing: Assumptions and Methodology, in *Writing in Nonacademic Settings,* L. Odell and D. Goswami (eds.), Guilford Press, New York, pp. 503-535, 1985.
2. D. A. Nadler and M. L. Tushman, A Model for Diagnosing Organizational Behavior, in *Readings in the Management of Innovation,* M. L. Tushman and W. L. Moore (eds.), Ballinger, Cambridge, Massachusetts, pp. 148-163, 1988.
3. L. B. Levine, Corporate Culture, Technical Documentation, and Organization Diagnosis, in *Text, Context, and Hypertext: Writing with and for the Computer,* E. Barrett (ed.), MIT Press, Cambridge, Massachusetts, pp. 149-174, 1988.
4. J. C. Mathes, Written Communication: The Industrial Context, in *Worlds of Writing: Teaching and Learning in Discourse Communities of Work,* C. B. Matalene (ed.), Random House, New York, pp. 222-246, 1989.
5. J. A. Lutz, Writers in Organizations and How They Learn the Image: Theory, Research, and Implications, in *Worlds of Writing: Teaching and Learning in Discourse*

Communities of Work, C. B. Matalene (ed.), Random House, New York, pp. 113-135, 1989.

6. F. W. Frank and P. A. Treichler, *Language, Gender, and Professional Writing: Theoretical Approaches and Guidelines for Nonsexist Usage,* Modern Language Association, New York, 1989.

7. Gender and Professional Communication, special issue of *Journal of Business and Technical Communication, 5*:4, 1991.

8. J. L. DiGaetani, The Business of Listening, in *Communication for Management and Business* (5th Edition), N. B. Sigband and A. H. Bell (eds.), Scott, Foresman, Glenview, Illinois, pp. R11-R17, 1986. (Reprinted from *Business Horizons,* pp. 40-46, October 1980.)

9. K. Davis, The Care and Cultivation of the Corporate Grapevine, in *Communication for Management and Business* (4th Edition), N. B. Sigband and A. H. Bell (eds.), Scott, Foresman, Glenview, Illinois, pp. R28-R32, 1986. (Reprinted from Dun's Business Month, pp. 44-47, July 1973).

10. J. E. Baird, Jr., and G. K. Wieting, Nonverbal Communication Can Be a Motivational Tool, in *Communication for Management and Business* (4th Edition), N. B. Sigband and A. H. Bell (eds.), Scott, Foresman, Glenview, Illinois, pp. R38-R45, 1986. (Reprinted from *Personnel Journal,* pp. 607-610, September 1979.)

11. M. O. Frank, *How to Run a Successful Meeting in Half the Time,* Simon and Schuster, New York, 1989.

12. J. T. Hackos, Managing Creative People, *Technical Communication, 37*:4, pp. 375-380, 1990.

13. D. C. Leonard, Understanding and Managing Conflict in a Technical Communication Department, *Technical Communication, 40*:1, pp. 74-80, 1993.

14. P. Buhler, Evaluating an Employee's Performance, *Supervision, 52*:4, pp. 17-19, 1991.

15. T. M. D. Santa. The Whys and Hows of Effective Performance Appraisals, *Technical Communication, 37*:4, pp. 392-395, 1988.

16. J. Kanin-Lovers, Making Performance Evaluation Work, *Journal of Compensation and Benefits, 5*:6, pp. 360-362, 1990.

17. W. C. Howell, Performance Evaluation Communications, in *Business and Management Communication: New Perspectives,* L. Driskill, J. Ferrill, and M. N. Steffey (eds.), Harcourt Brace Jovanovich College Publishers, Orlando, pp. 613-642, 1992.

18. M. B. Debs, Recent Research on Collaborative Writing in Industry, *Technical Communication, 38*:4, pp. 476-484, 1991.

19. D. S. Bosley, Designing Effective Technical Communication Teams, *Technical Communication, 38*:4, pp. 504-512, 1991.

20. C. M. Barnum, Working with People, in *Techniques for Technical Communicators,* C. M. Barnum and S. Carliner (eds.), Macmillan, New York, pp. 107-136, 1993.

21. M. M. Lay and W. M. Karis (eds.), *Collaborative Writing in Industry: Investigations in Theory and Practice,* Baywood Publishing Company, Amityville, New York, 1991.

22. R. E. Burnett and A. H. Duin (eds.), Special Issue on Collaboration, *Technical Communication Quarterly, 2*:1, 1993.

23. L. A. Jorn, A Selected Bibliography on Collaboration in Technical Communication, *Technical Communication Quarterly, 2*:1, pp. 105-115, 1993.

24. J. Prekeges, Planning and Tracking a Project, in *Techniques for Technical Communicators,* C. M. Barnum and S. Carliner (eds.), Macmillan, New York, pp. 79-106, 1993.
25. K. A. Schriver, Quality in Document Design: Issues and Controversies, *Technical Communication, 40*:2, pp. 239-257, 1993.
26. G. E. Schultz, A Method of Estimating Publication Costs, *Technical Communication, 34*:4, pp. 219-224, 1987.
27. R. A. Grice, Online Information: What Do People Want? What Do People Need? in *The Society of Text: Hypertext, Hypermedia, and the Social Construction of Information,* E. Barrett (ed.), MIT Press, Cambridge, Massachusetts, pp. 22-44, 1989.
28. P. Rubens, Online Information, Hypermedia, and the Idea of Literacy, in *The Society of Text: Hypertext, Hypermedia, and the Social Construction of Information,* E. Barrett (ed.), MIT Press, Cambridge, Massachusetts, pp. 3-21, 1989.
29. R. Krull, Online Writing from an Organizational Perspective, in *The Society of Text: Hypertext, Hypermedia, and the Social Construction of Information,* E. Barrett (ed.), MIT Press, Cambridge, Massachusetts, pp. 250-264, 1989.
30. P. Rubens, Writing for an On-Line Age: The Influence of Electronic Text on Writing, in *Worlds of Writing: Teaching and Learning in Discourse Communities of Work,* C. B. Matalene (ed.), Random House, New York, pp. 343-360, 1989.
31. H. A. Napier and L. P. Driskill, The Technological Context for Business Communication, in *Business and Managerial Communication: New Perspectives,* L. Driskill, J. Ferrill, M. N. Steffey (eds.), Harcourt Brace Jovanovich College Publishers, New York, pp. 195-226, 1992.
32. N. B. Sigband and A. H. Bell, The Electronic Communication Revolution, in *Communication for Management and Business,* (5th Edition), Scott, Foresman, Glenview, Illinois, pp. 70-105, 1989.
33. G. Clark, Ethics in Technical Communication: A Rhetorical Perspective, *IEEE Transactions on Professional Communication, 30*:3, pp. 190-195, September 1987.
34. M. E. Wicclair and D. K. Farkas, Ethical Reasoning in Technical Communication: A Practical Framework, *Technical Communication, 31:* 2, pp. 15-19, 1984.
35. R. J. Brockmann and F. Rook (eds.), *Technical Communication and Ethics,* Society for Technical Communication, Arlington, Virginia, 1989.
36. C. Walter and T. F. Marsteller, Liability for the Dissemination of Defective Information, *IEEE Transactions on Professional Communication 30*:3, pp. 164-167, September 1987.
37. R. W. Driver, A Communication Model for Determining the Appropriateness of On-Product Warnings, *IEEE Transactions on Professional Communication, 30*:3, pp. 157-163, September 1987.
38. L. Strate and S. Swerdlow, The Maze of the Law: How Technical Writers Can Research and Understand Legal Matters, *IEEE Transactions on Professional Communication, 30*:3, pp. 136-148, September 1987.
39. N. B. Sigband and A. H. Bell, Legal Considerations: Products, Promotion, and the Law, in *Communication for Management and Business* (5th Edition), Scott, Foresman, Glenview, Illinois, pp. 630-633, 1989.
40. R. B. Sypher, Communication and the Law, in *Communication for Management and Business* (5th Edition), N. B. Sigband and A. H. Bell (eds.), Scott, Foresman,

Glenview, Illinois, pp. R36-R42, 1989. (Reprinted from *The Handbook of Executive Communication*, J. L. DiGaetani [ed.], Dow Jones-Irwin, Homewood, Illinois, pp. 96-104, 1986.)

41. J. Paradis, Text and Action: The Operator's Manual in Context and in Court, in *Textual Dynamics of the Professions: Historical and Contemporary Studies of Writing in Professional Communities*, C. Bazerman and J. Paradis (eds.), University of Wisconsin Press, Madison, pp. 256-278, 1991.

42. J. L. Monday, Protecting Your Work—Professional Ethics and the Copyright Law, in *Techniques for Technical Communicators*, C. M. Barnum and S. Carliner (eds.), Macmillan, New York, pp. 337-358, 1993.

43. D. B. Clayton, Consultants' Communications, in *Business and Managerial Communication: New Perspectives*, L. Driskill, J. Ferrill and M. N. Steffey (eds.), Harcourt Brace Jovanovich College Publishers, New York, pp. 587-612, 1992.

44. Special Issue on Freelancing in Technical Communication, *Technical Communication*, *33:4*, 1986.

45. W. J. Buchholz (ed.), *Communication Training and Consulting in Business, Industry, and Government*, American Business Communication Association, Urbana, Illinois, 1983.

46. H. Holtz, *How to Start and Run a Writing and Editing Business*, John Wiley and Sons, New York, 1992.

47. R. O. Metzger, *Developing a Consulting Practice*, Sage Publications, Newbury Park, California, 1993.

Contributors

O. JANE ALLEN is associate professor of English at New Mexico State University, where she teaches publications management, a graduate-level technical and professional writing workshop, and courses in women's studies and women's autobiographical writing. Her book *Barbara Pym: Writing a Life* is forthcoming from Scarecrow Press, Inc.

PAUL V. ANDERSON teaches in the master's degree program in technical and scientific communication at Miami University (Ohio). He is author of *Technical Writing: A Reader-Centered Approach* and *Business Communication: An Audience-Centered Approach* and coeditor of *New Essays in Technical and Scientific Communication: Research, Theory, Practice.*

DAVID L. ARMBRUSTER is head of Scientific Publications at the University of Tennessee, Memphis. He has published a number of articles on internships and presents workshops and seminars on biomedical writing and ethical issues involving scientific publications. He is a fellow and past president of the Society for Technical Communication, and an active member of the Council of Biology Editors.

MARIAN G. BARCHILON is an assistant professor in the Department of Manufacturing and Industrial Technology, College of Engineering and Applied Sciences, at Arizona State University. Among the articles she has authored and coauthored are "Meeting the Demands of the New Workplace: Technical Communication Courses and Risk-Taking Skills," "The Changing Role of the Engineer as a Technical Communicator," and "How Economics and Technology Have Impacted the Engineer's Role as a Technical Communicator." She was the invited guest editor for a special section on downsizing in *Technical Communication.*

ROBERT M. BROWN is director of the technical writing program at Oklahoma State University. He has also served as a communications analyst at the RAND Corporation, as a reports analyst at the U.S. General Accounting Office, and as an independent writing consultant. In the summers, he trains report writers in industry.

STUART C. BROWN is assistant professor of rhetoric and professional communication at New Mexico State University, where he teaches history and theory of rhetoric, ethics, and professional communication. He is coauthor (with Duane Roen and Robert Mittan) of the textbook *Becoming Expert* and coeditor (with Theresa Enos) of the collections *Defining the New Rhetorics* and *Professing the New Rhetorics*. He is currently at work on an environmental rhetoric/reader for St. Martin's Press.

JOHN G. BRYAN teaches business, technical, and promotional writing; document design; and computer applications at the University of Cincinnati. He is chair of the committee on ethics of the Society for Technical Communication, and his "Down the Slippery Slope: Ethics and the Technical Writer as Marketer" appeared recently in *Technical Communication Quarterly*. He is currently at work on a casebook in professional writing.

LYNN H. DEMING is an associate professor of English at New Mexico Institute of Mining and Technology, Socorro, where she teaches in the technical communication program, a nationally recognized program whose graduates earn a bachelor of science degree. She has publications in *Technical Communication* and many conference proceedings. She was a technical writer/editor at the Physical Science Laboratory, New Mexico State University, and taught technical writing at Texas Tech University and New Mexico State University before joining the faculty at New Mexico Tech.

CHRISTOPHER J. FORBES, a former assistant professor in undergraduate technical communication programs at Washington State University and Northeast Louisiana University, is currently employed by Boeing Computer Services, Richland, at the United States Department of Energy Hanford Site in southeastern Washington. He has also worked as a technical editor and publications manager at the Westinghouse Electric Corporation Waste Isolation Division in Carlsbad, New Mexico. He has published articles in *Radioactive Waste Management and the Nuclear Fuel Cycle* and the *Technical Writing Teacher*.

JOHN S. HARRIS is a professor of English at Brigham Young University. He was founding president of the Association of Teachers of Technical Writing and has written three books on technical writing and two books of poems. He has also written extensively on firearms technology and aircraft design. His most recent book is *Teaching Technical Writing: A Pragmatic Approach* (Revised Edition), Association of Teachers of Technical Writing, 1992.

JODY H. HEIKEN is a technical writer/editor and manager of the undergraduate internship program at Los Alamos National Laboratory. She has edited several geology texts for the University of California Press and has presented papers on document management, online editing, internship management, and career paths in technical communication. She has served the Society for Technical Communication as director sponsor, publications manager, and currently, as assistant to the president for professional development.

RENEE B. HOROWITZ is a professor in the Department of Manufacturing and Industrial Technology, College of Engineering and Applied Sciences, Arizona State University. She teaches Engineering Communications, Impact of Communications Technology on Society, Technical Communication for Managers, Proposal Writing, and Management Dynamics. She has published articles and presented papers on techniques for quality improvement in technical reports and presentations. Her recent publications include an article on visionary leadership.

ROBERT V. PELTIER is an associate professor in the Department of Manufacturing and Industrial Technology at Arizona State University, and director of the Energy Analysis and Diagnostic Center. He teaches courses emphasizing energy systems design and conservation and conducts research in the areas of cogeneration and energy management and analysis. He is a registered professional engineer in Arizona and California and a certified energy manager. His recent publications in the area of technical communication include "Management Challenges for the Manufacturing Engineer" and "A New Role for the Technical Communicator: Facilitating Improved Supervisor-Employee Communication."

DANIEL L. PLUNG is manager of Management Information Services for the Westinghouse Savannah River Company. He was general chairman for the 1991 International Professional Communication Conference and serves on the Administrative Committee of the Professional Communication Society of the Institute of Electrical and Electronics Engineers (IEEE). His publications include two anthologies—*Guide for Writing Better Technical Papers* and *Marketing Technical Ideas and Products Successfully.*

CAROLYN D. RUDE is associate professor and director of technical communication at Texas Tech University. She also has experience as a technical writer and publications manager in the field of advocacy for persons with developmental disabilities. Her textbook, *Technical Editing* (Wadsworth, 1991), includes chapters on production and management. Her current research explores ethical dimensions of decision making.

DAVID L. SMITH is chief of the Publications Section at the Physical Science Laboratory, New Mexico State University. His experience includes trading on the Navajo Reservation, sales of oilfield drilling and production equipment in the Four Corners States, and sales of industrial manufacturing equipment in Mexico.

JAMES W. SOUTHER, now deceased, was professor emeritus of technical communication in the College of Engineering at the University of Washington, where he taught for 44 years. He published numerous articles and coauthored the textbook *Technical Report Writing*, published by John Wiley and Sons. Recently, he and Professor Myron L. White received from the Society for Technical Communication one of its first two Jay R. Gould Awards for Excellence in Teaching Technical Communication.

BARBARA WEBER is manager of the Documentation and Methods Analysis Group at El Paso Natural Gas Company. Her article "Technical Writing Skills: A

Question of Aptitude or Interest?" was published in the *Journal of Technical Writing and Communication* (1985: 1). She was copresenter of "CBT Authors Are Made, Not Born," in Washington, D.C., at the 6th annual Computer-Based Training Conference and Exposition in 1988; and her "Authoring On-Line Help Screens" was published in the August 1989 issue of *CBT Directions*.

CAROLE YEE is professor of English at New Mexico Institute of Mining and Technology, where she teaches technical communication, composition, and literature and chairs the Department of Humanities. She is also the associate editor for communication education and training for the journal *IEEE Transactions on Professional Communication.*

Index